RICHIE GINTHER
MOTOR RACING'S FREE THINKER

First Published February 2020
Copyright Text copyright Richard Jenkins
Page layout and graphics copyright Performance Publishing Ltd

ISBN 978-0-9576450-5-9

Author Richard Jenkins
Designer Sarah Scrimshaw

Front cover Main image: Monaco, 1960. Credit: Jorg-Thomas Fodisch/Ed McDonough
Rear cover Le Mans, 1966. Credit: El Sol/Ed McDonough

Printed by The Manson Group Ltd, Hertfordshire AL3 6PZ

Publisher Performance Publishing Ltd
Unit 3 Site 4 Alma Park Road,
Alma Park Industrial Estate,
Grantham, Lincolnshire NG31 9SE, Great Britain

French Grand Prix, 1961. *David Hodges/Ed McDonough*

Richie Ginther is one of only five Americans to have won a Formula One World Championship Grand Prix. He finished joint runner-up in the World Championship in 1963, he gave Honda and Goodyear their first Formula One victories, he set three fastest laps in World Championship races, he led 91 laps during his World Championship career, and finished in the points in over half of his races in Formula One. Then away from Formula One, he was one of the top sports car drivers in America in the 1950s.

He was one of the first, and still one of the finest, mechanically-orientated drivers in Formula One, completely at odds with so many of those before, during and after his career in that the car – not winning – came first. Development, understanding, and testing took precedence over pure speed (although he was blessed with that too). Ginther was a first-rate mechanic with a huge interest in how racing cars were constructed and then subsequently developed to be the best they could be.

He effectively invented the rear spoiler, helped develop the 1961 championship-winning Ferrari 'Sharknose' car, helped BRM win the 1962 World Constructors' Championship and was a very successful team manager and car developer in sports car racing in the early 1970s.

German Grand Prix, 1962. *Gunther Asshauer*

Despite all that, Ginther's legacy, with the rise of the internet in the late '90s, was none of the above. All the talk of Ginther now became how he was a hippy, a reclusive bum who eschewed the world and died an angry, resentful man. This significantly misrepresents his life, but material on Ginther has been lacking to combat the mistruths.

The last 20 years or so have allowed Richie's friends, family and fans to redress the balance to some degree through some magazine articles. Clearly, though, considering how many times I was asked about 'the trailer in the desert' in face-to-face or phone conversations while I researched material for this book shows that even those in the sport were unaware and often astonished that for many years he lived happily in a beautiful coastal home.

Considering his achievements in racing it was, at least at the start of this project, surprising to find that no book had ever been written on Richie himself. In truth, my belief – and this was backed up by many people – is that this book is at least probably 20 years too late in one sense. Most of those who raced against Richie or those who knew him best are either no longer with us or too poorly to recollect. As the journey into Richie's life went on, however, it became clearer why a book hasn't been forthcoming in years gone past. 'He kept himself to himself' was a common response from those who not only raced against him but were even on the same team as him as a driver or a mechanic.

But there are still those who carry the flame and with greater opportunity to source archive material, the voices of the past can still join the recollections of the living and Richie's story can be told for posterity. If this book achieves only one thing, it is to – finally – try to put all the erroneous legends about Richie firmly to bed. This book will not rewrite Ginther as a saint but it will allow for some background and some context as to Richie's life and career.

I have discovered many Richie Ginthers while undertaking what has been a greatly enjoyable task. The beatific, always-smiling Richie sits alongside the anti-social argumentative Richie. The Richie Ginther, sports car racer of the 1950s is a totally different beast to the Formula One driver of the mid 1960s. The team-manager Richie is almost alien to just five years previous, and then there is the final Richie of the last ten to fifteen years of his life who is unrecognisable to the man he used to be. It is almost as if Richie died and regenerated into a different character at different stages of his life. I have tried to be as balanced as I can and largely invite the reader to make their own mind up about Richie (or the various Richies as above).

One of the real joys of putting this book together has been the photographs that have been supplied by a number of people. The large majority of them have never been seen before, either in other publications or online. Most of them were taken by fans of the sport at a time that access to the pits and circuit was virtually free-for-all but, despite the photos not being captured by professional photographers, the quality of the images are outstanding. It is greatly satisfying that I can tell a story that hasn't previously been told with photos to illustrate it that haven't previously been shown.

Writing a book is never a singular activity and this would not have come together if it had not been for a number of people. Some

German Grand Prix, 1963. *Archive Nils Ruwisch*

Phil Payne, his wife and Stephen Payne with Richie, 1973. *Steve Payne*

spent only a short time assisting, some spent much, much longer, but they have all taken the time out to help where they could. So, in alphabetical order, I would like to thank Mario Andretti, Lesley Appel, Gerry Ashmore, Gunther Asshauer, Richard Attwood, Darren Banks (who was the soother of many a worry and eased the path for this book to be published), Eric Biggadike, Lionel Birnbom (Ottawa, Canada), Ian Blackwell, Rik Blote, Etienne Bourguignon, Tony Brooks, Allen and Susan Brown, Elizabeth Clare, Gary Critcher (photos from The Supercharged Collection), Peter Darley, Cleo Davidson (without whose initial email and encouragement, this book would never have happened), Hal Davidson, William Edgar, Jerry Entin, Nick Faure, Walter Fooshie, Elliot Forbes-Robinson, David Fox, Paul Foxall, John Gauerke, Graham Gauld, Catherine Ginther, Evi Gurney, Richard Heseltine, Derek Hill, Steve Hirst, Jim Jones at the wonderful Bourne Heritage Centre at Baldocks Mill, Bourne (a lovingly cared for museum which has a whole floor dedicated to BRM), Allen R Kuhn, Kate Lainton, Ronald Lathrop, Preston Lerner, Michael Ling, Pete Lyons, Ed McDonough, Chuck Miller, Milt Minter Jr, Doug Nye, Augie Pabst, Teresa Pavelsky, David Pearson, Patty Reid, Sigurd Reilbach, Arjan de Roos, Nils Ruwisch, Dick Salmon, Jon Saltinstall, Guilherme Sampaio, Tom Schultz, Mike Sims, John and Margaret Sismey, Jim Sitz, Jonathan A Stein, Judy Stropus, Dave Thompson, Brian Tregilgas, Sir Paul Vestey, Ted Walker and Kurt Zimmerman. A special thank you is reserved for Steve Payne who, without his vast collection of Richie Ginther material, articles and subsequent contacts – and then spending a massive amount of time to proof-read and critique as the manuscript developed – this book would not be anywhere near as (I hope) complete as it is. Any mistakes, factual or grammatical, left in are solely mine. Steve's enthusiasm was also key at times of doubt and stress when putting this all together. I also have to thank my parents, David and Angela Jenkins for their tremendous support, encouragement and interest in not only this book but in everything I've ever done.

In addition, I also have to thank the following editors or appropriate employees for allowing permission to use articles or quotes in this book: Casey Annis (*Vintage Racecar*), Juli Burke and Mike Fazioli (*Car and Driver*), Gordon Cruickshank (*Motorsport*), Ralph Drew and Erica Varela (*Los Angeles Times*), Aaron Jenkins (*Forza*), Steve Small (*Autocourse*) and Kevin Turner and Andrew van de Burgt (*Autosport*).

Of course, I also have to thank Adam Wilkins at Performance Publishing for allowing me the chance to write this book. Adam is a fantastic advocate of new writers and is not afraid to take a chance. I sincerely hope I have repaid his faith and support in me.

I have been very lucky to have been in contact with a lot of people who knew Richie, which sadly, is a dwindling number. I think that in another five years, this book may not have even been possible. However, I think it only fair to explain in the introduction, rather than the narrative, that Richie's son, Bret Ginther, gave his support for the book to be written but chose not to be involved with the project personally. Although that has meant an imbalance of photos and memories in certain areas, his decision, which has been pretty consistent since Richie's death, has been fully respected. I can only hope that I have done my best to record Richie's life and career appropriately so that Bret and his daughters can continue to be proud of their father and grandfather.

The final and, arguably, key thanks goes to my wife Amy. She has had to put up with so much when I've been writing this book, not least having to look after three young children which is a full-time job in itself. Despite having virtually zero interest in motor racing (which was not helped by me taking her to a hot, sunny Silverstone while heavily pregnant with our first child and simply expecting her to be entranced and enthralled by either a bunch of old blokes talking and similar looking racing cars whizzing around, which of course, she was not – it was not my wisest ever decision!), she has always been encouraging and allowed me the time and space to do this. She has watched me with, I guess, faint bemusement when I blather on that I have just spoken to 'such and such' on the phone and helped me when the stress got a bit too much sometimes. She has supported me from the beginning to the end and was a colossal help with the photos for this book. Quite simply, I could not, despite all the help of all the people above, have done this book without her. Thank you and all my love.

Hollywood Heritage

"Richie is a cerebral person. He thinks about things, but he also has a sense of the importance of history and the continuity of life"
James T Crow, Sportscar magazine

Richie Ginther, Spa, 1965. *Etienne Bourguignon*

Richie Ginther, or to be more precise, Paul Richard Ginther (he was still styling himself and signing official letters as Paul R Ginther until at least 1959), was born in Hollywood, California, on 5 August 1930 to Ernest John Ginther and Hazel Mae Sagle. Richie's family background, albeit a few generations previous, was German; his paternal great-grandfather Zekariah Ginther and great-grandmother Dorothy Lindeman travelled from Germany and settled near Hazeltown, Pennsylvania, in the early 1860s.

Despite Hollywood being his place of birth, it plays virtually no part in Richie's story. He often mentioned that he hailed from Glendale, and nearby Granada Hills, Santa Monica, and Culver City were to become more significant in the Ginther story than his birthplace. The exact reason for his preference for his middle name and the subsequent choice of hypocorism has remained unclear, but he was known as Richie from a very young age.

Richie was the youngest of three children, with his elder brother George Ernest arriving on 7 July 1927 and sister Bonita Mae, who was born just over one year later, on 13 July 1928. Despite being quite close in age to his elder siblings, Ginther said to his second wife Cleo (Davidson as she now is) that he felt quite solitary as a child. Part of this was because he was born with a heart murmur, which had he been born today would have been checked and controlled. But this was Depression Era America and, as such, Richie grew up to be a sickly child, his illness stunting his development.

As a result, he was discouraged from taking part in the more athletic sports and, as if to enforce this decision, fate intervened when, on one rare occasion Richie did take part in a football (gridiron) match, he had his front tooth knocked out. It was replaced by a gold tooth and, along with the fact that Ginther was small in stature, saw him repeatedly picked on and bullied at school. Traumatic events in a child's youth can affect them in numerous ways, but in Richie's case it appeared to both make him somewhat insular but, more importantly, determined to overcome adversity.

The Ginther family initially moved to Dayton, Ohio (or rather, moved back to be near George Ginther, Richie's paternal grandfather, and the wider family), relatively shortly after Richie's birth, before moving back to California and Santa Monica in 1935. His sickness did not help the family finances at such a crucial and fiscally difficult time in America's history. Cleo tells that the strain on finances caused by Richie's ill-health drove an irreversible wedge in the relationship between mother and son, "His mum, Hazel, repeatedly told her son that he owed her due to him needing more care as a boy. One day Rich, fed up, came back from the Korean War and simply said 'Okay, how much do I owe you then?' Very coldly, she actually sat down and figured out an amount! Rich then went to work hard and lived as frugally as he could until he had the amount. Once he paid his mother off, he never spoke to her again". Hazel Therien, as she then was, died on 19 October 1981, aged 79, in Carson City, where she moved to be closer to Bonita (Bonnie). Her obituary makes no mention of her son being a famous racing driver, merely that she was a retired restaurant manager and a member of the First Christian Church of Mill City. (For completion,

Ferrari headed letter written by Richie. Note that it is signed as Paul R Ginther.
Steve Payne

Bonita died on 22 January 1993. Despite being only 64 at her death, she was the only child of Ernest and Hazel to reach her 60s.)

Ginther, aside from the guilt put upon him, appears to have had a difficult relationship with his mother. With his father busy at work, Richie often mentioned in later life to Cleo that he never really had any guidance from his parents and did not, mainly through sickness, take part in a lot of typical childhood activities. His childhood was not the life of *The Hardy Boys*, for example, full of adventure and action. One thing Ginther never forgot was that, as a young boy, his mother told him that hummingbirds had long beaks specifically for pecking people's eyes out, which whatever the reasoning behind it, seems a particularly strange thing to tell any child, let alone your youngest offspring.

Michael Ling, in his article in *Automobile Quarterly* that was published in 2000, is one of the few writers to have interviewed Richie's first wife Jackie Ginther (and, to a lesser degree, their son Bret) at some length. The view from Jackie is the same as Cleo in terms of parental relationships. Richie was extremely close to his father and not really close to his mother. But Ling, through Jackie, suggests that Hazel Ginther was actually over-protective, possibly far too much so considering the hummingbird story, of her son, probably due to his sickness at an early age. The other thing that appeared to drive a wedge in their relationship is Hazel's focus on social standing and the effort to keep up appearances. She was slightly obsessive in projecting a grandiose portrayal of Ginther life than was reality. A sick child probably did not help social climbing in the slightest. Perhaps the greatest sign of Richie's family rift is how little they feature in any article or any interview about Richie's life and career, with the exception that Richie's brother was Phil Hill's classmate. There's no mention of Hazel at any stage other than the article below.

Maybe the distance between Richie and his mother was, as Ling and Jackie Ginther said, just down to much over-protectiveness. As Richie recalled to *Sportscar* magazine in 1972, "It was constantly impressed on me by my mother that I must not do anything that would tax my strength. I mustn't run. I mustn't roller skate. I mustn't ride a bicycle. I mustn't play strenuous games. I had to be careful, always. Don't do anything; your heart won't stand it. Well, I was a boy. This was a severe constraint. On the plus side, though, I learnt exercising control, patience, restraint and self-discipline which did help in later years."

Because Ginther was not allowed to run and play, he had to do things he could do by himself. If his parents had lots of books, music or other artistic things, then Richie Ginther may have had a different life. But his father used his hands and he was a practical man. So Richie learnt from an early age to put things together and take them apart, developing an appreciation for mechanical objects and what leads to the individual parts working together.

However, like any family facing financial challenges, there were luxuries from time to time. As a treat on every American Independence Day, on 4 July, Ernest Ginther would spend any spare money on fireworks. Richie adored fireworks as a child and did so for the rest of his life. Once, as Cleo and her brother Rik Blote recall, it nearly saw him miss a race. The evening before a race at Daytona Beach in 1965, Richie was in a boisterous mood with some friends and left their hotel to go out for a meal. As they pulled out of the hotel driveway, Richie let off a huge firecracker and tossed it out of the window. However, he had failed to notice a police car coming up behind them and it exploded below the undercarriage of the police car. The result was an overnight stay in jail and a severe reprimand for Richie, but he was allowed out to race.

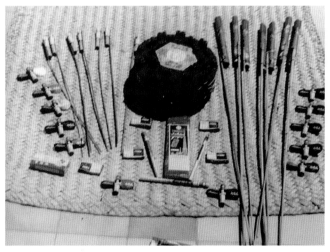

Richie Ginther's arsenal for the 4 July celebrations. *Paul Huf/Cleo Davidson*

This experience did not dissuade him from his love of fireworks. Like his father before him, even when money was tight, Richie would spend a lot of money on fireworks for a large 4 July celebration. When he lived in his coastal home in Baja, Mexico, the house had a concrete parapet overlooking the sea. As a result, the fireworks could be seen for miles with people congregating on the beach to both watch and then, with encouragement from Richie, bring their own fireworks to make one large arsenal for all to enjoy. Cleo Davidson recalls, "It was great fun. Every summer, though I have always had long hair, I'd have one or two short tufts where sparks landed on my head and I'd have to wait for the hair to grow back!"

Generally, though, money was tight and every cent counted. This kind of family dynamic might have possibly pushed Richie to work more as a boy and certainly meant he had a lot of obstacles to overcome to succeed. He sold *Life* magazines outside his father's place of work for a one cent profit. His paternal grandfather, George, was a blacksmith who moved the family from Pennsylvania to Dayton in Ohio, but the need for work saw Ernest, who initially followed his father by also working as a blacksmith, move his young family westwards to California on two occasions, once in the late 1920s and then again in 1935. In the latter move, Ernest then settled down and worked as a toolmaker for the Douglas Aircraft Company in Santa Monica. In an interview in 1972 with *Sportscar* magazine, Richie was very much inspired by his ancestors and interviewer James T Crow wrote, "Richie is a cerebral person. He thinks about things, but he also has a sense of the importance of history and the continuity of life. His ability to work with his hands and to understand mechanical things is important to him not only because this is the way he makes his living but also because it is a part of a continuing tradition. His grandfather was a blacksmith, his father a tool-and-die maker and Richie regards himself as an engineer though he holds no degrees from institutions of formal learning. Talking about his son, Bret, now ten, he says, "I hope I can pass some of this tradition onto him, as my father did to me, and my grandfather did to my father. When a toy breaks, for example, I don't say, we'll buy a new one, I say, we'll fix it'." Cleo, Richie's second wife said one of Richie's prized possessions is a hammer that his grandfather made, which Richie kept all his life and is still in Cleo's possession.

As Richie grew up, he was keen to work, and now healthier, eager to make up for lost time. In 1944, he found work at a gas station, initially as an attendant and then subsequently as a mechanic. An initial passing interest in motorcycles and then cars became much more of an obsession and with Richie picking up a lot of practical and mechanical skills from his father, used the $80 he had earned from pumping gas all summer long "with no movies and no milkshakes" to buy a 1932 Chevrolet Coupé, which he subsequently learnt to rebuild so that it was customised and ready when he gained his driving licence a few years later. As Richie told *Car and Driver* in 1961, "That Chevrolet meant everything to me. Nothing exotic was done to the Chevy, I just added dual pipes, that's about all."

In an interview with Kitte Turmell many years later, specifically aimed at teenagers who were looking to buy their first car, Ginther confessed that he was not the careful driver he was renowned for

The assembly line at Douglas Aircraft, Santa Monica, 1938. **US Navy National Museum of Naval Aviation**

decades later: "Sure I got carried away with driving when I started. I drove too fast and did not watch out for the other fellow. Lots of laws did not make sense to me. But then I learned that good driving is common sense and it's smart to obey the laws. You expect that others will."

Richie later admitted, in an interview with Jerry Sloniger for *The Autocourse* annual in 1961, his mechanical experience at this time was quite limited: "I had no formal engineering training, apart from taking all the mechanical shops I could in school. I took machine shop and auto shop and mechanical drawing and things like that. Right after school I went to work for Douglas Aircraft in tool and die and you have to read blueprints and understand why things are done a certain way – not just how. You learn a lot about materials for instance."

Richie recalled to Pete Lyons in 1988 for *Car and Driver* magazine that "Out of the three children, I was the one interested in mechanics; it was always what I saw myself doing; I always enjoyed and still do enjoy machinery; especially specialised machinery; cameras, guns, fighter planes, race cars; something with a single intent." Long-time friend Jim Sitz remembers what happened when he showed his camera to Richie: "When I first met Richie in 1955, he was absolutely fascinated by my new wonder camera, which was the Swedish Hasselblad. Richie obviously knew a fine piece of

equipment when he saw it. He fiddled around with it a bit and kept telling his mechanic all about it!"

Apart from machine and auto shop at school, normal schoolwork bored him and, by his own admission, his grades were pretty terrible. It was probably a good thing that the Douglas Aircraft job which came about largely through his father, was there as a fallback option; Richie working in the same jig and tool division of the company as Ernest.

The fact that the Ginther family moved to Santa Monica so that they could be close to Ernest's place of work was a fortuitous move as it turned out for Richie's future life and career. A very short distance (in fact, just two-and-a-half blocks away, four consecutive left turns from Richie's home) from the family home was a young man who owned a Jaguar XK120. For Richie, who had worked his way through the Chevrolet and then subsequently a Ford V8 ("That car was extensively modified but in a conservative manner. It had cast iron heads, not aluminium and a modest cam. It was kind of an old-fashioned car but everything worked together as a unit,") and a Dodge Sedan, a chance to see and also help work on the Jaguar with the owner was a huge attraction. The owner was no less than a man who would become entwined in Richie's racing life and someone would be a motor racing World Champion less than fifteen years later – Phil Hill.

International Motors

"Phil [Hill] has always been instrumental in
whatever I've done. If I had not met Phil,
I don't know what I'd be doing now"
Richie Ginther

Richie's first race – giving it all at the Sandberg Hill Climb. *Robert E Canaan/The Revs Institute*

It was not by chance that Richie met Phil. Hill knew George Ginther through school and also worked at Douglas Aircraft with Ernest and, in February 1948, Richie also joined the workforce at Douglas, where he worked for eighteen months. But he was never really happy and got quite exasperated by the clock ruling everything in terms of being timed, how quickly he made things, how much break he had, what time he arrived, what time he left and so on. But of the three Ginther males, it was Richie who was the car fanatic and, subsequently, when Hill competed in sports cars, Richie became one of his mechanics. Motor racing historian Doug Nye remembers that Phil Hill recalled to him, when discussing Richie, that he didn't particularly warm to George, mainly because George chose to drink quite heavily almost as a hobby. Phil had first-hand experience of how drink had destroyed family and friends' lives and, aside from Richie's mechanical prowess and enthusiasm, Phil also took to the younger brother's personality. Richie's frustration with the clock at Douglas would also have a significant impact in later life.

In an interview with *Car and Driver* in 1961, Richie made it very clear where his pathway to racing had started. "My interest in racing stemmed from knowing Phil. Phil has always been instrumental in whatever I've done. If I had not met Phil, I don't know what I'd be doing now; maybe I'd be driving as fast as I could in a straight line on the salt flats or maybe I'd be working in a gas station or digging ditches. He was so enthusiastic! He was the first one who ever started telling me how to drive a car, you know what I mean, how to drive it fast. We got plenty of speeding tickets. What I'm doing now, it is all his fault. But, you know, he has an interest in old cars. Well, that hasn't rubbed off on me yet."

Richie then followed Hill in working at International Motors, the Californian dealers for MG, Jaguars and Mercedes-Benz cars, among other sidelines. International Motors had a devotion to racing high on its priority list as the local agent, Roger Barlow, raced in California Sports Car Club and Sports Car Club of America events.

International Motors was, arguably, the main place to go if you wanted sports cars in Los Angeles and Southern California. It was the first foreign car showroom in the whole of the United States after World War Two and attracted immense interest, not least from the world of showbiz.

The owner was Roger Barlow, who was very much ahead of his time in terms of selling automobiles and noticing, appreciating and capitalising on foreign cars in the American market. Barlow wrote for *Autocar* magazine both before World War Two and after hostilities had ended. He also wrote for *Road & Track* magazine, specialising in French, Italian and British cars. Barlow founded the Californian Sports Car Club to promote and take part in racing around California in the late 1940s racing himself in sports cars, often in his Simca Special 8 roadster.

International Motors had two locations. The first was 5670 Sunset Boulevard where the showroom was based, and the second was at 8741 Alden Drive where the service workshop was based. The former would have such makes as MG, Jaguar, Healey and Talbot-Darracq and also sold Nordec superchargers. Alden Drive, however, would be the shop that Ginther would go to.

The showroom at International Motors, Sunset Boulevard. *Steve Payne*

Jim Sitz, a lifelong friend of both Phil Hill and Richie Ginther, remembers Roger Barlow and International Motors very well. "I first met Roger in the summer of 1949, where he had just opened the facility at Sunset Boulevard. He was a pioneer in the imported car business. He started to import cars in the same year that World War Two ended, initially with British cars, but kept an eye on other countries too. He was a man of vision and had real flair to promote the cars in the movie community with all the connections he had.

"I also knew his partner, Louie van Dyke, who was carefree and had worked at MGM Studios (he was the son of the film director Woody WS van Dyke) and invested in the new firm and used his contacts to help the firm. The movie, *Drive a Crooked Road* was released in 1954 and starred Mickey Rooney as a car mechanic and racing driver. A lot of the scenes and action were filmed at International Motors and revolved around it.

"It truly was International Motors in reality as well as name. There was Bernard Cahier from France as a salesman. He had a cute little accent which was popular with the ladies and in 1954, he was hired to become European Correspondent for *Road & Track* magazine. John von Neumann from Vienna was on the sales floor. In the shop you had two Americans in Phil Hill and Richie Ginther and an Englishman, Phil Payne. The service manager was Taylor Lucas who drove a Hotchkiss in a few races. Then there was Elliot Forbes-Robinson whose son would later drive for Richie; Jim Thrall the mechanic and then a sales lady from Ireland called Fay Taylour, who raced motorcycles and racing cars before the war.

It really was the place to go and buy the best cars. The Jaguar and Simca cars did well, partly as they were racing and winning, which boosted their reputation. The showrooms were glamorous and the likes of Clark Gable, Gary Cooper and Bing Crosby all bought cars there. There really was no other place like it. They did very well in 1951 with Aston Martin cars. They imported a pair of coupés in gunmetal, pre-sold one to the musical director at the MGM studio, a man named Johnny Green, and then they demonstrated the other one which was driven by Phil Hill for a test for *Road & Track*. Hill liked it so much he bought it! Forty years later I kidded Hill of what a hot shot salesman he was, buying a $5800 car!

"Now I previously mentioned Cahier and *Road & Track*. The magazine was based just ten miles away and so the two were close and interconnected; what was good for one was also good for the other. Both firms struggled to succeed at one point and, in fact, the magazine almost went under in December 1952 as it owed $80,000 to the printer, but it soldiered on. *Road & Track* not only gave International Motors exposure, it also greatly helped Phil Hill with his exposure via his track tests. Of course, International Motors gave *Road & Track* access to cars to both test and advertise, so it worked hand-in-hand really. I'm sure it helped Richie a little bit too as they remembered him from his International Motors days.

"Richie Ginther and Hill made a number of road trips all across America to deliver cars to their customers. I am sure this helped both of them in their own way with driving in years to come. It's certainly the reason the pair did the Carrera Panamericana together as they became very used to driving with each other over long distances.

"Roger really was truly a remarkable man who made his name in creating documentary films, winning an award for one about the New York World's Fair of 1939. He celebrated his win by buying a Talbot Lago from a lady who had escaped the troubles in Europe.

"He became the Mercedes-Benz importer in 1952, but the whole Mercedes-Benz venture turned out to be a mistake, with insufficient buyers. Eighteen months later, International Motors, next door to Grauman's Chinese Theatre, closed its doors in March 1954. Ironically, this was about the time the film with Mickey Rooney was released in the cinema, so really bad timing!"

After joining the business in 1950 on Phil Hill's recommendation, Ginther was assigned to race preparation and in particular to Bill Cramer, who also raced against Hill in sports cars.

Richie recalled in an interview some years later: "Phil was a mechanic at International Motors and so I went to sports car club meetings with him. He had a long delivery to make and I took some leave and went with him. We drove a Rolls-Royce to Palm Beach. Then we picked up an older Rolls and drove them both to New York. Then we flew to Houston, picked up a Simca 8 sport and drove to Los Angeles. Phil knew I was getting tired of Douglas and we talked a lot on the trip. When we got back, he got me a job as a mechanic at International Motors. That was in July of 1950."

By this time, Richie was part of Phil's racing crew, acting as mechanic, pit board man and supporter. Phil Hill's win at Pebble Beach in 1950 in a Jaguar XK120 launched his career rapidly skywards but as has been recalled in a couple of books, the eager

A Bugatti for sale at International Motors. *Jim Sitz*

Roger Barlow and Phil Payne outside the showroom. **Steve Payne**

Richie and the determined Phil almost accidently combined to lose an impressive win. The best account comes from the opus *Inside Track: Phil Hill, Ferrari's American World Champion – His Story, His Photography*, a collaboration between Phil, his son Derek and historian Doug Nye: "My pal Arnold Stubbs – who was becoming quite a good driver – led in the Cramer Brother's V8-engined MG special. I was making progress and passed some people. Stubbs went into the pits, leaving Mike Graham's Allard-Cadillac leading two XKs, Bill Breeze in second, with me right on his tail in third. Then Allard shot up an escape road, so Breeze was first and I was second. I could smell the brakes on Breeze's car and sure enough I got ahead and he retired next time around.

"Coming past the pits, Richie held out a chalkboard pit signal reading 'LONG LEAD'. Who was this guy Long? Stubbs had just been in sight on the main straight when I thought he was leading, so had Long been ahead of him? I was desperate to win the race so I drove harder and harder. I was sliding wide in the turns, bouncing off straw bales and even visited the escape road. At the pits, Richie waved another chalkboard signal, this time reading 'ONE'. Again I agonised feverishly over its meaning. One lap to go? Still not a sight of this guy Long's leading car, so I figured it was all over. But next time round there was no chequered flag, and only then did I realise I must be leading. 'Long lead' had described my lead. How dumb could I get? There were seven laps left to run. My Jaguar was clutchless and by this time brakeless. My brother-in-law Donnie Parkinson was up into second place and gaining but I pressed on until Al Torres finally waved the chequered flag."

1951 would prove to be a tumultuous year for Richie. He moved from International Motors to Bill Cramer's Chrysler-Plymouth dealership after impressing Cramer so much that Bill offered Richie a job at his own firm. It might seem strange that there is so much focus above on International Motors when Richie was there for just one year, but the links with Cahier, von Neumann, *Road & Track* and the road trips he shared with Phil Hill all were significant in his later racing career. If he hadn't had joined International Motors, he may not have joined Phil at the Carrera Panamericana and may not have started his own attempts at racing.

Richie began his racing career competing in the Sandberg Hillclimb Ridge Route in April 1951, driving Cramer's MG TC

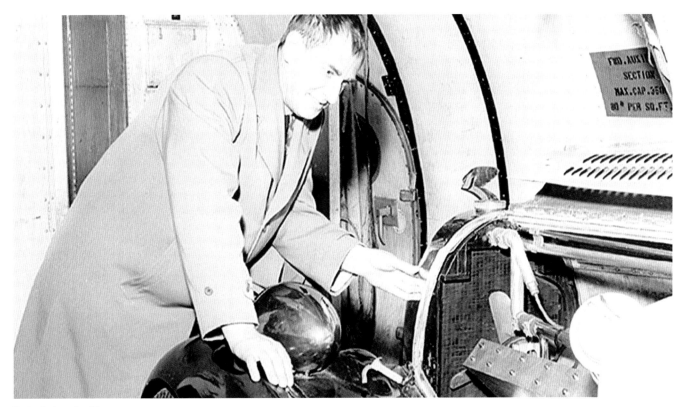

Roger Barlow. *Jim Sitz*

2 Junior Ford V8 but suffered an early crash, before setting the fifth fastest time. Ginther, in an interview with Pete Lyons in 1988 recalled, "I actually attribute the later success to the practice. If you spun, you could race again, rather than it being the end of your effort. I spun two or three times and always got another chance, each time learning the route more and more". In the last days of May, he made his own sports car debut, again in a Cramer-entered MG with a small-block Ford V8-60 engine, at Pebble Beach. He competed in the Del Monte Handicap, a ten-lap race. Here he was successful, finishing second on the road behind Phil Hill in his 1939 Alfa Romeo 8C-2900B, but was later demoted to third due to what the organisers deemed an illegal pass by Ginther performing the utterly heinous act of passing on the right!

However, he took home his first ever trophy from racing – he won 'Mechanic of the Meet' where he helped three different drivers, including Hill, prepare their machines. In a 1972 interview with James T Crow, Ginther said that he still was very proud of that and also that he still had that trophy in his possession.

Every racing driver has varying reasons as to why they began racing. For many, it is because of family interest, other drivers are swept off their feet by their first race meeting. For Richie, it was slightly different. As he explained many years later to *Car and Driver*, although racing was a serious business requiring attention and work, the reason he took up racing was because "It's one of the few lives of adventure left. Everyone wants adventure; some guys get it with girls; some get it with money, some get it with gambling. We're all looking for a more adventurous way of life. For me, driving is the most convenient adventure."

But then followed a hiatus from not only racing, but all he had known thus far. Drafted on his 21st birthday, Ginther joined the United States Army, serving both as a helicopter and automobile mechanic in a two-year stint that included a spell in Korea. But his time there, as harrowing as it would have been on occasions, also set him up for his future career as he explained to the *Autocourse* annual in 1961: "I went to aircraft mechanics school and the engine mechanics school. I learned a tremendous amount. Things you accept but don't go into. All this has aided me when it came to being a test driver for Ferrari."

However, there would be yet more upheaval for Ginther, early into his Korean service. On 19 November 1951, his father, Ernest, died of a heart attack aged only 50, largely caused by heart disease. Although Richie hinted in a 1961 interview with *Car and Driver* that there might have been more pressures on Ernest, without specifically naming him, than were originally obvious. This was, to put it in context, when Richie was discussing about his own life expectancy while driving a racing car: "Our odds of getting killed are worse than some guy working at Douglas Aircraft, but a lot of those guys spend their lives worrying about who is going to get their job and then they die of a heart attack." Tragically, both of Ernest's sons would die from heart disease before they were 60. George Ginther, a US Navy veteran who saw action in World War Two, was only 48 when he died on 10 December 1975.

A two-year spell away from home serving their country could sometimes have ramifications for a number of young men, but in Richie's case, his return saw no real difference in his working life. In fact, a new and successful chapter in his life was about to begin.

West Coast Racing

"Phil Hill has been the American star of the
Ferrari factory team for three years. But I'm also concerned about
Richie Ginther in his 4.1-litre Ferrari"
Stirling Moss

Richie with the Ferrari 340 at the Carrera Panamericana, 1953. *The Hill Family Archive*

After Richie's return from Korea in 1953, he linked up again with Phil Hill, who, like Ginther, not only lost his father in 1951, but, tragically, his mother as well. Hill used Richie as his riding mechanic for the 1953 Carrera Panamericana, driving a Ferrari 340 Vignale Mexico coupé entered by Allen Guiberson, but a crash between Puebla and Mexico City ended their adventure and almost ended their lives. On the second day, Hill went into a curve too fast, spun off the road backwards, rolled down a twenty-foot embankment before landing on some rocks, crucially, the right way up.

Hill recalled it in some detail to Eoin Young, which Young then recorded in an article in 2001 for *Classic Cars*, "We'd just topped a steep rise and here was a mean, curling, downhill turn, a right-hander. My foot was on the brake pedal, but we had a lot of fade and not enough brake left to do the job. We began to slide towards the edge, and mentally I was considering how far down we'd fall – because at our speed we were sure as hell going over. Now some drops are sheer, down hundreds of feet and you don't stand a prayer – and we did not know about this one. We slid off backwards, bouncing end over end down the jagged rock slope of the mountain for maybe forty to fifty feet – boom, bang, bang, bong! When we stopped bouncing, the Ferrari's top was caved in. I shouted 'You OK, Rich?' and he said yeah, he was, and we got out fast. Mexican spectators had removed the corner sign and were perched on the rocks watching it all unfold!"

Many years ago, Ginther also commented about the incident and this is his take on the events: "The Mexican Road Race came about when I was awaiting discharge up at Fort Ord. I got a weekend pass and came down to Los Angeles and saw Phil. He mentioned Mexico and said, 'Why don't you come to Mexico with me?' or something like that and I, of course, agreed. I had only raced twice before I went in the service.

"Phil and I flew to Dallas, where the car was being prepared, in November of 1953. We helped finish the work on the car. But the thing is some of the major teams were down there a week ahead of time, and our car was trucked down to Juarez, the El Paso border town, and we then drove the car down the Pan American Highway. What we did was create a logbook driving down to the starting point, Tuxtla Gutierrez, running the course backwards. That was our practice for the race. When we came upon a particularly difficult section, why, we'd go beyond it, turn around and come back so as to go through it in the racing direction. It took a while to get to Tuxtla, at least a week, I don't remember exactly, but that's the only way we could do it. Ours was a limited effort, and it almost turned out pretty well for our sponsor, Allen Guiberson.

"The race stretched ahead of us, 1909 miles: eight legs in five days of racing, and elevation changes from 328ft at Tehuantepec, the lowest point, to 10,482ft at some spot between Puebla and Mexico City. To give you an idea, the course went through Ocozocuautla (after Tuxtla and Tehuantepec), Oaxaca, Yanhuitlan, Tehuitzingo, the high ground just mentioned, Las Cruces, Leon, Zacatecas, Durango, Parral, Meoqui, Chihuahua and Ciudad Juarez. The factory made our coupé that first year specifically for the race. It had aerodynamic devices on it for brake cooling and attempts at

streamlining. It was quite fast, but we were totally outclassed by the factory-backed competition. Predictably, we did not do too well that first year.

"Puebla is where we stayed that first night and did whatever had to be done to make the car raceworthy again the next day. Then we were coming down out of the mountains towards Mexico City, and there was one spot which was pretty dangerous, and we probably did not have it marked that well on our logbooks. So, anyway, Phil lost it going into the turn and we went off the side backwards. The car went upside down and came back and righted itself on its wheels on a pile of rocks. You then saw two doors burst open and two people just split away from the car in 180 degrees from each other. We were both OK, neither one of us hurt or anything. And both of us were obviously pretty scared. We stayed there kind of looking down at the car there was a lot of smoke from being upside down, oil spilling on the headers, but no fire. Then we heard something else coming. This one was coming in such a manner that we knew it was not going to make the corner, either, even though other cars had gone by after our accident. I can't remember who it was, somebody in a big Lincoln and so, soon there were four of us sitting, down there on the rocks, and for quite a while before the people came back down there to pick us and the cars up. [Author note: I can't verify this as I can't see a Lincoln car that crashed out after Hill and Ginther in the race results, however I think he is referring to George Clark and Chuck Royal's Cadillac Series 62 car that crashed just yards away from Hill and Ginther's stricken car.]

"Juan Manuel Fangio's Lancia won that year, 909 miles in 18 hours, 11 minutes. I did not do anything after that, worked around cars as much as I could, but as far as my race-driving career, nothing really progressed during 1954."

The duo, although generally prepared and quite savvy, were a little unprepared for the differences this epic event had over the sports car racing they had done thus far. They had to endure or learn from a number of incidents; the truck carrying their car broke down, they had problems with batteries, wheels, spark plugs and tyre consumption but, worst of all, was that their race route notes were written down clearly and concisely, with what they thought was well-detailed, well prepared observations, before they realised that the direction they would be racing on the roads they had studied was actually the opposite to their prep work!

Richie recalled a few years later about the general experience: "Riding with anyone in a race that dangerous can be frightening but I had known Phil for at least six years by then and I knew his reactions just as well as I knew my own. I teased him by saying Uncle Phil's taking me racing! I'd been up and down every canyon road along the whole Pacific Coast with him in Ferraris, Alfas, MGs and so forth, so I trusted his driving completely. I was not much use to him however. It was all new to me and Phil had not made any log from when he did the race the previous year".

The duo returned in 1954 in a Ferrari 375 MM Vignale Spyder (another Guiberson entered car) and finished second, twenty-four seconds behind Umberto Maglioli and over a minute-and-a-half ahead of Hans Herrmann's Mercedes. The calibre of the field they beat convincingly included a number of established grand prix and

Indianapolis 500 drivers; Sergio Mantovani, Consalvo Sanesi, Keith Andrews, Bill Vukovich and Roberto Mieres to name just a few. "I was a lot more help to Phil that year," recalled Richie to *Sports Car Journal* in 1957 and in a later interview in 1970: "We took it down from Juarez and did much the same as the year before, plus we had the log book from the year before and we had updated it coming back the other way; so we were prepared. It seems like we were the first car through that year and one of the things I can really recall is the Tehuantepec straightaway.

"That's very near the coast on the west side, very near the ocean and we were moving along, going at whatever the speed the car would do, at 160, 170, 180mph, and the road was right at sea level so it was good and strong and Phil was straddling the centre line. That was our safety margin as the road did not leave too much margin on either side for, say, a tyre failure. So there was a local Indian lying with his feet at the edge of the road and his head at the centre line. We missed that guy's head by a foot or so and he's sound asleep with his sombrero over his face. I turned around and looked back in time to see him horizontal, only about a foot off the pavement. Every muscle came alive, flexed all at once, and he was still just as parallel as he had ever been. The last I saw, he was disappearing off into the jungle.

"We knew what was coming. When I'd see a blind turn rushing up, I'd signal the speed at which it could be taken. This meant we would

go through either fast, slow or flat-out, because we did not figure it out in miles per hour. When Phil got in the groove and starting whipping through I might motion slow down if I thought he was pushing a trifle too hard. That way we were able to work as a team. You don't really think about how fast you're going. The start is all chaos and you're too excited to be worried. Fifteen minutes later, you're starting to get settled and you're doing 160mph. We did back off on the long Tehuantepec straight because we did not particularly like being guinea pigs for some tyre manufacturer and that's where Maglioli passed us in the 4.9. Because we drove off the cliff the previous year, all I could often say was slow down!

"Then, that second year, when we came to that section of road near Puebla, near Mexico City, I was a total damper on the whole thing. When we came to that turn that we'd gone off of the year before, I was absolutely numb. I'm sure there was some kind of acknowledgment to each other when we were past, if it was just a raising of an eyebrow, or just glance. But we were really too busy to elaborate.

"That year, there was some doubt about the race being held or, I can't remember what it was, because the car was being prepared on the West Coast. Not by Phil and me, but by somebody else. They decided to run the car at March Air Force Base in a road race. Then after that race was over, they decided it was going to Mexico. That was the 4.5 with the fin on the tail and, if you recall, it was white and blue.

"We won several legs that year, outright, and set a few records on an overall time basis, and at the end of the event we were within striking distance of Umberto Maglioli, who won in a privately owned Ferrari. We went through thirteen states and the federal district of Mexico that year and, of 151 cars, only 85 finished. Maglioli completed the distance in 17 hours, 40 minutes and 26 seconds of racing time over five days, not counting the overnight stops, which were required. We were second. In 1955, I began to get rides of my own and I did not have to go back, although I would have."

This result was the springboard for Richie to try and establish himself as a driver, as he says above, and although he raced a few times in 1954, including in a Triumph TR2, in 1955 he stepped up his sports car efforts in an Austin-Healey 100 which he prepared himself; "The Healey is a wonderful competition car to start out with and I brought home a lot of Class D firsts with that machine," said Ginther in 1957. His efforts proved worthwhile as, among other early successes, he won the Stock Austin-Healey Class at the Singer Owners' Club Hill Climb at Agoura. But racing in sports cars had not been the original plan for Richie, for he was due to accompany Hill to Europe as a mechanic, co-driver and maybe an occasional driver for Allen Guiberson. Guiberson did not want to enter Le Mans but was keen on the shorter continental races planned after the event. Phil decided to enter Le Mans anyway, but with his old Carrera Panamericana sparring partner Umberto Maglioli in a works Ferrari 121 LM. Richie would attend as a mechanic and visitor. This plan was scuppered early with the Le Mans tragedy curtailing any other planned racing for them, and so the pair of them concentrated on racing on home soil.

Richie and Phil Hill, Carrera Panamericana, 1954. *Aramedis Ed McDonough*

Richie and the Ferrari 375 MM. **The Hill Family Archive**

However, the Le Mans tragedy left a real impact on Richie and his approach to racing. In an interview with *The San Francisco Examiner* in November 1958, Richie reflected, "I hope I never lose the sense of responsibility driven home to me by that disaster. I try to remember that any carelessness on my part might claim the lives of others." Certainly, given the fair way he raced and the focus by him on mechanical sympathy seems to reflect that he never truly forgot the horrific scenes which left 84 people dead. Also in 1959, in an interview with *Road & Track*, Richie said a similar thing but used his own experiences: "The crash at the Carrera Panamericana and a big spin into a ditch at Santa Barbara keep sticking in my mind; it constantly reminds me that there is just a fraction of a second that exists between control and disaster".

The crash at Santa Barbara, in particular, never strayed far from Richie's mind because, for him, it was one of the most embarrassing moments he had as a driver: "I was handling an Aston Martin in the rain and Bob Drake was dicing with me in another Aston. It was pouring cats and dogs and we were on our last lap. Bob had caught me and coming around Turn Nine onto the pit straight we were virtually side by side. Here we were, in two identical cars, dashing wheel to wheel for the chequered flag and I thought this was amusing. I looked over my shoulder at Bob and gave him a big smile.

"Suddenly I was going sideways. I had failed to pay strict enough attention to my correct line out of the turn and here I am heading straight for a pylon and about six parked cars. So I just let it spin around and off the road, I went backwards into a ditch. I'll tell you, I felt, and still feel, pretty damned stupid about this."

Richie smiling for the camera. **Allen R Kuhn**

The start of one of the sports car races at Bakersfield, 1956. WR Turner is in car 30, Richie in 211, William Darnold in car 241 and Troy McHenry in car 56.
Archive Bjorn Schlichting

Richie placed well at various tracks including Bakersfield and Pebble Beach and soon after this he caught the eye of John von Neumann. Von Neumann, who to be totally frank could have a whole book written about him alone, was an Austrian émigré to California who, among other interests, worked at International Motors alongside Richie, before setting up his own successful service shop and dealership, Competition Motors, in North Hollywood in 1951. At the time, Von Neumann entered a plethora of cars in multiple classes in a variety of Southern Californian races and was also a Porsche importer. He signed Richie to drive the Porsche 550 in a swathe of Sports Car Club of America (SCCA) events but had first made his name by driving MG cars. Von Neumann started off by selling Hillman, MG and Simca cars before going on to become the Western importer for Ferrari, Porsche and Volkswagen which all come into play later in this book.

Von Neumann first properly met Ginther in 1954 when Richie was helping Phil Hill out. Hill was working on von Neumann's Ferrari and Richie mucked in. Von Neumann was put out about who this interloper was until Richie showed him how he had tuned it. He impressed von Neumann enough by how he kept the cars in top condition and had a genuine interest in them. So von Neumann got him to work as a tuner, then as a tester and then subsequently as a driver, by saying to Richie, without any prior warning "Rich, this weekend you can drive the 550 Porsche at Santa Barbara." Ginther recalled the moment: "Well, I did not know he had two 550s! I was astounded, delighted, dumbfounded. I'm not very good at expressing myself in situations like that and I don't think Mr von Neumann knew how much it meant to me."

Richie's long-time friend Jim Sitz said, "I always regarded von Neumann as one lucky bugger. But Richie thought the world of him

John von Neumann's workshop. *Jim Sitz*

Richie and Cy Yedor, Paramount Ranch, 18 August 1956. *Jim Sitz*

Richie at Santa Barbara, 1956. *Jim Sitz*

and thought that he was smart. Jackie, Richie's first wife, did not share that opinion at all," and Richie's second wife Cleo, formerly also married to von Neumann herself, does not share the same kind of fondness that Richie did for the Austrian. Jim continues, "John was certainly the chaser of women, with some reputation of conquests all over Hollywood and beyond. He was a rake, really. He was terribly selfish when it came to women. His lust for them cost him dearly. His divorce from Eleanor was very expensive and he lost the Ferrari dealership to her; all a result of him chasing after a Las Vegas showgirl. I remember him coming to the 85th birthday party for Briggs Cunningham in January 1992 and seeking ladies there, and ignoring his then wife, Monica, who was really nice and very attractive, a tall black woman who could have been a model. [Author note: Monica von Neumann, who died in 2019, aged just 53, was indeed a model and dancer before marrying von Neumann; she worked for Yves St Laurent and Christian Dior. She was still married to John at his death in 2003.] Yet, he was the opposite with Richie; he could not do more for him if he tried, helped him with a mechanic job, helped him get a good racing car to drive, helped him with his house with one of his ex-wives to boot, helped Richie after he retired and just was always around if Richie needed him. John was also around when Richie probably did not need him as well." More of that later.

By the autumn of 1955, Richie was competing in the Porsche 550 alongside von Neumann and Jack McAfee versus Ken Miles in his MG Special. He also impressed Manning J Post, later to become a big name in Californian politics, but at the time was a Volkswagen dealer in North Hollywood. Richie drove Post's Ferrari 500 Mondial at Glendale towards the end of the 1955 season. In 1956, Ginther took wins at Stockton, Eagle Mountain, Pomona, Santa Maria and twice at Paramount Ranch. He came second in races at Bakersfield (twice), again at Pomona (again twice), Buchanan Field, Santa Barbara and Sacramento to quickly establish himself as one of the best sportscar drivers on the West Coast. As well as this, he came fourth in the Road America 4 Hour race, sharing a Cooper Bobtail T39 with Lance Reventlow and sixth in the Governor's Trophy in a Ferrari 857S, entered by friend and the victor of the Road America 4 Hour race, Carroll Shelby.

The edition of California's *Valley News* on 14 August 1956, when previewing the forthcoming races at Paramount Ranch refers to Richie as "one of the area's top names" alongside Miles, Bob Oker and Bill Krause. By 1957 *The Los Angeles Times* went further, calling Ginther "one of the nation's top sports car drivers" when announcing he was to drive an Aston Martin entered by Joe Lubin at an early-season race at Paramount Ranch. However, competitor Chuck Daigh had a more balanced assessment to Michael Ling for the *Automobile Quarterly* article; "Richie was what I call locally good, not spectacular. But he was a good mechanic and that placed him above other good drivers of his era as he understood what was happening with the car."

Chapter Three

Augie Pabst raced at a similar time as Richie but often in different circles; Pabst was back in the Mid-West while Richie was largely on the West Coast, but there were enough races for the two to lock horns against each other. "We got along fine but he was a very heavy thinker. He did not seem – ultimately – a very happy man, not all that social, especially so after he went to Formula One, as he was a bit more relaxed before the move. He helped me out as best he could. He was an excellent mechanic and a very good driver. I remember that he repaired my car once after I blew my warm-up plugs on my Scarab and he did a first-rate job. But I never really got to know him all that well," said Pabst.

Pabst was referring, in part, to a situation at a race at Vaca Valley Raceway in 1959. The story is told in much more detail in Tom Schultz's *Meister Brauser: Harry Heuer's Championship Racing Team* book but in short there was some resistance towards Pabst and the Meister Brauser team, partly due to their success and partly due to the fact they weren't from the West Coast. Ginther would have none of this and approached Pabst. Richie drove Augie around the circuit in his road car, showed him the racing line and gave him other tips. Augie was also told to ignore any jibes: "These guys are laying for you. They want to show you how tough the West Coast racers are." Richie also helped have Pabst's Ferrari serviced for free a few weeks later as it needed an engine change. When I was compiling interviews and information together for this book, Augie Pabst was one of the keenest people to get involved, spending some time (and I would imagine, money) on a transatlantic phone call. Considering the above and how Ginther treated him, it is no real surprise Augie remembers him with affection.

When taking note of the significance of Richie's wins, it is worth remembering the calibre of the drivers Richie raced against; Miles went on to have a very successful sports car career, while Carroll Shelby, Chuck Daigh, Lance Reventlow, Phil Hill, Bob Drake and Pete Lovely all raced, with variable success, in Formula One.

The next couple of seasons saw him continue in sports cars, more often than not in a Ferrari 500 TR entered by von Neumann, but Richie also raced Ferraris entered by John Edgar. For the first time, Richie expanded his racing beyond his home state. One of his biggest wins in 1957 was at the new Lime Rock circuit near Salisbury, Connecticut, where he won the fifteen-lap Gran Turismo race after a race-long duel with Gene Greenspun of New York. Putting Greenspun under pressure for ten laps, Ginther took the

Richie with mechanic Paul Primeau. *Jim Sitz*

lead when Greenspun made a mistake and crashed, unhurt, into a guardrail. The win at Lime Rock actually earnt him a Los Amigos entered Ferrari 500 TRC drive at the 1957 Le Mans, his first outing there, after Luigi Chinetti, the American Ferrari importer at the time, did a deal with journalist Gerard 'Jabby' Crombac for Richie to partner Francois Picard. They were second in their class before mechanical trouble ended their race when the water pump sheared after ten hours.

It was a mark of Ginther's ability, as both a racer and as a mechanic, that he started to race cars for a variety of entrants. The advantages for them to have Ginther involved were obvious. Richie could give them quality technical feedback, a genuine idea of real race pace and, most importantly, a chance of a win to boost sales and interest in their cars. The aforementioned Joe Lubin was a Beverly Hills based Aston Martin and Cooper dealer and enthusiast who owned the Cooper distribution contract for the West Coast as well as a dealership on Firestone Boulevard in Los Angeles.

Wolfgang Denzel was a BMW shareholder who designed sports cars from old Volkswagen frames and parts. His creations found their way from Austria to America in the mid-1950s as drivers favoured the oversteer the car would give when going through a corner because, when the car started to drift, it gave almost a perfect neutral steering sensation. Richie came fifth in a Denzel at Cotati in May 1957.

John Edgar was an enthusiastic entrant of varying machinery, which included marques such as MG, Alfa Romeo, Ferrari, Maserati and Porsche. He was a champion of supporting talent and the likes of Phil Hill, Carroll Shelby, Pete Lovely, Masten Gregory, Chuck Daigh and Bruce Kessler, as well as Richie, all raced his cars. He was also a motorsports photographer and having the means to do so, became a sports car team owner for the sheer love of it, although wins would always be useful for bargaining power when dealing with the likes of Luigi Chinetti and other dealers based in California.

There were many others, but few of them match Tony Parravano in terms of a colourful life. Parravano, born in Italy and long-time Illinois based, made a fortune in construction after a post-World War

Richie at Palm Springs, 1956. *Archive Bjorn Schlichting*

Richie in the Ferrari 550 Mondia, Sacramento. **Webb Canepa/Revs Institute**

Two housing boom in Southern California. Tony was a good friend of racer Jack McAfee and soon caught the racing bug, buying mainly Ferrari and Maserati cars. Parravano had no inclination to race himself but wanted to support McAfee's career with the enjoyment and prize money that a winning owner received.

The money he spent in the mid 1950s was astonishing. In 1956 alone, it was estimated he had spent $500,000 with Maserati. In today's prices, that's some $4.7million. Maserati, naturally, was so delighted with Parravano's investment that he received the 1956 Italian Grand Prix winning Maserati 250F. However, it soon fell apart like a pack of cards for Parravano, when the Internal Revenue Service discovered that Parravano had paid virtually no corporate tax. Richie raced his Ferrari 750 Monza at New Smyrna Beach in February 1957. Three months later, Parravano fled to Mexico with the vast majority of his racing cars, attempting to smuggle them south of the border to sell for future funds. Five of the nine cars he tried to smuggle through, including the Ferrari 750 Monza, were seized and later sold off to help pay back the IRS. After eventually surrendering in 1960, Parravano disappeared three days before being scheduled to stand trial for tax evasion in April 1960 and has never been seen since.

Another win in 1957, albeit closer to home than Lime Rock, was victory at the first ever over-1500cc sportscar race at the brand new Riverside International Motor Raceway (as it was called then). The

event, which brought 27,500 fans to the fledgling circuit, was the second highest crowd in Southern Californian sports car history at that time. Driving a Ferrari 410 Sport entered by friend and fellow competitor, John Edgar, Ginther won the 26-lap, 137km race at an average speed of 85.15mph, with his nearest challenger, Bill Murphy, almost a minute behind. However Richie had a bit of luck as Chuck Daigh was leading in the Troutman Barnes Special with three laps to go before he suffered a punctured tyre and also when another key challenger, Bob Drake in Frank Arciero's Ferrari 375 Plus crashed early on and, although Drake finished ninth in the end, his chance to win had gone. Despite it being one of his most notable wins to date, Richie was always self-critical if he felt he had not been at his best and this was one of the occasions, as he told *Road & Track* magazine: "People in the pits came up to me and said that I'd driven a good race, but I felt that I'd driven poorly. It was hard for me to remain civil. There are times, even in winning, when you don't drive a good race. There are times when you finish third and feel you drove very well, which was how I felt last year when I came behind Chuck Daigh and Lance Reventlow in the Scarab cars at Laguna Seca." John Edgar, who was responsible for financing the new Riverside track, was overcome with happiness and did not care if Richie had not driven well. So much so, that he entered Ginther in the 410 for two more races that year; another at Riverside and then the Nassau Trophy in the Bahamas.

Ginther racing at Riverside. *Allen R Kuhn*

Richie celebrates winning at Santa Barbara. *Jim Sitz*

Richie at Ponoma. *Jim Sitz*

In an interview to *Sports Car Journal*, Richie expanded a lot more on the race and the car. "It was actually my first time out in that Ferrari and I treated it with plenty of respect. The 4.9 is actually not as rough as you'd imagine. For example, it does not require nearly the amount of physical effort most people think it does to get it round the circuit. But you are definitely under mental pressure at all times. When the car loses adhesion it happens gradually, but you use up a heck of a lot of road through a turn if you foul up in the slightest degree. You can't just whip it around the way you can with a Testa Rossa. The 4.9 demands respect and that's what you've got to give it. Of course, it's very fast. I was hitting close to 160 on the back straight before I went through the timing trap. They clocked me at just over 150 and I had eased off at that point. I actually think I could take a brand new 250 Testa Rossa out there and go even faster than I did in the 4.9. You could really blast in that car!

"In terms of gears for that race, coming down the long back straight I dropped from fifth to fourth to third. All the way round turn nine, up the front pit straight and through the esses in third. Down into second for turn six, back into third again over the hill then to second for the last tight turns. I entered the back straight in second and moved on up through the gears to fifth. You know, I was lucky to have even finished the race on Sunday, let alone win it. At the quarter mark, I lost third gear and figured just to make the pits. But the box held and the other gears were okay, so I kept on going."

But there were plenty of other successes too. He also won again at Santa Barbara, in a Ferrari 625 TRC car and finished second in the highly competitive Nassau Tourist Trophy in a John Edgar entered Ferrari 410 sport and finished in the same position in the same car a couple of days later in the Nassau Memorial Trophy, this time behind Stirling Moss.

In 1958, he took win after notable win in the Ferrari 500 TR. Among his higher profile victories were at Pomona in February, when he pipped Bob Oker's Aston Martin DB3S by seconds after an 88-lap duel, the pair lapping at an average of 86.6 miles. One month later, in the same car, he won at Phoenix, Arizona, in the Thunderbird Sports Car 100-mile race. At that event, Richie also tried out the new Scarab sports car. The Scarab car was to be driven by Bruce Kessler, but partly through interest, and partly to help

Lance Reventlow (the man behind Scarab) to gauge how competitive the car was, Dan Gurney did a few laps in practice, but then Richie jumped in for five more laps. It was a sign of Ginther's prowess at that time that he went more than two seconds a lap faster than Gurney and an incredible six seconds faster than the old lap record. Later in the year, in June, he won three times at Laguna Seca in the production car race, the modified big car event, and then finally the feature big car race, all in a Ferrari 250 GT. He also drove that car to wins at Palm Springs and Riverside again.

It was not just Richie's racing that was going well. His personal life took on a new aspect when, in 1956, he met Jacqueline Marie 'Jackie' Holter, who was working as the secretary of the California Sports Car Club. Holter, Nebraskan born and six years younger than Richie, moved to California as a five-year-old and initially had more interest in another type of horsepower; that being the equine version, as she rode and exercised horses. Landing the secretarial role saw her strike up a friendship with many people and especially so with Richie. They were engaged in 1957 and then subsequently married on 9 August 1958 in Los Angeles. Richie had just turned 28 and Jackie was four months shy of her 22nd birthday. "Jackie always had misgivings about racing but never really put her foot down. I was already a part of racing when I met her and she accepted it. I guess she was part of it as well in one sense. It would have been different if I had taken it up after meeting her; in fact I would say it would have been impossible," said Ginther. Jackie certainly took a huge interest in her husband's racing career initially. She lovingly complied two huge volumes of scrap books on pretty much every race Richie did; articles, photos and so on. Arguably, in terms of coverage, it's one of the most detailed Ferrari based archival resources ever complied but sadly it ended up in a car boot sale after Jackie's death (she died, aged 66, on the 27 December 2002) before being rescued by a Ginther fan and memorabilia collector.

It must also be remembered that during this time racing – and winning – in sports cars, Ginther was also working. Initially, this was as a mechanic on von Neumann's cars in the dealership's service department before becoming the service manager and then, at von Neumann's dealership at 1767 Cahuenga Boulevard in Hollywood, one of the main Ferrari sales representatives of California.

Richie had a reputation as a competent, hard-working man who demanded a lot from people and even more from himself. He had a brilliant smile but if he was in a downbeat mood, his comments became very caustic. He certainly did not suffer fools gladly. When asked in 1957 by a *Valley News* journalist, Chuck Sexauer, why he raced for free, Ginther's reply, as Sexauer himself noted, was indignant: "Only Americans have this peculiar attitude towards sports car drivers. They look upon us as if we are fools. Listen, in Europe, a sports fan looks upon the top racing sports car drivers as the Americans look upon Mickey Mantle or Ted Williams [both baseball legends]. They are heroes, respected and admired. The Europeans give the racing driver the prestige that a standout footballer or baseball player has here. Sometimes sports car racing in America just hasn't grown up."

All of this racing, like the other drivers he raced against, was done on an amateur basis. West Coast sports car racing, though, was immensely popular, with crowds of around twenty thousand, and for those drivers linked to dealerships, the prestige of doing well and the subsequent sales they generated for doing so made it not only one of the fastest growing amateur sports in America in the late 1950s,

but easily the most lucrative amateur sporting pursuit as well. Augie Pabst, who raced sports cars successfully, in the 1950s and 1960s remembers the attraction to him as both a spectator and a racer: "Sports cars were thrilling to watch. My personal memory was when I watched the first race at Road America and it was something I just wanted to do – had to do – thereafter; I am sure others were the same. There was Bill Kimberley in his Ferrari, there were Cadillacs. There was close racing, different noises and just so much that made it thrilling. It was the same when driving; you enjoyed the opportunity to race, not just drive. It was a great experience. I always remember that you'd drive the car in the race, take the mufflers off and then drive home in the same car that you might have just won in front of all those crowds."

Certainly that era has continued to garner interest and literature over 60 years on, and likely will yet for a few more decades. Whether this is down to the era being the first introduction to the sport for so many, due to the close distances and cheap prices enabling them to watch live sport, or whether it is because any amateur car enthusiast could race competitively, or whether it is because iconic drivers like Richie, Phil Hill, Dan Gurney, Ken Miles and Carroll Shelby, to

Richie driving at Ponoma. *Allen R Kuhn*

name just five, all came via the same path to greater success or a mixture of all three and more, it doesn't really matter.

If anything, though, the fondness of the era might simply be that many of the tracks involved in Richie's era have long since gone and people naturally yearn for what is lost forever. Torrey Pines, a disused army base, was replaced by two golf courses as San Diego felt that would attract more tourism. Windsor Airfield in Nassau was replaced by an international airport. Precious little remains of Oakes Field, the second location in Nassau, whilst Santa Barbara, Buchanan Field and Minter Field were also swallowed up by their respective airports. Cotati was knocked down in the 1970s and Riverside in the 1980s for real estate. Paramount Ranch, which doubled as a film studio location, is now a park. Hourglass Field, which was shut, somewhat controversially, because of a drag racing crash which injured three people, now has a community college on its site. Pomona Raceway still exists, but now as a drag racing strip, with hardly any of the road course remaining. Willow Springs, however, continues to host road racing, but is in the minority as a surviving track of the mid-late 1950s.

The fact Ginther won, and won in front of such large crowds, was real manna from heaven for von Neumann and the dealership regarding publicity and performance. To use one example, *The San Francisco Examiner* of 20 November 1958 effectively became a puff piece of journalism extoling the virtues of Richie and his wares: "Richie Ginther, one of our favourite automobile racers is in charge of the Ferrari booth. He is a personable little guy and he will be glad to take your order for either a Ferrari GT coupé or a Ferrari Berlinetta, or both. Each car seats two and sells for $12,450. That's pretty reasonable when you come to think of it. There's a Rolls-Royce in the show priced at 25 Gs."

The *Honolulu Star Bulletin* earlier in 1958 even reported his personal sales figures for the previous year but they did also ask a very stimulating question of "Why do you drive racing cars?" Ginther's reply was frank and honest: "To prove to myself that I can do it. I drive also to satisfy the ego, to get publicity and so forth".

Richie puts on his helmet before racing at Ponoma. *Jim Sitz*

But Richie was not truly at ease as a salesman. Because of his day-to-day management of the dealership, other drivers would get in touch wanting to drive the cars and owners would constantly ask Richie about potential drivers. Richie admitted to Murray Roche of *Road & Track* magazine that as much as it was part of his job, he found it the most difficult part and did not really like it. If he felt the person being discussed was not ready to handle the Ferrari power, he tried to bow out of the discussion as discreetly and quickly as he could but this was not always easy for him. Richie was never a man for small talk and niceties, he had a candour with a cutting edge and that did not always work in business.

1959 saw yet more success. An early win came at Pomona in the Ferrari 335 Sport, leading for twenty laps after taking the lead from Bill Krause on lap five. He took a win in the 625 TRC V12 at the Lago de Guadalupe event in San Borja, Mexico, ahead of the very young Rodriguez brothers (Ricardo and Pedro), both of whom would later become, briefly, Ferrari Formula One works drivers themselves. At Sebring, co-driving with Howard Hiveley, he took a class win in the Grand Touring class, while there were two more wins at Hourglass Field, San Diego, followed by his biggest win of the year, the Kiwanis Grand Prix held at Riverside.

Richie at Ponoma. *Jim Sitz*

Chapter Three

His entrant was still von Neumann, but it was Eleanor von Neumann, now divorced from John who, as part of the divorce settlement, got the Ferrari dealership, the racing cars and Richie as a salesman and driver. Eleanor Bigelow was already deeply entrenched within the dealership and within racing; her daughter, Josie, also raced. She had a passion for cars herself and was a successful dealer in her own right. Eleanor kept the team going but saw the advantage of having her faster cars being driven by the fastest driver she had whereas John von Neumann had often selected the best Ferraris for himself, rather than Richie. As a consequence, Richie won more prolifically at what would end up being quite a crucial stage in his career. Jim Sitz recalls Eleanor in a good light: "I would deal with Eleanor at both Porsche and Ferrari operations, and she worked hard at their success and was a key part of their success. She was not just the wife of somebody, she was somebody in her own right."

Back to Riverside, a race held in blistering heat which Richie won in 1hour 46min at an average speed of 88.75mph around the 150-mile event, with multiple laps under two minutes and five seconds. Once again, his early challenge came from Chuck Daigh in his Scarab, but a vapour lock on lap sixteen condemned Daigh to a long pit-stop and an arduous, hot afternoon making up ground thereafter (Daigh placed sixth in the end). Of the 47 laps of the 3.275-mile circuit, Ginther led the last 32 and won by 2min 25sec from Sammy Weiss, another Californian automobile dealer in his Porsche 718 RSK. It was not without its tribulations for Richie though and, as he explained after the race to Murray Roche of *Road & Track* magazine, he was not happy, despite earning $100 for it, with the qualifying situation of one lap from pits to finish straight:

Eleanor von Neumann. *Jim Sitz*

"That's the last time that I want to pull right out of the pits and take off without warming my brakes up first; at turn one, I almost lost it. I think it damaged the brakes to affect them the whole way through the race, so I was surprised with my lap time. [Author note: Ginther qualified first in 2min 6sec.] I thought it would be around two minutes ten seconds or two minutes twelve seconds, which was really all I was trying for."

Winning earned Richie $2420 and then $320 for lap money ($10 for each lap led), but it also firmly established him as one of America's best sports car drivers. So much so that, in an interview with *The Los Angeles Times* in October 1959, Stirling Moss, still at the height of his racing career and on the back of four straight wins in either Formula One and sports cars, mentioned only two people that he thought might challenge him at the upcoming United States Sportscar Grand Prix: "I think the cars are fairly comparable. It will be pretty much up to the drivers. Phil Hill has been the American star of the Ferrari factory team for three years. But I'm also concerned about Richie Ginther in his 4.1-litre Ferrari". This was high praise indeed and if one of Europe's best considered Ginther to be a credible challenge, then it is little wonder Ferrari pricked their collective ears up about their Californian salesman and service manager. In the end, it was Hill who triumphed with Moss retiring quite early. Richie pretty much dominated the race, leading for the first 35 laps before transmission failure ended his race.

Come January 1960, though, Ginther's name was no longer on the entry list for the annual Palm Springs Road Race. He was no longer a car dealer either; he was now a Ferrari works driver.

Ginther takes the win at Hourglass Field, 1959. *Allen R Kuhn*

Richie leads Ken Miles at Ponoma, 1956. *Jim Sitz*

Ferrari America

"I guess I love the machinery and I have a different view
on driving to so many other drivers; many drive to lead the race,
but for me, there's no question about it, I drive to finish"
Richie Ginther

The start of the 1961 French Grand Prix. *Ferrari spa/Ed McDonough*

The story goes that Ginther only got the Ferrari drive by accident. While working as a developer and engineer one day, he shook the car down for a test. In doing so, Enzo Ferrari noticed how quickly he was lapping and hired him as a driver on the spot. One such version of this tale has Ginther wearing just a suit and tie with no crash helmet, but in truth Ginther's frequent sports car success in the US, a market that Ferrari were particularly keen to exploit, plus Phil Hill's feedback about his engineering and driving talent to Ferrari insiders, were more realistic factors. Ginther himself referred to Phil and Luigi Chinetti being key influences for him securing the role in an interview with *The Autocourse* 1961 annual. The move could have come earlier than 1960 as Richie had visited Maranello in 1959 when he took the 412 MI car to the factory to have the disc brakes upgraded and had brief discussions with Enzo Ferrari about some kind of driving role. However, as Richie recalled to *Car and Driver*, "Although it's plausible that I would have been angling for a move to Ferrari and I tested sports cars whilst at the factory on business, it was just plain wrong to suggest that was my only reason for being there. I was always told that I was more important to Ferrari as a representative than as a driver."

However, this was not as lucrative as his time in America; no direct sales after a weekend's victory anymore, anything but. Richie was paid just $3000 a year to test for Ferrari. Enzo Ferrari believed that, when it came to money, to be given a chance to be a works driver for the Ferrari team made fiscal earnings immaterial. Compare the wage he now received to the Riverside win in 1959, where he won $2740 in just one race in prize money alone.

It is interesting, though, that he accepted the low-paid role when you consider that in an interview with Murray Roche of *Road & Track* in late 1959, Richie said the following: "I do enjoy my job in the dealership. There have been lots of times I could have gone to Europe with hopes of a factory try out. There is very little in the world that I would rather do than race in Europe, but I guess I'm not willing to make the sacrifices necessary for the chance to drive on the European circuit. My wife, Jackie, and my home mean too much to me. My finances would not cover the starting expense of becoming a new factory man. However, if the right terms and right chance came along, I'd probably grab it."

A large clue as to why he changed his mind was revealed in an extensive interview with *Car and Driver* in September 1961, where clearly something or a combination of things had changed to push Ginther towards a move. "Truth was I was tormented by the tensions of business life and I wanted to trade my desk chair into a more soothing seat even if that's inside a Ferrari. I was at my wits' end before. It was just over my head. I felt I was not doing the job right. I was running the whole business; selling, service, book-keeping, handling complaints, ordering from the factory. If I made a mistake on ordering, I would have had $12,000 worth of car staring me in the face.

"I had no experience in all that. I was just unhappy and it was affecting my married life. In January 1960, I went to Argentina to drive with Wolfgang von Trips. I stayed a month and relaxed and I realised how unhappy I was. So I went back and quit. I did not care what I did and would have worked in a gas station. Now I'm much more at peace with the world and much more at peace with myself. I'm more relaxed now because I enjoy what I'm doing. Why, I'm even getting to a place where I can be around people I don't like!" The change in attitude may well have been a hark-back to his school days where he was not comfortable if he was not doing something with his hands; mechanical work and designing things had been his forté at school – advanced mathematics, English and business skills, while far from being a dunce, were not as strong attributes in Richie and must have eventually worn him down.

But Richie's friend Jim Sitz thinks that Eleanor von Neumann might just have tipped Richie off about her future plans and Richie realised that he probably had little choice but to move: "In 1959, Eleanor sent Richie over to Modena with the 412 to have disc brakes fitted. It seems that Mr Ferrari liked his testing and offered Richie a sports car drive for 1960. This caused Richie a dilemma as he was quite cushy in his job and he had just bought a new home in Granada Hills. But actually Eleanor encouraged him to pursue it. She said to him, 'Go for it Richie, what can you lose?'"

"As it turned out, though, the next race in Nassau was the last hurrah for the team as she had already made plans to start selling the operation. In the end it took a bit longer than she planned but she sold the operation to Otto Zipper, another enthusiast from Vienna. Soon after that she had a garage sale on the whole stable. Jack Nethercutt wanted the new 250 TR driven by Hill, but she made him buy the whole stable for $50,000. Not a bad deal really."

So, in March 1960, Ginther was effectively unemployed, although he had plenty of options both via racing and through connections from his sports car days. Interested in racing single-seaters, he tried out a Gemini Formula Junior car at Riverside in March. After finding out that Ginther had quit his role with Ferrari in the US, Luigi Chinetti offered Richie a chance to drive the works TR59/60 entered by the North American Racing Team in the 12 Hours at Sebring. Overall, it did not go well and the car retired with Chuck Daigh at the wheel. There was not, initially, much more guarantee than that, but Chinetti then managed to persuade Ferrari to give Richie a contract to do four races; Targa Florio, Monaco, Le Mans and the Nürburgring, more of which is below. There's no doubt that Ginther appreciated Chinetti for rescuing him from a life of pumping gas (although Jackie Ginther told Jim Sitz that, on balance, Richie would have been quite happy working as a mechanic during the week, racing at the weekend and being close to her and his family had his life turned out that way instead of grand prix racing). So Richie and Jackie moved over to Italy, staying opposite the Ferrari factory and tried to get used to their new way of life.

1960 started successfully with a second place at the Buenos Aires 1000km in late January (that he mentions above), as Ginther posted fastest lap when he and Wolfgang von Trips finished behind team-mates Phil Hill and Cliff Allison in the sister TR59/60. He was employed to drive in Formula Libre events but also as a standby for Formula One races. As he enthused in an interview to *The Los Angeles Times* on 17 January 1960, "I'm hoping I get a chance to race in Formula One as well as the other races; It's a cultured degree of motor racing." It did not take long for Richie to get his wish; by May, he was a grand prix driver. Entered for the Monaco Grand Prix in the mid-engined Dino 246P, he qualified ninth, one place ahead of team-leader Hill and one place behind von Trips. He then followed that up with a world championship point on his debut, finishing sixth, but suffered a gearbox failure towards the end of the race, finishing thirty laps down.

In truth, the rest of the year was a disappointment. Ginther failed to finish the Targa Florio, the 1000 Kms at the Nürburgring, Le Mans (he did well though as, at the halfway mark Richie and Willy Mairesse in a TRI60, were one of the main challengers to eventual winners Olivier Gendebien and Paul Frere), and the 200 miles of Riverside. He did at least manage two points-scoring finishes in the only other two grand prix he was entered in by Ferrari. Ginther later said (to *Car and Driver*) that the failure to finish the Targa Florio was a blessing in disguise: "That crash was actually one of the best things that could have happened to me. I bored into a turn too fast, hit some gravel and then a tree. I realised that I had a hell of a lot to learn. It scared me, it really scared me. Not because I crashed, but because I did not know what had caused it. If I had not crashed I might have gone through the season trying to look good and got into some serious trouble. As it was, it reinforced my belief in going slow and learning it rather than going fast and thinking I know it and getting hurt."

A sixth place at the Dutch Grand Prix, where he out-qualified both his team-mates, was followed by finishing runner-up to Hill in the Italian race at Monza, which, incidentally, was the last grand

prix victory by a front-engined car. He took the lead at the start (something that would become a regular feature for the next six years) and kept it for some while before Phil Hill overtook him, not bad for just Richie's third Grand Prix. In the end, he led for 24 of the 50 laps which was the first time he had led a World Championship grand prix race. However this was a somewhat hollow result and a processional race due to the boycott of the event by the British teams following the decision by the organisers to use both the road and oval circuit, deemed by them to be too dangerous for the drivers and too damaging on the cars. Ginther gave that decision short shrift; "The British cars did not come to Monza because they could not take the pounding. Now when they built those cars for the 1960 season, they knew there was a race at Monza. That's not right to then not turn up. One thing about Ferrari is you're driving pretty safely prepared cars."

There was even a brief – very brief – interlude away from Ferrari at the French Grand Prix, 1960. The Reventlow Automobiles Ltd Scarab, run by Lance Reventlow, assisted by Chuck Daigh, had enjoyed a lot of success on the West Coast themselves as well as Ginther. Ginther had some association with them in his own sports car days, testing their car from time to time and helping the team out. In 1960, they made an attempt, albeit one that with hindsight was rather naïve, to enter Formula One. They entered front-engined cars, which were becoming obsolete but also had a four-cylinder unit very similar to an Offenhauser engine, but was actually their own design, put together by Offenhauser employee Leo Goossen.

Monaco Grand Prix 1960, Richie's World Championship debut. **Ferret Fotographics**

Watched by the locals, Richie tries to put together the damaged Ferrari at the Targa Florio, 1960. *Hill Family Archive*

The engine was based on the one that Mercedes-Benz had enjoyed all-conquering success for five years previously, but the trouble was the desmodromic gear in the engine could not easily cope with the engine block movement. Subsequently, the gears would close the valves too much and it would end up with repeated engine failures. Daigh and Reventlow had failed to qualify at Monaco (ending up slower than some Formula Juniors in the support race) and both retired in Belgium.

Before the French Grand Prix, Reventlow, under immense pressure, decided enough was enough and quit driving. He was keen, however, to have an American race the car, so he got in touch with Ferrari to see if they could lend Ginther to them. In theory, it worked all round. Ginther's prowess versus Daigh and Reventlow Stateside was proven and he had already had encouraging results for Ferrari. For Ferrari, it was a chance to give Ginther race experience away from promoting him into one of its own cars. In reality though, the Scarab project remained a disaster; the cars had multiple engine failures during practice and ran out of both engines and spare parts which ended their weekend early. On top of this, the acrid aroma of burning oil prompted Richie to bring the car into the pits with a bearing he felt was ready to break. Thankfully, this little foray had not damaged Richie's reputation in any way. It certainly did not help Reventlow, and the Scarab car, solely with Chuck Daigh, would only appear once more.

On balance, 1960 had gone pretty well overall and 1961 certainly saw that continue. Interest in Richie certainly began to increase in both America and Europe. Although his race results brought

Richie, 1960. *Dr Benno Muller Archive/Jorg-Thomas Fodisch*

Ginther at Sebring, 1961. *BARC Boys/Ed McDonough*

a lot of welcome attention, Richie's main role was that of test and development driver. This kind of role had been around for a while; Norman Dewis was long-time test driver for Jaguar and Ken Richardson likewise for BRM but neither were given much race time. Ginther's involvement as a tester was just as detailed and important, but he was given racing opportunities too.

As quoted a few times already in this book, *The Autocourse* 1961 annual ran an extended feature on Ginther at Ferrari in 1961 called Tester to the Prancing Horse, where Richie was interviewed at some length and gave a lot of insight into the team, the role and himself and much of it follows below. There are also comments from *Car and Driver* magazine which also focused on him while at Ferrari and the quotes from Richie are combined below:

"I wanted to do testing and was very happy to get the job; I inherited the job of test driver and it has been very important to me in racing. I really look forward to going out on a test. I enjoy doing

Richie with Wolfgang von Trips during testing at Modena.

Jorg-Thomas Fodisch/Ed McDonough

a good job testing, when the only person out there is the engineer, as much as I enjoy doing a good job in a race when there are thousands of people. I don't have a set schedule as such; I go over two or three times a day; if they want anything all they have to do is have the gate keeper come across as the hotel is right across from the factory. We're getting used to hotel living but we don't like it. We're both very homesick for California but we are learning how to pack bags!

"There is a definite routine to testing, a routine totally separate from racing. I do all the testing, as do the other drivers, before the cars are sent to a race to see if they are right. The only thing we can tell on that sort of test, of course, is whether the gearbox, clutch, engine and so forth work properly. It's a routine at Modena, our test track. I take the cars that are going to a race out for about ten laps apiece and then tell them of any little problems. Now our test track at Modena is unique, of course. What makes a car go fast there does not have to work anywhere else, but the personality of the cars can be judged. If I have experienced something strongly enough then I can come in and say the toe-in isn't proper or something like that. Once you get used to our cars you can tell easily when one shock isn't equal. Right or left particularly. Fore and aft is more difficult. This is of great importance to me in racing and of great importance to them too. Being just a test driver would not interest me but being part of an engineering staff and testing does.

"Suppose we try something new and it works so we use it for a race. I know what it is and why it's there. For all the other drivers it's just something new for them to get used to. Test as much as possible; that's the only thing that does any good. I definitely intended to do the testing this year. It was my job from the first day, I mean many drivers dislike the idea of having to test. They consider it a bother and are far more interested in racing itself; whereas I have a lot of mechanical interest and it was a good opportunity to learn the cars. I am now familiar with the refinements.

"I am completely free at the factory. I can go into any department I please, including experimental, only because I never said anything to anybody. The temperatures or pressures, for instance, can't do any other builder any good but the point is, once the factory starts seeing that I am telling people about their cars it becomes more difficult for me.

"The mechanics are all individuals; they have a lot of pride, and feel that a driver is a driver and a mechanic a mechanic. This is sometimes a handicap as I like to get in the car and do something myself to understand it better. We have had some changes more recently and everything goes along fine. There's been some increasing confidence on both sides but learning the language has made a big difference. I picked up the Italian to pass my thoughts on over here. There were never any foreign languages taught at school in Santa Monica. All of the mechanics speak only Italian. Anything done with them or the engineers has to be done in Italian.

"Initially, I would know a key Italian word and someone knew a key English word. With a bunch of hand signals, we got the point over. Most of my Italian vocabulary is technical, no question. Conversation wise I'm very limited. Jackie, my wife, has quite a few books on grammar, language and that; she studies a lot. Sometimes I got frustrated enough with the language barrier that I picked up the tools and tried to do it myself when I could not get the point across. We've worked together though and sharpened our taste for wines."

It's worth interjecting at this point where Richie talks about the mechanics and the language to reinforce something that both Jackie Ginther remembered when recollecting to Michael Ling in his 2000 article in *Automobile Quarterly* and that Cleo mentioned to me: "When he was working for Ferrari, he would see some quintessential loud, brash Americans, touring the factory. Obviously they had many at the time with Phil and Richie driving. Some of them would recognise him, or so they thought, but when they tried to talk to him, he would throw his hands out apologetically, saying '*Mi dispiace, non parlo inglese*' which the mechanics loved".

Going back to the interview, it becomes clear why he was to later gain a real reputation as a mechanically-sympathetic racing driver, but also why he never became a frequent winner, let alone a World Champion: "Take Reims [the 1961 French Grand Prix]; there has been a lot of talk about oil pressures but I was aware mine was down from the start of the race and it concerned me. I dropped my revs right from the start. I took 500 off the redline and eventually another 500. Once I moved into the lead the writing was on the wall. The pressure was going down lap by lap and I was sure I would not finish. I stopped primarily because there was a drastic fault in the engine and I did not want to destroy it. As it happened I managed not to, by shutting off quickly enough. I hate to see anything broken.

German Grand Prix, 1961. **Paul Meis/Ed McDonough**

Richie drives past the grandstand at Reims, French Grand Prix, 1961. *David Hodges/Ed McDonough*

"I guess I love the machinery and I have a different view on driving to so many other drivers; many drive to lead the race, but for me, there's no question about it, I drive to finish. Maybe that's not the proper attitude, I don't know, but I do it. There are two ways of driving, no question. You can drive to finish, which to me is very important, or you can drive to lead and stand a chance of not finishing which I don't endorse. However, I always drive to win. That's the whole essence of racing.

"If something happens to your car when you're driving to the limit, it can just happen and that's that. But I can't endorse abusing the car to stay in front. Take these Ferrari cars; they are damn strong cars, probably stronger than any others that are really competitive and I want to lead, but if I have to over-rev to do it I just won't. The odds against the machine finishing are long enough and they fall off completely when you take it out on the car. If you start moving the red line up another 500, for instance, that's going fast the wrong way. Some race selfishly; they only want to race for the glory and not the true accomplishment. That's why I think the best driver in the world is Jack Brabham. He starts and finishes a race and wins the World Championship. Starting and finishing is much more important than turning the fastest lap. There's no doubt Stirling Moss is the fastest driver out there. But Jack Brabham just gets in his car, plugs along and at the end of the year he has the highest score.

"I am a study-driver in a sense. That's another advantage of testing. You can try different lines in the turns and look at your lap times to see what difference it made. You discover a lot of tricks

in testing to make a car go faster without going any faster yourself or frightening yourself or something. This is another phase where testing helped me. It's all knowledge."

It was not the first time Ginther had said something like this; he said the same in the *Sports Car Journal* in 1957: "I feel having a good mechanical knowledge of your car is a definite advantage. If you understand a car you try not to abuse it; and you end up finishing more races. When a car passes me and I know I am going as fast as I possibly can, I let him go rather than risk blowing the whole car up."

He repeated this mantra many times in his career and again, after he retired, when he looked back at why he did not win more races in an interview for *Car Life* magazine. "I was a little too conservative as a driver. I was not a charger. I used to lie back and pace myself and pick off the front-runners as they faltered. But whilst you can gain a lot of places that way, you can't win many races. I've worked on these cars and engines more than a lot of drivers and I think sometimes that maybe I know too much about them. If I thought I heard or felt something, I'd be inclined to back off and maybe even to drop out. I could always get a lot out of a car. I could nurse it along. I know I've finished races many other drivers would not finish.

"But I was not one of these win or else guys. And I guess I outsmarted myself out of some wins. I know I lost races I could have won, races others might have won. I guess I wanted to finish more than I wanted to win. I always knew it's a dangerous sport and I knew I could get hurt driving and I accepted these things, but I was not about to put myself in a position where the odds were against me.

Jim Clark (8) spins and Richie overtakes him at the 1961 French Grand Prix.
David Hodges/Ed McDonough

Dutch Grand Prix, 1961. *Ferret Fotographics*

Start of the 1961 French Grand Prix. *David Hodges/Ed McDonough*

Stirling Moss (14) and Richie battle it out at the Dutch Grand Prix, 1961. **BP Photo Archive/Nick Faure.**

"No-one likes to be hurt. I used to have conversations with myself about this. As long as I could analyse an accident I know I had done all I could to prevent it, I could put it away and accept the dangers. I learnt from each accident. I think as you begin to understand what might happen on the track you get smarter and more conservative."

This pragmatic and thoughtful attitude is one that is so at odds with racing in general and it is essential to the Richie Ginther story when trying to understand the driver, and even the person. It is key as to why he did not win more and why racing accidents bothered him so much. This attitude was rare in 1961 and still is today. Motor racing has always been about winning and, had Ginther been racing in a top car in 2019 for example, he would likely be pilloried on social media for having those thoughts.

But the difference between motor racing today and motor racing in 1961 is that a car breakage could easily lead to death. In 2019, it needs an almost freakish event, certainly in Formula One, for a driver to lose their life. Of course, nowadays most cars reach the

Richie at the Dutch Grand Prix, 1961. *Ed McDonough*

finish and one could imagine Ginther to be more than happy with the technological advances and the reliability of the cars if he were racing today.

Back to the Sloniger interview, Ginther also made a point about testing, compared to sportscar racing: "I like the responsibility of driving the car myself. In a sports car race you are driving with somebody and maybe they're doing a good job up in the first three places or something. If you go out and crash you've not only dropped yourself out but ruined all the work your co-driver has done as well." Although not mentioned by name, he was almost certainly referring to the Sebring 12 Hours in March 1961; the Ferrari 246 SP, he enthused before the race to the *Pasadena Independent* newspaper was, "The best car I've ever driven. It handles and goes better than any Formula One car I've raced". Ginther and his co-driver, Wolfgang von Trips, were leading by a huge margin when after two and-a-half hours, the car retired with a broken steering arm when von Trips was driving. The *Pasadena Independent* did not hold back as to the real reason; "Although not verified, there is a good hunch that von Trips ran off the road, and thus caused the broken steering link. He was pressing quite hard with the car when he took off the circuit."

1960 saw him work closely with Carlo Chiti to persuade, through testing and development, that front-engined cars were no longer the way forward. The duo's work led to one of the most iconic racing cars of all time, the Ferrari 156 'Sharknose' car, although that was after some development. When it first appeared, at the Monaco Grand Prix of 1960, it came across as being, to quote BRM's PR manager AF Rivers Fletcher, "rather clumsy, and it was big in the pre-war Auto Union manner." As Ginther recalled to Pete Lyons in 1988 for *Car and Driver*: "I did most of the testing on the first mid-engined car. My first impression was that it was the way of the future. But there was a lot of understeer and people said that it's

Richie shared the number 4 car with Olivier Gendebien and Wolfgang von Trips at the Nürburgring 1000 Kms, 1961. *MullerCologne*

German Grand Prix, Nürburgring, 1961. *Archive Nils Ruwisch*

because the engine's not up-front. Ferrari wanted to scrap it but I said to them 'Wait, there's something important – I can put so much power down exiting a corner.'"

Richie was also a genuine admirer of Carlo Chiti, the Tuscan born engineer who had left Alfa Romeo and joined Ferrari as its chief designer in October 1957. In the autumn of 1959, Ginther had been testing at the Autodromo Modena and set times close to the lap record, which impressed both Chiti and Enzo Ferrari. Richie liked Carlo's designs and his approach to work and made this quite clear to all at Maranello. Because the Modenese mechanics took to Richie in a positive way regarding development, it made the life of the Tuscan native Chiti a lot easier when it came to liaison with the mechanics than it would have done normally considering the complicated background to Italian history and politics.

Therefore, in 1961, the first year of the 1.5-litre Formula One era, Ferrari had a mid-engined developed car ready to go. The English based teams had tried to resist the 1.5-litre changes coming in and it took them some time to adapt; any circuit that was not twisty and slow, they had no chance.

By 1961, Ginther had built up a special bond with his mechanics. He told a story to Nigel Roebuck for *Autosport* in 1977 – which has never been fully verified and has only come from Richie himself – but it's a story that has been repeated in a few articles and a couple of books since, so it only makes sense to go into this book. If it indeed happened, then it's no wonder Ginther was listened to with some reverence:

"Well, they thought I had the sixth sense! This goes back to a test day we had at Monza in 1960. We were using the full circuit that day, which included the banking. I was supposed to do a series of laps and I came in before I was supposed to have stopped. I could sense something was wrong. And they said, not completely politely, 'It's not time yet to come in, don't you know?' I said 'Wait a minute, this thing is going to blow up; there's a vibration in there that isn't right.' Well, the mechanics fired it up again – wham, wham, wham – they ran the hell out of it and said everything was okay and I should go back out.

"Well, I did not want to do that. I thought it might be dangerous if I should blow whilst I was on the banking, so they put someone else in; 'Wild' Willy Mairesse. Poor old Willy. Before he went out, I said to all the guys, 'Hey that thing is going to blow in twelve laps'. And would you believe, on the twelfth lap, it blew up! Not the tenth, or the sixth, but the twelfth! I mean I had just picked a number from the air, but the guys all thought I was magic!"

The aforementioned Sebring race notwithstanding, 1961 was the year where Ginther's career moved to the next level. Given a much more regular grand prix drive, he took his chance with aplomb. Third places at Aintree for the British Grand Prix and at Spa for the Belgian Grand Prix were highlights (especially the latter event as he achieved fastest lap – a lap of 3min 59.8sec on lap 20) and his mechanical sympathy, as mentioned above, was shown by him finishing the majority of his races, something that, unsurprisingly given his attitude towards the car and racing, would become a

The start of the British Grand Prix, 1961. *BP Photo Archive/Nick Faure*

British Grand Prix, Aintree, 1961. *Ed McDonough*

recurring feature during his grand prix career. He only failed to finish in two races. The first was the French Grand Prix, when the car succumbed to oil pressure as mentioned previously in the Autocourse interview. The second was at the Italian Grand Prix when the engine failed, but in truth, nobody really cared much. Phil Hill became the first American World Champion but in tragic circumstances when Wolfgang von Trips was killed in the same race so in the midst of both triumph and tragedy, Ginther's retirement wouldn't have been of too much concern to him or the team.

He also took fifth place at the Dutch Grand Prix to finish a decent fifth place in the World Championship standings. For Ferrari, the season had been one of triumph overall, taking five grand prix wins, victory at Le Mans, the World Constructors' Championship and the World Sports Car Championship.

Briefly going back to von Trips' tragic demise, Phil Hill later recalled to Nigel Roebuck for *Motorsport* magazine in 1999 about the feeling in the team, the funeral and the general dislike for Laura Ferrari, wife of Enzo. Laura Ferrari, née Garello, was Enzo's wife from 1923 until her death in 1978. When their son Dino died in 1956, Enzo Ferrari became even more reclusive and Laura became more involved with running the company, including daily visits to the factory. She was an immensely strong-willed woman who would often clash with many individuals, but chiefly Girolamo Gardini, Ferrari's sales manager. Back to the funeral recollection from Phil Hill: "The whole Trips thing was a big trauma. I was with Ferrari for days afterwards, and there was all this, 'Oh, what are we going to do?' kind of stuff. You can't imagine what it was like. It seemed like everyone in the damn country was milling around Maranello, and there's Enzo Ferrari, with three days' beard growth, and wearing bathrobes all day – he'd been through it lots of times, and I always felt he regarded his drivers like a general thinks of his soldiers. Insofar as he was fond of any driver, I guess he was fond of Trips, but Ferrari was a great actor, you know. Did he go to the funeral? No, he didn't. He sent the old lady.

"I was dreading the funeral. For all the Germans, Trips was going to be their new World Champion, and then I had to go as this terrible disappointment. Anyway, Richie Ginther and I took my Peugeot, and drove up to Milan, where we just barely made it onto the train – I had to pull him aboard when it was actually moving!

The funeral of Wolfgang von Trips. German Grand Prix and sports car driver Edgar Barth is at the front on the right, with Phil Hill behind him.
Dr Benno Muller Archive/Jorg-Thomas Fodisch

Richie Ginther (6) and Ricardo Rodriguez (8) battle it out during the 1961 Italian Grand Prix. *Archive Nils Ruwisch*

We get to Cologne, and there is Amerigo Manicardi, who was in charge of Ferrari sales worldwide, and about the best guy in the place. He had been sent to take Mrs Ferrari to the funeral, and keep her out of trouble.

"The funeral was the worst thing you ever could imagine. They had Trips' Ferrari sports car there, and they'd built this platform on the back, to carry the coffin. And the kid that drove it didn't quite know how to do it; he just kept slipping the clutch, and by the time we'd got a couple of miles down the road, where the services were, it was about cooked. It was just a bad business all the way around. It was raining and dark, and we had to go along at the pace of this old woman, with the lantern hanging in front of her, you know. Awful, but we got through it.

"Trips' friends had little receptions afterwards, and while we were there, all of a sudden Mrs Ferrari said to me, 'Pheeleel, are you going back down now?' She'd decided she didn't like Manicardi – he didn't like her, either! – so she said maybe Richie and I would let her go back with us. 'Where are you going?' she said. I panicked – I said, 'We're going to... Stockholm!' She said, 'What a shame,' and meanwhile Manicardi's doing all these winks and everything!

"So we went back the same way we came via train and then back in my Peugeot 404 to Modena. We're going along, and all of a sudden Richie says, 'Duck! Duck!' Instinctively, I just did what he said. And he says, 'It's the old lady!' And we're supposed to be in Stockholm!' The next day we get to the factory, and we see Manicardi. I said, 'Christ! Richie saw you at the last second! I didn't even see you – I just ducked.' And Manicardi then told us that Mrs Ferrari had said, 'Manicardi! Isn't that Phil Hill's car?' And Manicardi said, 'I don't know – there's nobody in it!' And she said, 'Oh, that's all right, then.' That was what it was like, living with Mrs Ferrari."

Richie was also consistently competitive in sports cars in 1961, although an outright win eluded him. He finished second behind Phil Hill and Olivier Gendebien in a works Ferrari 1-2 at the Sebring 12 Hours, sharing the Ferrari 250 TRI/61 car with von Trips, Mairesse and Baghetti (although von Trips and Richie commandeered the car after their Ferrari Dino 246 SP retired with a broken steering arm), and also came third at the Nurburgring 1000kms (in a Ferrari Dino 246 SP this time) with von Trips and Gendebien. The Targa Florio, however, ended very early – so early in fact, that Ginther never got to drive a lap in anger as Phil Hill crashed on the very first lap. Running

Le Mans 1961. Ginther shared the drive with Wolfgang von Trips. *The Grand Prix Library*

out of fuel ended Ginther and von Trips' Le Mans effort on the 231st lap, while steering issues accounted for his retirement at the 4 Hours of Pescara.

Richie felt, as he recalled to Lyons, that his testing gave him an advantage when it came to races at times: "Jack Brabham was ahead of me as the first tester-developer-driver, but my testing put me ahead of so many drivers. At Modena, I could go half-a-second or a second faster than Phil without sneezing. He was only coming to verify what I'd already developed. I'd say a car had understeer, whereas Phil would say it was oversteering. That was due to him pitching the car. I would take the car to the point its first shortcoming showed up and then subsequently, that's what I would report. They'd fix the understeer and the car would be faster."

It was while Richie was at Ferrari that arguably his greatest legacy to motor racing came about. While testing a sports car one day, the car's handling was very unstable and the exhaust gas kept going back into the cockpit. Ginther remembered back to his time both at Douglas Aircraft where he used to have a small piece of aluminium welded upright across the rear deck, and as a mechanic on aircraft during the Korean War and how he used to rivet trim tabs. Ginther mused what might happen if they used a similar process on the car so they tried a similar exercise on the Ferrari after persuading Carlo Chiti and Medardo Fantuzzi to try the idea. The car handled well and the fumes disappeared and the rear spoiler was born. As he recalled in detail to Pete Lyons: "We took the new Tipo 246 sports car, which was a mid-engined car to Monza for the first time. I worked up to speed gradually, as you do, but when I was going fast as I wanted to, I was still unhappy with the times and with the car. At speed, it entered what I guess you call in jargon that came along later, 'The Twilight Zone'. Going down the straights, it felt like a Cadillac, very soft-sprung, very floaty.

"We left with no decisions. Typical of the Italian press, the next day in *La Gazzetta dello Sport*, why there was a telephoto photograph of the car being secretly tested at Monza. I knew what the problem was from the photograph. I went rushing out of my hotel room to the factory with the newspaper in hand and said 'It's flying' as the photograph had shown it tail up.

"So the engineers tried curing the problem with vertical stabilisers, with as many as three fins on the tail, as well as a headrest fin and I kept shaking my head. I'd take it out and try it; they did not do anything. But then they put the outside fins converging with the central one and it was much better. Only thing was that it was now slower on the straights. We removed all the aerodynamically dimensioned vertical stabilisers and took just a flat sheet of aluminium and attached it across the back. Just standing up straight; a vertical aluminium flap. I went faster than I had gone before and maintained the revs along the straight and that was without trying different heights.

"That went back to when I was in the military; when I was a crew chief as I had to understand how aircraft fly. You have trim tabs on the trailing edges of the control surfaces and you bend them until the aircraft flies straight. I kept saying that what we needed was a trim tab. So that's where the spoiler came from, as we know it today. It was practical experience, not science. I never considered myself as a scientist. I could not figure out how to do it at the front of the car until I saw Jim Hall's chin spoiler on a Chaparral a few years later."

The spoiler may well have been his greatest legacy to racing but the same year, 1961, also saw what Richie himself, and so many others, considered his greatest race. It was a race where he matched one of the greatest racing drivers of all time for lap after lap. The Monaco Grand Prix of 1961, the opening race of the season, is rightly remembered as an all-time classic.

Monaco Grand Prix - 1961

"I got a board saying, 'Ginther: Give All'! Jesus Christ, did they think I'd been stroking? You just felt, 'Jeez, what can you do about Moss?' And the answer, of course, was nothing"

Richie Ginther

Wolfgang von Trips and Richie Ginther, Monaco Grand Prix 1961. *The Grand Prix Library*

This chapter is not a detailed race report as such but just to summarise the race briefly for context: Ginther qualified second in the Ferrari 156, only behind Stirling Moss in a far superior handling, albeit much underpowered, Lotus 18 entered by Rob Walker. Richie made a fabulous start and led into the first corner ahead of Moss and Jim Clark in the Lotus before dropping to third behind Moss and Bonnier in the Porsche, thirteen laps later. Ginther and Phil Hill in the other Sharknose Ferrari 156 then played catch-up to Moss, bringing the gap down from eight seconds on lap 50 to three seconds 10 laps later. Despite the Ferrari's power advantage, it had barely been tested and handling woes were a frequent issue for the American duo.

Hill then developed a problem with the carburettor but was able to continue quickly enough to just about keep ahead of Ginther. Not for the first time, or the last, Ferrari was slow to react and let the quicker so-called junior driver past the more senior one. Ginther finally got the go-ahead to pass Hill with a quarter of the race to go and immediately made up the deficit to Moss, harrying him all the way to the chequered flag, finishing 3.6sec behind. To reinforce how quickly they were going, in qualifying Moss and Ginther had lapped in 1m39.1sec and 1m39.3sec, respectively. In the race their average lap time over one hundred laps was 1m39.5sec.

The race is quite rightly remembered as one of Moss's greatest grand prix wins but it was a sensational effort too from Ginther to match the Briton with intensity and speed lap after lap. Both Moss and Ginther consider it their greatest race and so, rather than me go through the grand prix about what happened or repeat the many race reports about this event, I am going to, in this case, let Ginther and Moss recall it in their own words with a comment or two from Phil Hill.

Moss: "Without a doubt, it was the hardest race of my life, and I consider it the best. But I very nearly did not get very far. I called my

Ginther (right) stands by his car before the start of the Monaco Grand Prix, 1961. *Etienne Bourguignon*

The start of the Monaco Grand Prix, 1961. Ginther leads. *Ed McDonough*

mechanic Alf Francis over and said, 'Is that a crack?' He said yes, it was, and off he went to get an oxyacetylene torch. The crack was right next to the fuel tank – which was full, of course. He covered the tank with wet cloths and started welding. Everyone was leaning over and watching what he was doing and then when he lay down on the road and lit this thing, everyone ran for it including me! Rather doubt anyone'd be allowed to do anything like that now."

Ginther: "At the start of the race, I made a perfect getaway and took the lead. After three laps I had five seconds on Moss, who was just ahead of Jo Bonnier in the Porsche. Stirling soon got into his stride though, and after ten laps, my lead was down to one second and even then I was getting threatening pit signals – the down arrow signal with a sign 'Hill-Trips-Ginther' telling me to drop back behind the other two Ferraris and let them try and deal with Moss. They did not want me – the new boy in the new car – to be the winner of that race. So I slowed down."

Moss: "Richie was going well in the lead but I knew Phil Hill would come into the picture, and I needed to get into the lead, and try and make a break and on lap fourteen I did it."

Ginther: "I let Hill and von Trips catch up and go by. In no time at all Moss was ten seconds ahead with all three of us Ferrari drivers mixing it with Bonnier's Porsche. Phil then passed Bonnier and tried to catch Moss, and I got by von Trips as his car was running badly so he waved me by and I set off after Jo, passing him about lap forty. I then began pushing Phil and we got Stirling's lead back down to about seven seconds at the half-way mark. I was up Hill's pipes, but he kept getting the up-arrow [author note: This meant Hill was allowed to stay ahead of Ginther] but his car was not working as good. I was sure I could get away from Phil if only I could get by, but I just did not have the power."

Moss: "I felt that… because I could never get clear of Hill and Ginther; I'd pull away a bit, but then they'd close up again; I really felt they were playing with me. It was not a race I ever thought I'd win; honestly, I thought the Ferraris were biding their time. I'd look in the mirror one lap, and there was Phil behind me. One lap later it would be Richie! I thought they were just buggering about, swapping places for the sake of it. No way did I realise they were getting frantic pit signals, because of course I could not see them. I really believed they were waiting until towards the end; I thought they'd get me on power, on the hill up to Casino Square."

Monaco Grand Prix 1961, Jo Bonnier's Porsche chases the two Ferraris.
Ed McDonough

Richie Ginther, Monaco Grand Prix, 1961.
Jorg-Thomas Fodisch/Ed McDonough

Ginther leads Stirling Moss (20) and Jo Bonnier (2) at the Monaco Grand Prix, 1961. *Ed McDonough*

Monaco Grand Prix, 1961. *Ed McDonough*

Richie Ginther, Monaco Grand Prix at Tabac, 1961. *Graham Gauld*

Phil Hill: "By lap 75, I was wiped out and when they held a board out to me, saying I should let Richie through, it made sense. I was not getting anywhere, so let him have a go. And it made sense in another way, too, because only he had the latest 120-degree V6 in his car; von Trips and I had the 60-degree engines and I knew, from running with Richie, that he had the edge on power."

Ginther: "Phil's idea of letting me by, it turned out, was to wave me past as we went into the tunnel, but not back off at all! We went in side-by-side but I just did not have the power to overtake and had to drop back as there is only one line through there. Then I almost got alongside him going into the hairpin, but he would not back off and I had to hit the brakes and drop behind once more. Eventually he made a mistake at the hairpin at the Gasworks and I went past and just disappeared. But I had lost a lot of time to Moss because my team mate just would not let me by. I thought that was not nice of Phil at all, and that's putting it kindly! I thought we were friends."

Moss: "I remember getting into the lead and thinking, 'Right, I'll hold on for as long as I can'. What I kept doing, through the race, was saying to myself, going into Casino Square or Tabac or wherever, 'OK, you're going to do a perfect lap from here'. Of course you never can do a lap that's perfect, but it was a test I kept setting myself to keep my concentration where it needed to be. It's a lot more difficult to maintain concentration when you're in the lead; it is much easier when you're chasing someone, when you've got a goal to go for."

Ginther: "With Phil out of my way, I made up a bit of time on Moss, but then every time I took a tenth or two off him, that delightful son-of-a-bitch found a way of getting it back. Around lap 83 or 84, well he just broke my heart. I was running at the limit and a bit more and he instantly responded! I had no idea of the times we were doing; all I knew, every time past the pits, was the gap. Then, finally, I got a board saying, 'Ginther: Give All'! Jesus Christ, did they think I'd been stroking? You just felt, 'Jeez, what can you do about this guy?' And the answer, of course, was nothing."

Moss: "That night, in my diary, I wrote 'Drove flat out all race' and underlined the all. That was the only time in my career I put

something like that in the diary; I really was flat out the whole way, and that's why I think it was the best drive of my life. I knew I was trying as hard as I could, that's all. All credit to Richie who fought like a tiger all the way. I don't think I had a single problem with the car, which is surprising, because cars, other than the Ferraris, were pretty unreliable in those days. Thing is, if I'd had a problem, I would not have won, simple as that. I don't remember any mistake or moment where I caught it; honestly not."

Ginther: "That was certainly the best race I ever drove and when Stirling said it was his, too, I felt incredibly proud. He was the greatest driver I ever saw – by a long way – and if I was able to push him to the best drive of his life, that meant something, believe me. That son-of-a-gun! In the Monaco programmes they credit me with the fastest lap for that year, but he equalled it the very lap after I did it! A lot was made about how Stirling beat the more powerful Ferraris but Monaco is a handling circuit and compared to the Lotus, the Ferrari did not handle worth a damn. I was so tired afterwards that when I tried to climb out of my car, my legs just went from under me.

"It had been a marvellous race and it certainly did my reputation a power of good. I was swamped with congratulations afterwards, except from Enzo Ferrari. He never said a word. As miserable as he was, I enjoyed working for him though as his heart was in racing and winning, but he had a strange way of accomplishing that. He was a dictator."

After Richie's death, Stirling Moss recalled to Chris Nixon for an article in *Thoroughbred and Classic Cars* that Richie was "a racer of the old school and a very simpatico sort of guy. Thanks to him, the Monaco Grand Prix was the best race I ever had in my life."

Richie said about Moss to Nigel Roebuck for *Autosport* magazine in 1977: "Moss was the greatest driver that I ever saw, by a long way. But I felt he compromised himself by never joining a team. In a way, I always admired him for that, but a private entry never gets the latest equipment. If he could have joined a team that could have accepted him, that he would have gotten along with and who would have worked with him like he deserved, then Stirling Moss would have been World Champion who knows how many times."

The race, however, was bitter-sweet for Richie and taught him a valuable racing lesson; one that both befits his personality and probably, along with his comments previously to *Autocourse* about mechanical sympathy, best explains why he never ended up with more wins. Sadly, the greatest race of his life also meant a seismic change in the greatest relationship (bar Jackie of course) of his life so far; his feelings towards Phil Hill were never quite the same.

In later life, Ginther spoke to his brother-in-law, Rik Blote, about the race: "I never really forgave Phil for blocking me. It did teach me though that to win, you need to do more than drive well. To finish as number one, at some point drivers often have to push their luck aggressively and risk everything. That's what Phil did that day. Now since I've always liked living, I disliked taking risks like that just to finish first in a motor race."

Gijs van Lennep, who would race in Formula One and sports cars in the 1970s with much success, got to know Richie in the early 1970's as van Lennep was a works Porsche driver. Gijs also knew Cleo from her father's involvement in the sport so met the pair of them a few times over the years. He recalled that Ginther, when remembering 1961, said: "Hill made his mistake and then kind of responded as if he had made a mistake on purpose to show the crowd how he was letting Richie past. Richie felt like punching Phil Hill for that."

It appears that although this race was the seed that sowed resentment in Richie, it did not come out straight away and it certainly was not obvious to the racing world at large. For the rest of 1961, it appeared not to manifest at all, as shown by the recollection by Phil Hill about their road trip to and from Wolfgang von Trips' funeral. It only appeared more in print after Richie's death. His interview with Chris Nixon at the BRM reunion that was later printed for 'Race of My Life' in *Autosport* magazine on 15 March 1990 was the first time the annoyance with Phil had spilt over in a published article. Richie would have known that he had not long to live at that point so it hardly mattered to him if he brought it up in his dying days. Michael Ling, when interviewing Cleo for his article in *Automobile Quarterly* in 2000, also mentions the relationship was not the same in Richie's eyes.

Phil and Richie's close friend Jim Sitz recalls: "I remember a big blow up between Phil and Richie during the Ford GT days. They were travelling together and Richie suddenly let it all out, showing his long time jealousy of Phil and the fame Phil had got through the years. It must have been building up on him. With Monaco, I always got two different versions of what happened. Phil always said he waved him by to chase Moss and it was as simple as that. Richie did not see it that way and he lost time because Hill was driving aggressively. It certainly began bad feelings.

"Phil did say to me that they did patch their relationship up somewhat later on after Phil finally got married. Richie met Cleo, Phil was now married to Alma and these two women had an effect on them both."

Both Jim Sitz and Doug Nye, who interviewed Phil Hill many times, recall that the incident itself that truly ended the friendship happened in a restaurant in 1964. What exactly was said was between the two men is unknown but it appears some off the-cuff-

Richie at the Station Hairpin, Monaco Grand Prix, 1961. **The Grand Prix Library**

Phil Hill and Richie Ginther, Italian Grand Prix, 1961. *Fred Taylor/The Grand Prix Library*

Phil Hill and Richie Ginther, Belgian Grand Prix, 1963. *MullerCologne*

remark set off the explosive outburst Richie was evidently capable of. All the resentment of Monaco 1961, being number two, Phil taking the credit (not for himself but by the motorsport media at large) for Richie's testing work and so on came to the fore as Richie launched a tirade against his long-time friend. Phil was so dumbstruck he never said a word, perhaps wisely.

Paul Foxall was a broadcaster who knew both men well: "I knew Phil anyway, and when I got in touch with him about tracking down Richie [for the BRM reunion in 1989], he could not have been more encouraging. When he heard of Richie's death in France, Phil was the first person to ring me to see if it was true. I met Phil years later at the Goodwood Revival and he just wanted to speak more about Richie."

Jim Sitz: "At the memorial service for Rich, Phil spent a lot of time with Bret and conveyed to him just how big a contribution his father had made on all the teams he drove for."

The short of it is, though, that Richie no longer idolised or had much time for Phil from late 1961 onwards. Cleo quite simply says "Richie did not like Phil." While it is clear Richie held the bigger grudge between the two men, to be fair to Richie – who appears to have had a near-30-year humungous chip on his shoulder – it appears that Phil did not really, at the crucial time, make many overtures to Richie about what happened at Monaco and it is not clear if he ever actually apologised to Richie; whether Phil felt he should have done so or not is immaterial. It is clear that the resentment was allowed to fester where a few choice harmonious

words might have done the trick, either on the day in Monte Carlo or a short while later. Maybe Phil could have reflected on Richie's outburst in 1964 and sought to try and work out what was wrong with his old friend but he might well have had justifiable reasons to not persevere.

Phil, on his side, never said much about the falling out. The only real interview he actually alluded to it was to Richard Heseltine in an interview with *Motorsport* magazine in 2005: "About the time he stopped driving, I was busy getting married and starting a family. He was busy getting a divorce. We had a falling out so I did not stay in touch with him much after that. Richie was a nice, easy-going kid who became more serious once he got into Formula One. He wanted to project himself as being professional, so I suppose he became more assertive as time went on. Having said that, he was never shy about speaking his mind."

Without Phil Hill, Ginther would never have been a racing driver. Phil got Richie a job at International Motors. Phil sought Richie as soon as Richie was back from Korea to help him as a co-driver and mechanic. They shared so much time on the road together both through work and racing. Working on Phil's car saw John von Neumann meet Richie to then change the path of Richie's career. Phil helped, where he could, Richie get the Ferrari works role. The two shared so many intimate times together and it is immensely sad therefore that Richie's greatest race spelt the end to a close friendship and that the two should have drifted – and allowed themselves to drift – so far apart in life.

Ginther's Rift

"Enzo said to me, 'Sign it or you'll never drive in
Formula One again.' I snatched it up and threw it
across the desk at him; right into his lap"
Richie Ginther

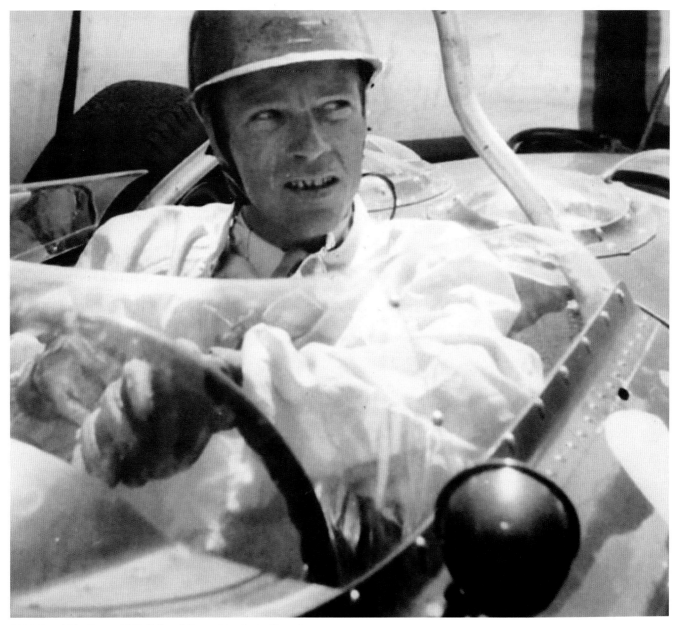

British Grand Prix, Aintree, 1961. *Hallawell Photos, Manchester/Steve Payne*

I t was with some surprise, and some considerable acrimony, that Ginther left Ferrari at the end of 1961 to join the BRM team. There are many reasons or theories for this, all of which will be looked at below, but Ginther had already alluded to the fact that a Ferrari drive was not for life in September 1961 to *Car and Driver*. "I respect their racing cars and could stay here for years. However the cars are fast but the pay is low; apparently the Commendatore hasn't fully realised that we're not all Counts like Wolfgang. Dan Gurney, who has a wife and two children would love to race here, but decided it was not worth the strain. If I ever feel that I'm being treated worse than I deserve, then I'll move on."

Of course, there will never be confirmation of what actually happened for certain and the fact that there are so many theories suggests the actual situation is far from clear-cut. However, many sources cite money, or the lack of it, as being the chief reason. Richie was offered, according to Michael Ling, a 1962 contract but on reduced pay. Bear in mind, according to Richie, he got $400 a month for racing for Ferrari. This was quite low for his profession; certainly nothing compared to what the drivers of the 2019 Formula One grid earn. It was not just confined to Ginther himself; Chris Amon recalled to Nigel Roebuck that he also got $400 a month in 1967!

So an already industry-low $400 was reduced significantly and it was also a contract that offered no guarantee of drives (hence the reduction) but was solely for a test driver role. If this is the case, then it's quite clear Ferrari rated him very highly for his testing ability but clearly felt there were better racing talents than Ginther around and, as Richie had said to many publications that he was not going to push the car to win at any cost, this, more than likely, went against Enzo Ferrari's beliefs and the commitment he wanted from a driver – as Phil Hill recalled to *Sports Illustrated* in 1976.

"To this day I do not know if he had any genuine feelings for us as individuals or whether we were just tools tolerated as necessary evils. When one of us did win it was more as if Ferrari felt the victory was doubly his; he had not only managed to build the fastest car but one that was good enough to foil his drivers' destructiveness. There was something about the mood at Ferrari that did seem to spur drivers to their deaths. Perhaps it was the intense sibling rivalry Ferrari fostered, his failure to rank drivers and his fickleness with favourites. Luigi Musso died at Reims striving to protect his fair-haired-boy status against the encroaching popularity of the Englishmen, Peter Collins and Mike Hawthorn. And Collins, a favourite while living in the hotel within earshot of the factory, began to get a Ferrari cold shoulder when he got married and went to live on a boat in Monte Carlo. He was dead within the year. Time and again I felt myself bristling as Ferrari used Richie Ginther and Dan Gurney to needle me. And certainly Trips and I were locked in combat."

We have learned that Ginther had a short fuse, something that would come out more at BRM but had already manifested itself somewhat at Ferrari and it looks like Ginther's naivety or basic refusal to be political at Ferrari stunted his progress. His comments to *Car and Driver* would have been noted by Ferrari that this was not a gladiatorial racing driver willing to die trying. So it's natural that Ferrari, ever the master Machiavellian, would have seized on these comments and pushed Richie into a role that he likely thought Richie would have been happy with and was best suited for. To be fair to Ferrari, Richie quite possibly was, but not for the amount of money he was offered.

Ginther's recollection of the meeting with Ferrari, as he recalled to Pete Lyons (*Car & Driver* 1988) and friend Gijs van Lennep (who later wrote in his obituary/tribute to Richie in *NRC Handelsblad*, 9 December 1989) was as follows: "They offered me the original contract, which was part-time pay and no guaranteed starts. I wanted an honest contract, so I said no. I was told that Il Commendatore wanted to see me and that it could all be worked out. So I was ushered in to see him across that great desk of his and he smiled and told me that he now had a new contract for me. Why, I took one glance at it and could see it was exactly the same contract that I turned down already. So I refused. He said to me, 'Sign it or you'll never drive in Formula One again.' I snatched it up and threw it across the desk at him; right into his lap. He did not say another word to me, but called in a flunky and told him to take the key to Signor Ginther's car and go and check the jack is still in it."

In Anthony Pritchard's book, *Grand Prix Ferrari: The Years of Enzo Ferrari's Power, 1948-1980*, another theory is offered in that Ginther was the victim of mistrust and paranoia floating around Maranello at the time, or at least this is what was alleged. However, this version of Ginther's departure from Ferrari must be seen in the context from who supplied Pritchard the information: Romolo Tavoni. Tavoni was Ferrari's team manager between 1957 and 1961, which included their successful, albeit tragic championship win, as well as Mike Hawthorn's 1958 Drivers' Championship but also took in the deaths of Luigi Musso, Peter Collins and Eugenio Castelotti as well as von Trip's death in 1961.

Tavoni, a long-time friend of Pritchard, is, at the time of writing, still alive at the age of 94, but the information given to Prichard may well have an agenda; to besmirch Eugenio Dragoni, Tavoni's replacement as team manager and who many would have believe was less popular than Tavoni. A little background is needed here to explain more.

At the end of 1961, eight Ferrari executives left Ferrari after a ferocious argument with Enzo Ferrari which centred on Enzo's wife, Laura. They felt that she was negatively influencing Ferrari in all kinds of company affairs. She was attending races and visiting the factory on behalf of Enzo, but as far as the eight were concerned, she was overstepping the mark between their roles and whatever they deemed as her position within the company. One thing is clear, Enzo Ferrari was not a man to discuss ways forward; it was his way or no way. Along with Tavoni, designers Giotto Bizzarrini and Carlo Chiti, commercial director Girolamo Gardini, four other employees left, many of whom became founding members of the ATS (Automobili Turismo e Sport) team shortly after.

So enter Eugenio Dragoni. Dragoni, originally a perfume salesman, later became the owner and manager of Scuderia Sant Ambroseus and in 1961, had run Giancarlo Baghetti in what was effectively a de facto fourth official Ferrari car. This had come about after, especially, the deaths of Luigi Musso and Peter Collins in 1958. As Phil Hill would say some years later to *Motorsport*, "The Old Man was getting criticised to hell and of course the Vatican pitched in, saying racing should be banned, and Ferrari was a killer of young men, and all that stuff." Enzo Ferrari wanted nothing more than Italians winning grand prix in his cars, but also emphatically did not want the vociferous abuse should one of his countrymen die whilst racing for him. Therefore, the Scuderia Sant Ambroseus solution worked nicely for everyone.

Dragoni was a polarising figure. Within Italy and Ferrari, he is remembered well. Mauro Forghieri, later to be one of Ferrari's most successful designers and team managers, credits Dragoni with a number of positive attributes in his book Forghieri on Ferrari but also puts the role of Dragoni (and Tavoni) in context:

"Being a Ferrari man meant executing his orders, for better or for worse. When the eight Ferrari executives were fired in 1961, there was a real revolution. The role of technical director was entrusted to me, I was very young, but Eugenio Dragoni was a very experienced man to help me from the point of view of sports management. He was chosen for a number of reasons, including that he had a lot of knowledge and power in the CSAI. As he was very wealthy, he also became team manager for free and wanted no bonuses or commission. With the arrival of Dragoni, Ferrari became a lot more professional as Dragoni used a level of ambassadorial skills.

"Dragoni gradually changed the image of Scuderia Ferrari and also discovered many young drivers such as Ludovico Scarfiotti, Nino Vaccarella and Lorenzo Bandini. But his reputation suffered with the argument with John Surtees. Really, it was Enzo Ferrari. Dragoni only executed orders and did the job he was employed to do the best he could."

Without delving too much into Eugenio Dragoni, as this book, after all, is not about him, his reputation in the English-speaking motorsport world is less favourable. Phil Hill simply described Dragoni, even with the benefit of elapsed time in 1994, as "That guy was just something else". Hill felt that Dragoni was blaming only him for the struggles of 1962, with the cowardice of Hill a chief reason (which sounds more like an Enzo Ferrari suggestion but in Dragoni's words), for their failure. It was a mixture of a whole range of things. The English teams had cottoned on to Ferrari's development, Carlo Chiti had left, Ginther had left and Forghieri was still finding his way. Hill's decision to leave Ferrari forever was cemented when he heard Dragoni say after an unsuccessful 1962 Belgian Grand Prix, *"Il tuo grande campione non ha fatto niente"* (Your great champion did not do a thing). But it was when Dragoni was involved in John Surtees' departure from Ferrari (as mentioned above) that the English-speaking press found its archetypal villain; Dragoni either being the culprit or the mouthpiece, whomever you believe, as the man who suggested John Surtees was no longer physically fit and able to drive for Ferrari in 1966 due to a crash in a Lola at Mosport in a Can-Am accident in 1965. Being hurt when driving a non-Ferrari car appears to have particularly upset Ferrari. Surtees vehemently disagreed and left the team while still at his peak.

Now the (extensive) background is over, back to Romolo Tavoni talking to Pritchard: "Mr Ferrari should have kept Richie for 1962, but in the autumn of '61 it was reported to him in a phone call by Eugenio Dragoni that Ginther was seen talking to Tony Rudd

Carlo Chiti and Richie Ginther. **Archive Nils Ruwisch**

of BRM in a restaurant at Modena. Mr Ferrari refused to renew Richie's contract because he thought he was planning to join BRM I learned that the meeting was purely social, but once he knew his contract was not going to be renewed Richie walked straight into a drive with the British team."

Former Ferrari employee Mauro Prampolini remembered Ginther as his favourite driver during his time there (due to his dedication to development) and said that Ginther decided to leave Ferrari long before Dragoni got involved and while Tavoni was still team manager: "Ginther left Ferrari at the end of the 1961 season, before the eight managers quit. He left along with engineer Vico Chizzola; they both left by their own accord. I believe that he had already signed a contract with BRM for 1962. I remember one evening crying, after learning that he would no longer race with Ferrari."

Either way, Ginther was out immediately. As he later recounted to Nigel Roebuck in 1977, "The Commendatore was so angry I was not even allowed to go round the factory to say goodbye. Fortunately, the mechanics came to my apartment to see me." Ferrari's finance manager Ermanno Della Casa later revealed that, when Richie quit Ferrari at the end of 1961 bound for BRM, he was frisked when he left the Maranello factory for the last time. Ginther retained his respect for Ferrari despite all this, saying to Pete Lyons in 1988 for his article in *Car and Driver*; "I admire the Old Man to this day [note this interview was done just before Ferrari's death in August 1988]. He's a dictator, he demands the highest standards."

The feeling remained across the racing world, however, that Ferrari had made a mistake in letting Ginther go. No less than a driver of Tony Brooks' calibre said in a preview for the forthcoming season in *The Observer* newspaper in 1962: "Giancarlo Baghetti and Lorenzo Bandini, though possessing considerable talent are still lacking experience. The Maranello concern must be feeling the loss of Richie Ginther to BRM. The little Californian was extremely valuable in sorting out the cars during pre-race testing."

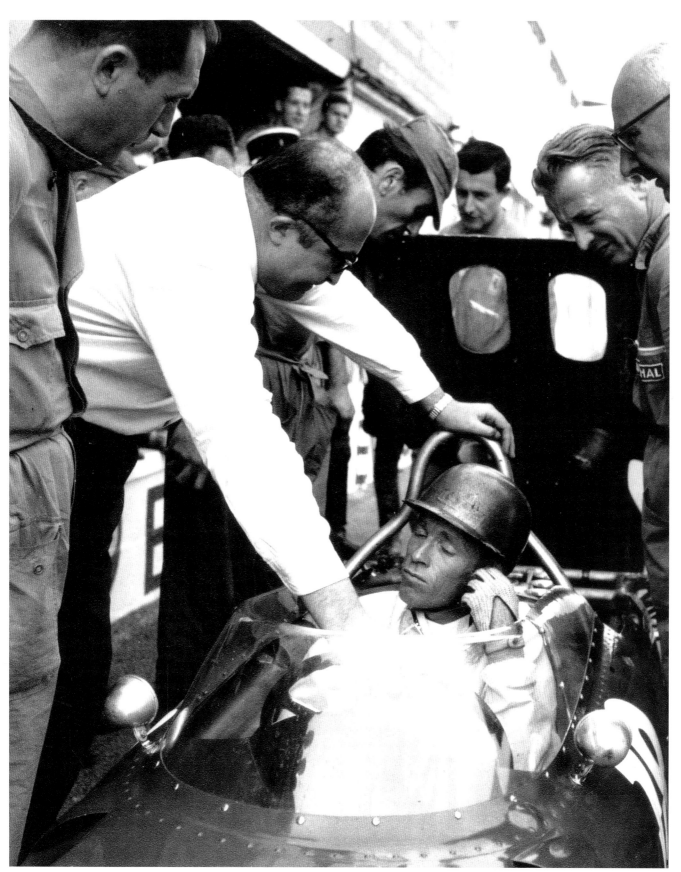

Chiti and Richie, French Grand Prix, 1961. **David Hodges/Ed McDonough**

Chapter Six

Richie's meeting with Rudd was always labelled as social, but the likelihood is there was some intent or interest in moving away relatively imminently. The drain of experienced names from the team would have been unsettling and Ginther's annoyance with Hill over Monaco must have been preying on his mind. Hill was now World Champion and Richie cannot have felt it would have been a truly fair fight to become the team's number one. Dick Salmon, the BRM mechanic who later wrote *BRM: A Mechanic's Tale*, recalled explicitly that Ginther was persuaded to leave Ferrari to join BRM, rather than just being available.

As it happened though, a number of sources have said that both Phil Hill and Richie Ginther were approached by BRM. The first source is an interview between motorsport journalists Nigel Roebuck and Jean-Louis Moncet, both of whom were particularly close to one of the doyens of the motorsport journalistic world, Gerard 'Jabby' Crombac, who was the likely source of the information. They said that both Hill and Ginther were approached by BRM in 1961. Ginther agreed, but Phil stayed for two reasons. Firstly that Ferrari increased his wage (this happened naturally, not as a result of the BRM talks) and secondly because Ferrari promised Hill that he would do all the sports car races for Ferrari in 1962, something Hill was much keener on doing than Grand Prix racing.

The next source is long-time Hill and Ginther friend Jim Sitz; "In November 1961, Phil and Richie met up with Tony Rudd. Both made a verbal agreement to drive for BRM as at that time, Graham Hill had not agreed to their terms as he wanted more money. Tony Brooks was thinking about retirement. As Phil was World Champion, he was offered double than what he was earning at Ferrari. I accused Phil of speaking to BRM merely to increase his worth at Scuderia Ferrari but he was emphatic that he was leaving and he just had to tell Mr Ferrari face-to-face. Well, Phil and Richie were quite different when it came to speaking to Mr Ferrari face-to-face!"

In Doug Nye's opus of BRM history, the potential driver merry-go-round is explored in some considerable detail, in particular in Volume 2, thanks to the thorough notes and correspondence kept by Tony Rudd. As fascinating as the six pages of the book devoted to the off-season are, I've summarised Rudd's notes below with some of my own observations.

By September 1961, discussion was fully under way regarding drivers for 1962. Rudd reported that a number of drivers are interested in driving for them and for once, BRM is in a strong position to have a good line-up. Driver payment was the key to negotiations though with Rudd reporting that, in 1961, Tony Brooks and Graham Hill were receiving in salary, prize money, starting money and so on, £25,000 [Author note; to put that in context, although it is nothing compared to what the majority of F1 drivers today get, £25,000 in 1961 is now effectively almost £860,000 a year, a hefty sum, similar to what 2019 Formula 1 driver Robert Kubica earns]. Raymond Mays had learnt that all the Ferrari drivers, including Richie, were paid £3000 plus starting and prize money at 50 percent. Rudd was keen for tighter control regarding driver salaries for 1962.

In early November 1961, Ginther agreed to join BRM. Richie had been targeted as BRM knew they could offer him real money at last, but he was what was required at that time; a technically adept and experienced test driver who could also perform in public on the Formula One World Championship stage. Ginther was told that the position of who would be the number one driver and even the number two driver was not settled but Ginther decided to sign.

Peter Berthon, BRM's chief engineer and long-time manager then got in touch with Graham Hill over a number of issues but made it quite clear the £25,000 was not happening again. Instead it would be £4500 contract, 50 percent of starting, bonus and prize money, £1000 for a win, £350 for second (championship races only) and £100 for third (likewise, only for the World Championship races). Berthon then turned the screw somewhat on Hill by approaching John Surtees, Jack Brabham, Innes Ireland, Jo Bonnier and Phil Hill.

Phil came over to Lincolnshire on 10 and 11 November. He told BRM that verbally he had agreed to stay with Ferrari but that no contract had been signed. He would sign for BRM if they could guarantee him £10,000 a season, provided he could leave Ferrari with a clear conscience. He flew back to Italy to see Ferrari on 12 November. On 14 November, he confirmed that he was staying with Ferrari and would be paid £15,000 – a huge rise for Ferrari, even for a World Champion, from what they previously had been paying. Had Phil said yes, then it would have been Phil and Richie together again. Maybe a new team, working closely together (with no von Trips or anyone else) and different surroundings might have solved, or maybe softened somewhat, the Monaco 1961 spat. However, if Hill was on £15,000, and Ginther on a lot less, that might have been another reason for Richie to feel Phil got better treatment and sowed even more resentment.

However, it is worth pointing out at this stage that Phil may well have been the reason that BRM signed Richie as well. Phil started initial discussions with Tony Rudd before Rudd met Richie. It is not clear if Rudd had always identified Richie or not as a potential target (the answer is a probable yes, Richie's stock was high from Monaco 1961), but historian Doug Nye has confirmed that Phil definitely recommended Richie to Rudd and did his best to promote Ginther's racing career as best he could. The exact timeline is unclear but irrespective, Phil's backing would have made Rudd feel a lot more comfortable about his new number two driver.

Graham Hill had been approached by Porsche with an offer of £5000 and 80 percent starting and prize money but in the end, in late November, he decided that, on balance, it worked best for him to remain at BRM. On 4 December, although he had already decided to leave BRM at the American Grand Prix, Tony Brooks officially retired from motor racing. Tony Brooks, generally, is one of motor racing's 'good blokes'. It was one of this author's most enjoyable moments in writing this book to speak to this delightful man for some while about Richie. But in a stinging letter to Sir Alfred Owen, he did not hold back about how miserable he found the 1961 season for a whole number of reasons, but the chief one was driver equality. The key paragraphs are as follows:

"The equality agreement, which was discussed in great detail before the contract was signed, was flouted time and time again and culminated at Monza in the giving of my V8 BRM to the other member of the team. A certain party admitted it was completely contrary to what we had agreed before the contract was signed but said that conditions had changed since we discussed it. I can visualise a repetition next season of this season's nonsense if action is not taken. I have never experienced the situation at BRM with any other team and I have met some very difficult people.

"I would very much like to see you do well and Richie Ginther is a good and likeable driver. I would like to think that he would not be compelled to put up with the situation experienced by myself and that he would be happy to remain with BRM and always be psychologically at his best."

So, in effect, BRM was sorted by the beginning of December, or so they thought. Peter Berthon announced a third driver, in February 1962, who was a young South African called Bruce Johnstone, who was to be a test/reserve driver and mechanic. What Berthon had failed to mention was that Bruce's mother was the best friend of Peter Berthon's soon-to-be wife, Althea! (In the end, possibly due to the departure of Berthon soon afterwards, Johnstone endured a difficult year, racing only once, at his home grand prix in the last race of the season which ended up being his only World Championship event). The family link is also not really fair on Bruce as he was consistently one of the best drivers in the South African Formula One Championship in the very early 1960s and with fellow countryman Tony Maggs impressing many in Formula Junior as he won the European Championship (shared with Jo Siffert) in 1961, BRM wanted to tap a potential gold-mine of driving talent.

Anyway, back to Richie. Despite all of the above political and financial shenanigans, the reason to leave Ferrari may have actually been influenced heavily by Jackie Ginther. She later confessed to Michael Ling for his *Automobile Quarterly* article that she had been too young to really appreciate living abroad. She did not pick up as much Italian as Richie and as a result felt somewhat isolated and lonely. She was also homesick for her family and, unlike in America where she was already involved in detailed work and motorsport before she met Richie, she was now, in her eyes, solely 'Mrs Ginther' and not seen as a person in her own right. All of these stresses tragically led to a late term miscarriage in 1960. So Richie would have been both considerate of Jackie's feelings and the joint heartache of losing a baby. When these discussions came up about staying at Ferrari almost eighteen months on from the miscarriage, Jackie was two to three months pregnant and Richie knew a move away to keep Jackie happier would have been of benefit to all concerned, including the unborn child. That said, Jackie believed, as she recalled to Ling, that Richie would have stayed at Ferrari if the offer was not insulting.

There's a lot of smoke and mirrors above, but to summarise it the very best I can I believe the actual chain of events to be:

- Ginther decides, by his own choice, to leave Ferrari due to a combination of low pay, the death of von Trips, his annoyance with Phil Hill, his position within the team and Jackie's pregnancy.
- Ginther does indeed meet up with Tony Rudd and agrees to sign for BRM as their number two driver either to Graham Hill or to Phil Hill, his grudge with the latter nothwithstanding.

Richie, Jackie and Puck, their dachshund.
Dr Benno Muller Archive/Jorg-Thomas Fodisch

- However, likely prompted by Jackie, Ginther decides to see Ferrari to discuss his options and seek a payrise. When his contract is officially given to him, he already knows he has a BRM drive. Therefore when the subsequent contract does not resolve the outstanding issues of pay and his role within the team, Ginther can be as dismissive as he likes towards Enzo Ferrari.
- The Dragoni story is irrelevant to Ginther leaving, if indeed the events happened as they did. This all seems pinpointed on Dragoni due to the political hurricane swirling around Maranello. Neither is the departure of Carlo Chiti, Romolo Tavoni or anyone else a factor in Ginther's decision.

Ginther retained amicable links to Ferrari, however, for the rest of his life. When he appeared at Hockenheim to celebrate Goodyear's 100th Grand Prix win in 1977, he spent most of the time as much a guest of Ferrari as Goodyear, even sitting in Niki Lauda's 312-T car. When discussing them in 1967, Richie was largely positive: "Ferrari has been in the racing business for so long and so successfully, his organisation has a lot going for it. The Italians seem to have an inherent ability to build competitive cars. I did have a feeling at times that they might be a bit over-confident and not receptive to new ideas and changes."

Rik Blote, the brother of Ginther's second wife, also recalled that, although he believes Richie left Ferrari to join BRM by his own volition, Richie must have left on good terms with Ferrari as Ginther received a Christmas card from Ferrari every year. It's hard to see that happening if the contract had indeed been thrown back in Enzo Ferrari's lap.

Bourne to Race

"Richie Ginther is not a sentimental figure. He's a Cheshire cat; always seen with a broad fixed grin. Cheshire cats are never sentimental but Richie possesses bags of natural charm"
Louis Stanley, author

Dutch Grand Prix, 1964. *Gunther Asshauer*

t BRM's base in Bourne, Lincolnshire, England, Ginther linked up with another Hill, this one called Graham. Coming from the high drama and high emotions from Maranello, working at BRM appeared, on the initial face of it, to be a more relaxed affair. As it happened, there was immense pressure on everyone. BRM had continually promised much and failed to deliver year after year. Sir Alfred Owen, the owner of BRM, had said to Rudd that if the team did not win, then Owen would disband the team for good. Rudd, who was now team manager and chief engineer worked hard to source the best people he could obtain.

Ginther's technical knowledge, mechanical sympathy and genuine fast pace would have made him an attractive proposition. Maybe it was only that Rudd was garnering Ginther's technical feedback in that Modena restaurant but if that was the case, then being able to sign Ginther shortly afterwards was an unexpected bonus.

Rudd was a very practical man who, as mentioned a number of times in Doug Nye's BRM books, had no management style at all. Using a plethora of respect and strong personnel skills to get the best out of Graham Hill, Rudd also had design nous to create the P57 and equally had an eye for talent to sign Ginther to both drive and develop the car and all this combined saw the team flourish. Ginther was, by his own admission, a perfectionist and a pessimist and was more serious than humorous when it came to the business of racing. Hill was very much dedicated himself, but able to deflect his stresses somewhat into his larger-than-life positive persona. In short, BRM had a very workable, very favourable duo with complementary skills to enhance their chances of success. Hill won the World Championship for Drivers and BRM won the Constructors' Championship; the International Cup for F1 Manufacturers.

It did not start well though for everyone. On 18 March 1962, while testing at North Witham Airfield in Lincolnshire, a loose banjo-coupling connection on the fuel pump outlet sprayed fuel onto the car and the back of Richie's neck. Interestingly, instead of just stopping and jumping out, Richie drove the car for some while and got badly burnt as a result. Richie reacted very differently, rightly, at the end-of-season South African Grand Prix, when during practice the electrics caused a fire behind him. Richie jumped out of the cockpit and ran down the nose of the car and because he was a small and light man, he did not even make a dent in the car!

Richie, now engulfed by fire at North Witham, owed his subsequent racing career and quality of life to two BRM mechanics. The first was Arthur Hill who smothered Ginther's flames out immediately and then, secondly, Dennis Perkins who rushed Richie to Stamford hospital. He made a full recovery but it ruled him out of the non-championship Brussels Grand Prix at Heysel Park and the Lombank Trophy at Snetterton. However the fact that Tony Rudd offered to house Ginther at his own home while he recovered from his injuries was a testament to how popular he had already become.

John Sismey worked in motorsport for many years but spent some time in the early 1960s as a mechanic at BRM: "They just went up there to try something and I think the car was still unpainted, so they took a minimal crew up there. Richie was cruising around and it was the first time we'd tried the fuel injection. It was very high pressure

Tony Rudd, Richie and Graham Hill before the 1962 British Grand Prix, Aintree.
Brian Tregilgas

and something was not quite tight enough. There was a leak of fuel which ignited from the exhaust and it burnt the back of his neck. He came in straight away, and they took him to the hospital which was about twenty minutes away. Tony Rudd came into the workshop and told us what had happened and encouraged us to go and see him. So my wife Margaret and I did just that. I remember that he said to another of my colleagues [Author note: The colleague was probably Dick Salmon who recalls the following comment in his book] 'Well, thank God it happened in Britain. If it had happened at Monza, all the Ferrari mechanics would have run in the opposite direction; you all ran towards me!'"

Tony Rudd recalled to Eoin Young in 2001 in *Classic Cars* magazine about the whole experience: "We were testing and vibration had unscrewed a banjo in the fuel system and petrol was spraying over Richie and the engine. It ignited but instead of switching off and bailing out, he drove the burning car to us and then jumped out with his overalls ablaze. His mechanic, Arthur Hill, knocked him down and rolled on him to extinguish his burning overalls while I used a 50lb extinguisher to put the fire out on the car. I rolled Richie in my overcoat and Dennis rushed him to Stamford hospital which had a specialised burns unit.

"Richie made good progress. I used to go and see him each evening. He was great fun and had a wealth of stories of his days as a Ferrari tester. Sir Alfred Owen came to visit Richie in hospital and the outcome of their conversation was a reorganisation of the BRM team. I had just been dogsbody to Peter Berthon when Richie went into hospital. When I collected him eighteen days later, I was monarch of all I surveyed at Bourne, chief executive and team manager of the Owen Racing Organisation."

Before Rudd's comments are interpreted as such that Richie was responsible for the whole reorganisation of BRM, there needs to be a little context. As already mentioned, Sir Alfred Owen had got very frustrated about the complete lack of success from the team, especially when Cooper had won the 1959 World Championship on a fraction of the budget. He had already decided that if success was not forthcoming, he would pull the plug on the team at the end

Richie in the BRM, 1962. *Lesley Appel*

Dutch Grand Prix, 1962. *Roy Lane/Ed McDonough*

Richie at the German Grand Prix, 1962. *Gunther Asshauer*

of the season. Ginther's injuries, though, had shocked and subdued everyone, not least Sir Alfred. His sister Jean Stanley had persuaded Sir Alfred to carry on as they were potentially in a brilliant position, but that one person – that being Tony Rudd – had to be in charge. Owen spoke to both Graham Hill and then Richie while the American was in hospital and decided that Berthon was out and Rudd was now in charge.

Elizabeth Clare was one of the nurses who treated Richie during his stay at Stamford and remembers his stay well. "I was a nurse at Stamford & Rutland Memorial Hospital when Richie was brought in for treatment to the burns he had suffered in his testing accident at North Witham. We didn't know who he was when he arrived but, when we were told, it was quite exciting to have a celebrity patient. It certainly made the headlines in the local newspaper, the *Stamford Mercury*.

"He had quite severe burns to his neck and back, which we had to keep spraying rather than bandaging them. As a private patient, he would normally have had a side room to himself, but because the hospital had only six private beds and was very busy at the time, we had to put him in a shared ward for two people that already had someone else in it who was being treated for kidney failure. I recall Richie wasn't too happy about it!

"The shared ward was right next door to the private ward, which was run by a Ward Sister who treated the unit like her own realm –

especially if someone significant was in for treatment. For example, when the nearby Burleigh Horse Trials were on, she never went off duty. I think Richie received most of his treatment in the private ward, even though his bed was outside of it. He spent most of his time walking about, keeping himself to himself mostly, and I don't recall him having many visitors at the hospital. He didn't particularly like being in hospital and left as soon as he could."

Rudd housed Ginther who, through boredom, became a handyman, chauffeur and family friend. Jackie was now back in the US, heavily pregnant. He fixed the television, any children's toys that were broken and even relaid the carpet to minimise wear. Lesley Appel, one of Tony's daughters, remembers Richie with great fondness: "Richie more or less lived with us while he was at BRM and was very much loved by us. He was genuinely lovely and, of course, I was only at most six or seven years of age but we have never forgotten him. He collected us from school in our Austin A40 car, and was always taking something apart from the television to the stair carpet. He said to us that as he had served in Korea as a United States Air Force electronics crew chief that he liked taking things apart. My dad even jokingly thought about delaying his return to racing so he could fix more of the house! He was great fun to be around as a kid. I can remember how awful his back looked. Mum would not allow him to recuperate in a hotel. He was at my sister Philippa's christening in odd socks which would be in 1964. He loved doing the school run but I think only in the afternoon. We had stools in the boot of the A40 and thought his driving was great fun, always great to have a grand prix driver drive you back from school. I remember when he had the accident and the burns; I heard he was bundled in the back of a car and taken to hospital and I think that was when I saw his back. For a while he had to lie on his tummy."

Richie was clearly not a fan of the A40 as he told, as per Doug Nye's BRM Volume 2 book, Sir Alfred Owen that it was not appropriate transport for the BRM Chief Engineer and Team Manager. 'Quite right' said Owen, 'I will see to it that he gets a new car'. Richie mentioned this at the International Trophy at Silverstone on 11 May. On the 13th, Rudd was asked to bring in the A40 and was presented with a brand-new Hillman Super Minx as a result.

Although Ginther brought a lot to the table for BRM, his influence was not quite as dramatic in Lincolnshire as it had been in Italy. John Sismey: "He came to us, of course, with a reputation as a tester and he did contribute a bit but I don't think he was as important for us as he was for Ferrari because Graham Hill was a very good tester as well. Graham wanted to go through the whole range of springs, roll bars and dampers and all that to get it right and he used to note everything down in his book and Richie almost went along with what Graham set up."

Ginther, was by now a father, when wife Jackie gave birth to Bret Evans Ginther (Richie's only child) on 10 June 1962. Richie took two podiums (third in France and second in Italy) that year in, injuries excepted, what should be viewed as a largely encouraging season overall, despite another crash in the Dutch Grand Prix, albeit this one was not his fault at all: a sticking throttle had slowed his car down and before he could move out of the racing line, he was collected by Lotus driver Trevor Taylor.

Richie felt that 1962 had been a disastrous year for him personally, despite the fact that he had helped BRM win the Constructors' Championship and helped team-mate Graham Hill win the driver's championship. He later recalled to Eoin Young: "My first year was terrible. I had a heck of a time, what with the car catching fire when I was testing, crashing fairly hard at Silverstone, having the throttle stick wide open at the Monaco start, gearboxes breaking, it was not a good year at all."

Indeed, there was a catalogue of issues throughout the year. Richie endured engine failure at the BARC Aintree 200, the Rand Grand Prix and the United States Grand Prix; gearbox failure at the Reims Grand Prix and Belgian Grand Prix; and piston failure at the International Gold Cup. Even the Italian Grand Prix, where he finished second, was not without its problems as he had an engine failure in qualifying.

Richie crashes out of the Dutch Grand Prix, 1962. **Gunther Asshauer**

British Grand Prix, Aintree, 1962. *Brian Tregilgas*

Belgian Grand Prix, 1962. *Archive Nils Ruwisch*

He finished at the British Grand Prix in thirteenth but was in line for a potential points finish before a combination of throttle assembly and electric pump issues saw him lose several laps. Although there were strong drives, a pole position at Oulton Park and fast times, there were only the two aforementioned podium finishes (his only World Championship points-scoring finishes) and a third place in the non-Championship Natal Grand Prix to show for it. Graham Hill had amassed 52 points in total (albeit 10 were removed from the official score as only the best five results counted for the World Championship back then), Richie had mustered just ten.

Even the third place in France at Rouen was a disappointment as, realistically, Richie could have well have won. Ferrari could not take part due to a metalworker's strike in Italy. Leading contenders Jo Bonnier, Graham Hill, Jim Clark and Jack Brabham all retired. Dan Gurney won for Porsche, but Richie would surely have been up there challenging for a victory had it not been his car's failure to start and then having to push the car unaided, as per regulations, into the pits, where it was found that the starter motor had broken. Ginther lost 75 seconds, and a good three-quarters of a lap to everyone else there. The amount of retirements sped him up somewhat and he was gaining seven seconds a lap on Tony Maggs in second place before a throttle linkage problem slowed him down with five laps to go. In fact, on the last lap, ever the mechanically

sympathetic driver, he had to control the throttle wire manually with his right hand which is a remarkable feat when you consider the gearbox was also on the right-hand-side.

Although Ginther does not refer to the throttle incident at Monaco above in any great detail, this was another reason 1962 was such a wretched year for Richie. At the start of the grand prix, when the throttle stuck, he could not slow his car down at the Gazomètre Hairpin and crashed into Maurice Trintignant and Innes Ireland, while Dan Gurney's Porsche and Trevor Taylor's factory Lotus were also involved. The right rear wheel flew from Ginther's car and struck the head of marshal Ange Baldoni, who was the Automobile Club's commissaire-contrôleur. He was very seriously injured and taken to the Princess Grace Polyclinic of Monaco. After being given first aid, he was transferred to the Saint Roch hospital in Nice where, despite an operation, he died, aged 52, on the morning of 12 June. Baldoni was also the assistant manager of the Monaco Bus Company depot. Ginther was utterly blameless but would likely have been distraught that Baldoni's death had come through a crash caused by him and a part of his car striking the fatal blow.

John Sismey recalls that Richie was getting more and more nervous before the start of races, maybe with reason after the incident at Monaco. "We were at Oulton Park in 1962 where Richie was very quick indeed and got pole. There was quite a nasty accident in the previous race before this one (Alan Hutcheson in

French Grand Prix, 1962. *Etienne Bourguignon*

Richie at Belgium, 1962. *Etienne Bourguignon*

The Monaco 1962 crash. Innes Ireland (chequered flag helmet) tries to rejoin the race. Richie (foreground right) is out. Behind him, Maurice Trintignant is also eliminated. Tragically, the wheel that came detached is about to fatally injure Ange Baldoni. **The Grand Prix Library**

the touring car race saw his Riley 1.5 roll off and crashed out; he escaped totally unhurt) and in those days, the crowds could go on the grid along with everyone else. I was with Richie and this guy – a journalist – came up to me and said 'Hey John, did you see that accident, he was lucky to get out of it, the car was a total write off' and I was aware Richie was right next to me so I said to this guy 'Bugger off we're busy' as it was unnerving him; you don't want to talk about accidents and especially not before a race. Richie turned round to me and said in his Californian accent 'Jaahn, Don't ya meet some assholes in racing?' That just shows how keyed up Richie was before a race; Graham was not particularly, he was more relaxed. But Richie was always quite keyed up".

As for the Silverstone incident Richie mentions above, David Fox was a spectator marshal that weekend for the International Trophy and he takes up this particular crash: "I was part of the Peterborough Motor Club (PMC) spectator marshalling team, and we were allocated the sector from Club up to Abbey. The job was hardly taxing and consisted of standing in front of the crowds some 10 or so yards from the edge of the track. Our job was to make sure no-one wandered beyond the spectator railings. In actuality, it meant that I, as a young enthusiast, was able to get closer to the track than most. Truth be told, I was only 14 at the time, but was a tall lad for my age!

A pensive Richie at the British Grand Prix, 1964. **Steve Payne**

"Anyway, I was about half-way between Club and Abbey for the F1 race. It was very damp as the field roared past with Jim Clark pulling away. On the fifth lap, I saw Ginther in the BRM sliding way out of line, coming out of Club and hurtling into the bank at the exit. He quickly got out, and his now-crumpled car was roughly manhandled away from the bank. The race continued, and what a race it was, with Graham Hill shedding BRM stack exhausts and finally pipping Clark at the line.

"Then, we PMC chaps were told to go down to Club Corner, where the stricken BRM still sat, so to keep the crowds back whilst the wreck was recovered. This we duly did, joining several policemen and a lone WPC. The crowds did indeed surge forward, and I remember the WPC repeatedly and very politely saying, 'Please stand back, thank you.'

"Finally, a breakdown truck arrived, along with several BRM mechanics and Ginther himself, who appeared somewhat forlorn. It was then that one of the mechanics noticed a crumpled fabric Dunlop banner draped around the left-hand side of the BRM, and he could not resist saying, 'Thanks, Richie, you wrapped it up nicely for us.' I never did learn what he mumbled in response to that mechanic, but if Ginther looked unhappy before, he was now completely crestfallen."

1962 also didn't see much joy away from BRM when, in a brief interlude with Graham Hill also joining him, Richie drove an Aston Martin at Le Mans. Aston Martin had won Le Mans and the World Sportscar Championship in 1959 and decided to quit while they were ahead at the top of their game. Under a bit of pressure from their own car dealers, who were struggling to sell cars without any racing connection, Aston Martin created a special prototype car, a 4.0-litre GT car called the DP212 and arranged for the BRM duo to drive. The DP 212 had some considerable speed, but again, for Richie at least, another retirement, as the car suffered an oil pipe failure on lap 78.

It was 1963, driving a BRM P57, that saw Richie enjoy, arguably, the most successful season of his career. Jim Clark dominated the season in the Lotus 25, but Ginther came joint runner-up in the World Championship standings, which, and it's easily forgotten, was the second best performance by an American in a World Championship at that time and even now, over 55 years on, is still the third best season by an American; even Dan Gurney, who overall had more success, only finished fourth in 1961 and 1965. Of the ten races in 1963, he finished eight of them and in those eight, never finished lower than fifth. He once again excelled at Monaco, finishing second to Graham Hill in the opening race

British Grand Prix, Aintree, 1962. *Etienne Bourguignon*

Richie at the Belgian Grand Prix, 1962. *Etienne Bourguignon*

Monaco Grand Prix, 1963. Graham Hill (6), leads Jim Clark (9) and Richie (5). *Nick Faure*

Graham Hill is pushed off by his mechanics at Monaco, 1963. Richie (far left) watches on. Directly behind Hill and not watching her husband leave is Bette Hill, Graham's wife. **Nick Faure**

that appeared to signal domination for the BRM team, but Clark and Lotus soon hit back.

Although, as Tony Rudd recalls in his book *It Was Fun!*, a very savvy Richie nearly won. "Graham again had symptoms of a low oil level towards the end of the race, so he was taking it very easily around the corners. Richie was going well and catching him fast. I did not want them to get into a dogfight, so I just showed Richie his lead over third place man Bruce McLaren and not the distance between him and Graham. Suddenly, Richie spotted the helicopter ahead, filming the race leader and he realised he was very close to Graham. When he learned, after the race, that Graham had a problem and that he could have won, Richie had something to say! Fortunately he did not bear me too much ill will and we had a very pleasant lunch at Bideau's on the Monday before I flew back to England." Richie would not have begrudged Rudd, but he didn't forget how he lost the chance of his first win as we shall see later on when it came to contract negotiations.

Richie took more second places in championship events at both Monza and Watkins Glen and also took second place at the non-championship Oulton Park Gold Cup. Richie also became much more of a threat to the opposition throughout the year. He led for

ten laps at the early-season Lombank Trophy at Snetterton before leaking seals on the right-hand rear wheel cylinders caused the brakes to lock. Richie also led for two laps at the Glover Trophy at Goodwood, and one lap at the Aintree 200 and in the World Championship. He made a superb start and led for the first lap at the German Grand Prix at the Nürburgring, which was the only World Championship lap he ever led in a BRM. He was not on the level of his team-mate or Jim Clark, but he was consistent and often played a crucial supporting role in second, third or fourth place.

BRM unveiled a monocoque racing car, the P61, at the third race of the year at Zandvoort, for the Dutch Grand Prix, but it ended up having a number of minor problems. The chief one was the handling of the car and practice proved quite a struggle. Despite finishing fifth in his P57, Ginther also complained of handling problems in his old car which were resolved the day after the race in testing at Zandvoort when it was found that the shock absorbers were badly worn. Still, the hard-earned points meant that Richie was, albeit after only three rounds, second in the World Championship to the soon-to-be dominant Jim Clark. Graham Hill may have won the first race of the season but now it was his turn to suffer mechanical failures.

Dutch Grand Prix, 1963. **Gunther Asshauer**

The South African Grand Prix, 1963. Ginther (6) laps Carol Godin de Beaufort (14) in the Porsche 718. **Ken Stewart/David Pearson (www.motoprint.co.za)**

Ginther at the Italian Grand Prix, 1963. **The Grand Prix Library**

One of the two races Ginther failed to finish at was the French Grand Prix, the reason being sheer bad luck. Richie had made a superb start and, despite starting on the fifth row of the grid, had made up seven places on the first lap, and a further three on lap two to sit in second place behind Jim Clark, but when Dan Gurney went a fraction wide when Richie passed him, a large stone was thrown up by Dan's wheels into Richie's radiator. Richie would have likely finished second to Clark had this not happened, rather than winning, but on balance it was really the only disappointment of the season.

The only other race was the last event of the year at South Africa. Ironically, Ginther, in lieu of his position in the World Championship, was offered the chance to drive the P61 monocoque car by Sir Alfred Owen. Although Richie was, according to Doug Nye's BRM Volume 3 book, 'very appreciative' he decided to tell Tony Rudd he wished to stick with the P57: "Ideally, I'd prefer my old mount. It's only failed me once this season and even then it was not the car's fault. We've been most successful this year when we've run the two old cars without the monocoque, leaving us free to concentrate on 100 percent preparation of the old cars." This time it was Rudd's turn to be appreciative, but unfortunately it did not work out. The old mount finally failed Richie when the half-shaft failed on lap 43.

Ginther's ability to hold a grudge, as he did with Phil Hill, flared up again at BRM. John Sismey explains; "It was during practice at the Nürburgring in Germany, and Richie came in for us to fuel him up as, of course, it was an extensively long track. Back in those days we would have two people to stand and fill the car up; one on one side and one on the other; we'd get the large funnel, take the petrol cap off and put the fuel in. Well, I was on one side and Cyril Atkins, the chief mechanic on the other. Richie went out of the car and waited around. I finished at my end and Cyril at his, so Richie asked if he was able to get in. It was my responsibility to say it was good to get in, because of course, there was a much greater pressure back then to make sure it was good to go; if something broke, then the driver could lose his life.

"So I said it was fine to go and off Richie went onto the service road that led to the main track. In a matter of minutes, if that,

Richie Ginther smiling at the Nürburgring. *MullerCologne*

Richie came back; Cyril had gone at that point. 'John,' he said in his Californian drawl, 'What's this?' He showed me the fuel cap that had not been tightened and just looked at me. I apologised but he said to me 'No, John, it's not you. The person responsible was the chief mechanic. The CHIEF mechanic! I never want him working anywhere near my car ever again.' Obviously the issue where he had been burnt would be in his memory but it was so important for the driver to trust us. Once you've lost that trust, you're finished."

Talking of Phil Hill, John Sismey also recalls an incident at the Nürburgring in 1962 which was just a memory of how twitchy drivers could be. When conversation turned to Ginther's grudge from Monaco 1961, we were left debating whether there was a malevolent side to Richie to get some comeback on Phil in whatever form: "In those days the paddock was low down and you pushed the cars onto the kerbed back to go onto the apron to the grid. We were pushing Richie's car up and Phil Hill's sharknose Ferrari was just ahead of us. As they emerged onto the apron, the Ferrari's left front wheel fell off; they'd not put the nut on. Well, Richie just looked at me. They covered it up but we all saw it so that would not have helped Phil at all. Phil was standing about near us but with his back to me. Richie said 'John, you've got to clap your hands behind Phil, he'll do a vertical take-off!' Well I knew how keyed up Phil got so I did not do it…"

1963 also saw a varying diversion for both Hill and Ginther at Le Mans. In the end, it was Ginther's most notable result at an event he often challenged for overall victory but never came close to actually winning. The Rover car company had spent around fifteen years developing a gas turbine car, starting the process just after World War Two. They had produced a number of road cars but the particular aim for 1964 was to become the first turbine car to achieve over 93.2mph around the clock and winning 25,000,000 Francs for doing so. This prize had been created in 1957, so it showed how developing a turbine car to go fast enough took some considerable time.

Richie pushed off by his mechanics, including (top left) John Sismey.

John Sismey

This particular carrot at the end of the stick was the incentive for Rover's chief engineer, Spen King, to contact Sir Alfred Owen. Rover would double its efforts and develop the 150bhp engine, combining with The Owen Organisation, owners of BRM, who already had a relationship with Rover via its 3.0-litre production engine, and who would then built the chassis and suspension. The chassis of Richie's damaged car from the crash at Monaco 1962 was supplied with a custom-made aluminium body and the turbine mid-mounted into the car. Peter Berthon was then instructed to develop a specialised transmission for the car.

There was some pressure for the project to succeed for the British duo; Chrysler was already fast developing its own range of turbine cars for sale. If Rover could achieve here, it would not stop Chrysler but it would definitely put the focus back on Britain for engineering talent and, publicity wise, it would be a massive fillip.

Ginther was a key element in the car's development. Ginther would test and Walter Wright, then with Dunlop, would accompany Richie in the car to note on brake performances bearing in mind there was no engine braking, and between them they came up with the right tyre for well-balanced braking.

Mark Barnard of Rover recalled to Michael Ling how Richie's development skills were crucial in identifying problems with, it must be remembered, the first real racing turbine car. "We went top speed testing at Elvington, which was an old Royal Air Force base, with a long runway. On one particular occasion, Richie returned very quickly to the mechanics after leaving what was effectively the pit area. No words came out of Richie's mouth, he just motioned for me to get into the passenger seat. So Richie proceeds to drive down

Ginther celebrates at Le Mans with Graham Hill, Ludovico Scarfiotti and Lorenzo Bandini. ***The Grand Prix Library***

the runway. At some stage [at] around 120mph, I felt a distinct blast of furnace-like hot air sweeping down my back. This was because the hot turbine exhaust was brought forward from the exhaust by the back flow of the air over the windshield. A clear delivery of a problem without a single word spoken. So we proceeded to construct an extension of the exhaust system."

Once again, Richie's experience in Korea helped. In practice at Le Mans, Richie had noticed that the car was suffering aerodynamic lift at the rear end. It was a carbon copy from his Ferrari days and instantly, an aluminium duck-tail rear spoiler was added to the car. Both Ginther and Hill supplied feedback to help other aerodynamic developments with changes to the wheel fairings and windscreen.

John Sismey: "Richie was totally, totally relaxed at Le Mans. He still wanted to know what was going on with the car, which is understandable, but he was not as tense. Maybe it was because there was not as much significance. The car was a double-nought as it was effectively a demonstration car. They could not agree. Rover wanted to enter it as a 2.0-litre car, but the other 2.0-litre engine cars said 'Okay, prove it's a 2.0-litre', which of course, they could not.

"Well, it started half-a-minute after everyone else. Graham started but had to park his car behind everyone else. Richie said how easy it was to drive with such great handling but the most notable thing was the silence. You did not hear the car coming, you just heard a kind of sssssssssssshhhhhhhhh noise when it went past the pits, rather than the ear-splitting noise of the other cars. The other thing Richie told me about driving it was that you had to accelerate when entering a bend. Now obviously you still had to brake, but there was no direct drive, just a torque converter so you could try and build the engine up whilst you were braking as it did not affect the braking; there were no pistons to be compressed, so Richie said that was the biggest thing he had to learn, but once he got the hang of it, he said that it was so stable.

"I remember that when he got out after his pit-stop, he stayed around with us for about half-an-hour, let his adrenaline drain and get his head down. He performed beautifully there; as did Graham. They thoroughly enjoyed it and there was a much more relaxed atmosphere. There was only one thing that bothered Richie and that was that, bearing in mind Graham Hill was quite tall, the seat had to

Graham Hill and Richie Ginther, British Grand Prix, 1962. *Etienne Bourguignon*

British Grand Prix, 1962. **Brian Tregilgas**

be set more for Graham than Richie. So Richie had to have a kind of booster cushion and could only just reach the pedals! Although he did cause us to be a bit put out at the start as we were all ready for the start and then Richie suddenly asked for a wooden block to be fitted as a rest for his clutch foot. He did not mention this during testing or practice. We did it, but it was a panic literally at the last minute I think we could have all done without!"

In a race dominated by attrition, the car officially finished unplaced, starting thirty seconds after everyone else and only focused on this particular prize. But had it been part of the conventional entries, it would have finished a very respectable seventh and would have also finished ahead (or did) of all twelve British piston-engined rivals. The minimum speed was never really in doubt. The car averaged 108mph and, as Ginther said afterwards, 'It went like a bomb'. Hill and Ginther joined Ludovico Scarfiotti and Lorenzo Bandini, winners of the race in a Ferrari 250P, on the podium.

Although Richie himself already said that he was not going to risk everything to win, either pushing his car or himself, he made an interesting remark in *The Observer* newspaper of 16 September 1962, when describing his team-mate Graham Hill and his focus on motor racing; interesting from the aspect that as much as Ginther took his job seriously, he clearly felt others took it further. Hill was a man who loved an audience and who often loved to play up as a result. Some might have seen Ginther as the more serious of the two but, as Ginther said, "Two days before a race he disappears into a cocoon of concentration. He is so absorbed he cuts friends, colleagues and mechanics out. At this time, he has no sense of humour at all. His place in life is motor racing. I don't like to say it is his whole life, because he has a fine wife and lovely children, but he is as dedicated as a man can healthily be."

But as John Sismey says, "Richie got into 'the zone' as well just as much as Graham. He was not really approachable. Well, we (the mechanics) knew better to talk trivialities to him anyway but I always thought he was more twitchy out of the two drivers we had."

Hill enjoyed a good relationship with Richie and had praise for the Californian: "I'd say he's the most improved driver on the circuit this year," when speaking to *The Los Angeles Times* in October 1963. Ginther enjoyed a trip back to racing in his home state in the latter months of the year to race Otto Zipper's Porsche 718 RS 61 in a few events, which included the aforementioned *Los Angeles Times* International Grand Prix at Riverside and the Monterey Pacific Grand Prix at Laguna Seca, both won by Dave MacDonald, who would tragically lose his life in a horrific accident half-a-year later at the Indianapolis 500.

In his article in *Sporting Motorist* in 1965 about Richie, AF Rivers Fletcher of BRM describes Richie in very positive terms and especially his relationship with Graham Hill. However whilst there is much truth in what Rivers Fletcher wrote, it must be remembered that, by and large, he was BRM's PR man, so obviously this was more a BRM promotional piece and any negatives would be largely brushed out: "Richie was always cheerful and even if his car failed, he seemed completely happy if Graham won. Richie makes friends with everyone immediately with a big grin and infectious and noisy laugh. I remember going to the movies one day in England with a number of the grand prix circus; it was a good party and Richie's laugh could be heard everywhere. Richie is completely without temperament and one of the few drivers who is approachable in practice or even just before the start of a Grand Prix; a team man who is invariably popular with the mechanics and is easy with the VIPs and the press.

"He always did a lot of test driving with us and it was a great help to have another viewpoint on the roadholding of our cars, in that Graham and Richie wanted their car set up in different ways and each was able to learn something from the other man in this way. It is often said that you can find the most about a driver from the mechanics, who all loved him, they all think the world of him. He never has any grumbles and if he has any criticisms they are put with kindness and modesty."

For more balance, John Sismey, one of those mechanics mentioned above recalls, "I always found Richie to be tense. Quick to anger, very quick to anger in fact, and did not suffer fools gladly at all. Richie got on alright with Graham but Graham loved an audience. Richie was very intolerant of people he did not like; very irritable. Graham was in his element with black-tie events and the like and Richie just was not anywhere near as comfortable at these events.

"But they would try to wind each other up in a friendly way. I remember that the day after we won the World Championship, I was walking through Durban and saw this photo of Richie on the grass spinning. Well this came as a surprise to us as none of us were aware of this and in fact, we went through the lap times and we could not really find it so it must have only been a second or two, so I bought the photo. We were all in a good mood when we met up later and I gave the photo to Graham Hill. 'What's this then, Ginther, know anything about this? I don't know, out of control again?!' he said. Well, Richie had a big grin on his face and just said 'Well, I just got bored!'"

Peter Miller, in his article on Richie for the Men at the Wheel series, describes Ginther as rather scruffy, wearing an old sports coat and open neck sports shirts whenever he can; he is no socialite. In short, the complete opposite to the normally well-dressed and personable outgoing creature that was Graham Hill. Ginther, according to Miller, was also a creature of habit on the track, wearing a Bell Helmet and one-piece goggles.

1964 saw Ginther again teaming up with Graham Hill in the P261, finish every World Championship race that year; in those days – and even now – a quite remarkable achievement. It showed a mechanical affinity with the car that few other rivals had. Yet again, he finished second at Monte Carlo, the third time he had

achieved this with Hill again beating him into first place. But somewhat surprisingly, given the fact that Ginther and Hill had finished runners-up in the World Championship, there had been discussions by BRM, according to Doug Nye's BRM Volume 3 book, on replacing Ginther with either John Surtees or Masten Gregory. The former was down to the belief that BRM wanted a more aggressive (which is fair enough considering Richie's sympathy to the cars) and natural winner. This was quickly rebutted by Graham Hill when he was asked about the prospect, not because of any loyalty to Richie, but because he did not want anyone else coming in that would likely take the team's concentration away from his role as the team's number one. Gregory, was seriously considered as he was fast, not good enough to be a number one, but he was a more aggressive driver than Richie.

So Richie was kept on, but like Hill, he also knew his worth. In Nye's book, there is a letter from Tony Rudd to Alfred Owen: "We have had a visit from Richie Ginther, who feels due to his better season last year, he is entitled to ask for a total contract fee of £7000, which will include Le Mans. I will put all his arguments before Mr (Raymond) Mays when he returns from his holiday, but Richie has also made the point that in previous years his share of the starting money has been less than Graham's. He also pointed out that he would have won at Monte Carlo last year had it not been for team orders that he was to stay behind Graham."

Nonetheless, BRM started looking to the future. After all, Hill was now 35, Ginther 34. BRM managing director Raymond Mays started looking around, in conjunction with Keith Ballisat (a former racing driver who was now racing manager for Shell Oil), for a young driver to join the team, which ended up being Richard Attwood, who impressed the most over Mike Beckwith, David Hobbs and John Taylor.

Richard Attwood, as well as his time at BRM, also crossed paths with Ginther in racing at both Le Mans and in grand prix racing for the next couple of years: "Richie was a private chap; I never really got close to Richie at all. I was the third driver for BRM in 1964 but the only race I did that year was the Goodwood Easter Meeting because Richie was back in America at the time. He kept himself to himself but he was quite an affable guy. I do remember him being

Ginther signs autographs. *Gary Critcher – The Supercharged Collection*

Ginther multitasking. Carrying a bag, smoking a cigarette and driving a BRM Formula One car! *Gary Critcher – The Supercharged Collection*

Belgian Grand Prix, 1963. *Gunther Asshauer*

Monaco Grand Prix, 1964. *Etienne Bourguignon*

Monaco Grand Prix, 1964. *Etienne Bourguignon*

very chirpy at Le Mans in 1964, maybe because there was a bit less pressure on him. But, socially, he did not mix. Graham [Hill] did, but of course he was much more open and outgoing and Richie kind of went into the shadows. I kind of got the impression though he was actually quite happy in the shadows and out of the limelight." It must also be noted that part of the reason Richard Attwood could remember so little of Richie despite being in the same team as him was as Tony Rudd remembered to Doug Nye in the BRM Volume 3 book that Richie was always quite distant with Attwood during testing.

However, it was not a year without its troubles. In fact, in terms of his marriage, somewhat terminally so. Richie was under serious pressure from Jackie to retire from racing now that he was a father, partly due to the danger aspect, but also because she did not want to raise a son alone, which she was effectively doing. Richie ignored her wishes, mainly because he felt that to best maintain the family lifestyle was to continue to be a racing driver, rather than run a garage or machine shop. General consensus among friends and relatives appears to indicate that, if he financially could have done this, he would have been more than happy to retire. The emotional cracks seemed to affect him more that year than before, but also affected Jackie. Tragically, on 23 March, the news came through to BRM that the Ginthers had suffered their second miscarriage. The stress, upset and differences in opinion had come to an awful head.

Jackie Ginther's transition from lovingly compiling scrapbooks and being heavily involved in Richie's career to someone who worried and spoke of little else other than wanting Richie to stop racing appeared to have been accelerated by her visit to the 1960 Monaco Grand Prix. Richie was fine but Cliff Allison, Richie's team-mate, had a big crash in practice, being thrown out of the car after hitting a kerb and landing, unconscious, with a broken arm, in plain view of Jackie. She was also very deeply affected by the loss of Wolfgang von Trips, Richie's team-mate in the Italian Grand Prix of 1961. She had already withdrawn from going to races and even staying nearby. She was now living in America, where she had lived, by and large, since 1962 to raise Bret the best she could. The Richie of 1961 who was mindful of the first miscarriage seems slightly different to the Richie of late 1963, quite possibly due to the success of the season he had just had – after all, he was at his peak. But of course, this is unfair to Richie who would have deeply mourned the loss of, had fate been different, a third child.

Before the 1964 World Championship season started with that Monte Carlo race, there were a plethora of non-Championship F1 events held at Syracuse, Goodwood, Snetterton and Aintree. It was at the latter that Ginther had his biggest crash of his career thus far, crashing at 110 miles per hour in a practice run. As per Doug Nye's BRM Volume 3 book: "I had been much faster than Pete Arundell's Lotus which I'd just overtaken. He waved me by but when I braked for the corner the brakes seemed to snatch, slewing the car to the right. I knew it would not make the corner so I let it run onto the grass. I remember nothing after that." He managed to hit the grass edge of a track going into Melling Crossing, the curve that was at the end of the longest straight on the circuit. The resulting crash looked more horrifying than it actually could have

Richie and famed motorsports journalist Denis Jenkinson at the British Grand Prix, 1962. *Etienne Bourguignon*

Richie inspects the car at Aintree, British Grand Prix, 1962. *Brian Tregilgas*

British Grand Prix, 1962. *Brian Tregilgas*

been. The car went airborne, rolled, skidded and travelled sixty yards before stopping. Ginther's injuries weren't too serious (three broken ribs on the left-hand side and a cut chin) but it ruled him out of the race and then also, because the car had extensive damage, out of the BRDC International Trophy at Silverstone two weeks later. Coming soon after Jackie's second miscarriage, Ginther appeared to be more shaken up by the crash than previous ones and maybe lost a bit of confidence in the car as a result.

Then, later in the season, in a Formula 2 race at Reims, Ginther was involved in a crash that saw Peter Arundell, the British driver for Lotus, left with grievous injuries. Arundell himself recalled in *Motorsport* magazine's July 1984 edition what happened: "I was in a tight slip-streaming bunch, where you could be first one lap and seventh the next; I kept my eye in the mirror for a fraction too long, got onto the rough at the kink on the straight, corrected, slowed slightly and was hit by poor Richie Ginther. Jochen Rindt later said I went fifty yards in the air, over the level of the trees. I parted company with the car at the top of its climb and landed on my head and shoulder, while the car landed on all four wheels, relatively undamaged. I might have been OK had I been wearing seatbelts but, on the other hand, my weight might have caused the car to land the other way up."

German Grand Prix, 1963. *Archive Nils Ruwisch*

In truth, there was little Ginther could have done as it all happened so quickly, but there was no doubt it affected him for the rest of the season as the full extent of Arundell's injuries and subsequent complications with his recovery became apparent. If Ginther had, as he said in 1958, not forgotten the responsibility that his actions could lead to the death or injury of others, then it would have been little surprise that he appeared to become a bit more withdrawn.

Arundell's right femur was broken and he was in a coma for two weeks. When it came to the operation to fix the leg, an infection set in, then osteomyelitis and, although Arundell did eventually return to racing, he was never the same driver having lost about a year-and-a-half of racing whilst at his peak.

As a brief aside from Ginther's troubles, the hierarchy at BRM made it quite clear that at the top of the BRM tree were the management; the drivers were only just above the mechanics in terms of how lowly they were looked upon. Ginther was always called 'Ginther' or 'Mr Ginther' and never Richie. However, there is a little nugget of information from BRM management which comes from a pen portrait of Richie in *Grand Prix 1964* by Louis Stanley. Stanley was, among many things, an outspoken, pompous man. John Sismey recalls going to Louis Stanley's house and seeing all the photographs on the wall: "There he was with presidents and prime ministers and other great people and in every photo, he had made it look like all these great men and woman were pleased and privileged to see him and not the other way round!" He looked down at virtually all drivers and mechanics but in this case, he's hit the nail on the head: "Richie Ginther is not a sentimental figure. He's a Cheshire cat; always seen with a broad fixed grin. Cheshire cats are never sentimental but Richie possesses bags of natural charm." It was one of Stanley's more positive pen-portraits which probably says more of Richie than it does Stanley. His BRM team-mate Graham Hill was called, among other things "so tactless he cannot tell the difference between tongue-in-cheek and foot-in-mouth."

However, the first win never came with BRM. There seemed to be a general feeling at Bourne, throughout his time there, that Richie was never going to win a grand prix. He had been signed as a number two and for his testing ability. He was never supposed to be a World Championship challenger, despite what Richie may have thought. He was, in the eyes of the hierarchy and the mechanics, a good second-tier driver. Richie, by his own admission in later interviews (Pete Lyons, 1988) found BRM, at times, to be quite frustrating. "We could have saved some significant weight by removing metal bodywork that was under the plastic windscreen. They refused as they said it would not look right. They would not lighten it because to them, it would not look like a classic racing car. The final straw came at Reims in 1964 in practice. There was no horsepower at a horsepower track. They had the engine apart every night but there was still no power. I said that I would not drive it in the race. Tony Rudd brought out the dyno sheets and said that it performed better than Graham Hill's engine. But I could not hold a tow behind the privateer cars. I demanded the spare car but they said it was even worse. Well, I went from fifteenth to third very quickly so I knew I was right. They had a blind adherence to preconception as opposed to a willingness to try new ideas."

Rudd recalled to Eoin Young that it was not quite like that. "I had, well we all had, enormous respect for him as a man and as a sympathetic thinking driver, but maybe because of the accidents, his race performance was in serious decline. He was extremely good on slow twisty circuits, but he did not like the fast, open airfield circuits like Silverstone or Zeltweg. It was the Austrian Grand Prix there in 1964 which sealed his future fate at BRM. He did not win there when he should have probably done so and so we soon signed Jackie Stewart."

Maybe the assumption that Ginther was not a winner is slightly unfair. At Monaco, still quite sore from his Aintree injuries as mentioned above, Richie came second, one lap behind Hill, but Richie had a lack of fitness and blistered hands to contend with as well as a right foot which became badly burnt due to the cockpit overheating after the steel bulkhead soaked up the radiator and oil tank temperatures of over 100deg C. With Ginther constantly on the throttle and the brake, the right foot took a real punishing. But, as impressive as this drive was, he would not have won there anyway unless Hill had retired due to team orders. The rest of the season, generally, saw him mostly second-best to Graham Hill. Richie was beset by fuel pump problems at Zandvoort which likely denied him fifth place, but other than that, Richie seemed unable or unwilling even to push the car that little bit more to challenge Hill.

The nadir came in Britain. Richie finished three laps down and, despite having a more than capable car to pull well clear of (the albeit very talented) privateer Bob Anderson in a Brabham-Climax, finished behind him in a subdued and lowly eighth place. In Doug Nye's BRM Volume 3, Tony Rudd recalled that weekend: "Richie's eighth was unacceptable. He seemed not only unable to explain how he had been lapped three times, but almost unwilling to even talk about it. He was honest enough to state that there was nothing in particular about the car that he could pinpoint in the way of

Belgian Grand Prix, 1963. *MullerCologne*

explanation. But I had become increasingly disappointed by his lack of performance and this was effectively the final straw.

"I had always looked upon Richie as the other third of my sources of inspiration, alongside Graham and my own aspirations. All the fire of his tigerish drive for Ferrari, chasing Moss at Monaco in 1961, had gone. He had collided with Peter Arundell's Lotus the previous weekend at Reims, but even before that, he had not been the same old Richie. I always felt it was a happy team at BRM, but lately Richie had seemed chippy, quick to flare up and increasingly withdrawn.

Pam, my wife, told me that Richie was increasingly worried about his wife, Jackie, and their relationship. She was a devout Roman Catholic and he said much of their time together was spent arguing about religion and how their young son, Bret, should be raised. Pam urged Richie to invite Jackie and Bret to Europe for the summer and she [Pam] would look after the boy so Jackie could accompany Richie to the races. She joined him at Spa, but whatever his demons were, they did not immediately desert him. After the British Grand Prix, we made Jackie Stewart an offer as Richie's replacement which he said he would think about."

Perhaps his best chance of a win, despite all of this, came at the Austrian Grand Prix that Rudd mentions, eventually won by Lorenzo Bandini. It was an accomplished drive by the Italian, but with Hill, Surtees, Clark, Brabham and Gurney all retiring, Ginther had arguably the fastest car remaining. However, Ginther did not make a particularly strong start whereas Bandini was always near the front. Six seconds was all that divided them in the end, but arguably his best chance of a victory with BRM had gone.

German Grand Prix, 1964. *MullerCologne*

Richie at the Belgian Grand Prix, 1964. *Sigurd Reilbach*

German Grand Prix, 1964. *Sigurd Reilbach*

The reason for the six seconds varied, according to Doug Nye's BRM Volume 3 book. At half-distance, sensing a win was possible, Ginther was gaining on Bandini at a second-a-lap and had reduced the gap from sixteen seconds to ten. Then on lap 58, Phil Hill crashed in his Cooper. Hill's car turned over and caught fire. A rather shambolic attempt by the circuit to put the fire out followed as the ambulance went round the circuit in the wrong direction and fire extinguishers did not work which added to the delay of getting Phil out safely. Ginther lost the six seconds he had made up and went slower than before his charge. Rudd believed that Ginther was seriously worried that Hill had been injured and had sacrificed a win for his friend.

Ginther, who obviously would not have let on to Rudd about his falling out with Phil, said that he knew Phil was OK but actually the car would not accelerate out of the hairpin on the exhaust stubs in second gear. Whether this is true, or secretly he did not want to admit that he was worried about Phil is unclear. According to Richie, if he used first gear, he had too much power and the car was undriveable. Ultimately though, that lost six seconds cost him his first win.

Both Nye and Michael Ling mention that the previous amiability that Ginther had in 1962 and 1963 vanished completely in 1964, as Rudd has said. Richie not only became less driven to get good results but more confrontational. It's natural that arguments with Jackie about his career and the injury to Arundell did not help but Rudd recalled to Ling and Nye: "When he came back to Europe, Richie had lost his form, his enthusiasm and psychologically was at a disadvantage. He did not feel he had fair equipment but I was able to prove to him most of the time that it was all level and above board. He took Jackie and Bret to Monza and they had a family holiday in Italy. Pam and I offered them to come and stay with us where hopefully we could retrieve the old relationship and finally dispel any ideas he might have that Graham always received preferential treatment, but he never warmed to the idea. I tried hard to interest in him in other plans. He was always polite but no longer interested and, to his credit, he finally admitted he had lost his edge."

Rudd's overall opinion of Richie, though, was favourable as he recalled to Michael Ling: "Richie was very good on twisty multiple corner circuits such as Monaco, Oulton Park and Watkins Glen. He had a deep and reasoning interest in the engineering problems that occurred, including the engine and gearbox. Graham Hill was more focused on handling and suspension and, ultimately, winning the World Championship. Richie was fascinated by the four-wheel-drive car we tried to develop and the turbine cars and became very involved in their development to their benefit and this lightened my workload in the process. I sometimes think that if we could have afforded a full-time non-racing test driver that Richie would have been in his element. As it was, his seat at Honda was the perfect solution for him, them and everyone".

Rudd, recalls in his own book, *It Was Fun!*, "I also had a long talk with Richie about his future. He realised he had lost his edge, but he was still an invaluable development driver to us. We got valuable information from him, especially with the gearbox and with the central exhaust layout."

At the end of the year, Ginther left BRM in much (overall) happier circumstances than he left his last team. BRM had been hunting Jackie Stewart for some while and won the race, ahead of Lotus and Cooper, to sign him. Stewart felt that racing alongside Jim Clark would only be detrimental to his burgeoning career, but BRM was competitive enough to learn the next step of his motor racing journey. Ginther recalled to *Car Life* magazine his thoughts on BRM "BRM has a massive operation, more technically skilled people than Ferrari and greater technical resources. BRM has more people and more money to pour into racing, period. But the problem with BRM is that it does not have the broad racing experience of Ferrari."

The year ended with an assignment Stateside. Richie had done some testing work in the autumn and winter of 1964 on a Cooper Monaco-Ford sports car, often nicknamed 'King Cobra'. Carroll Shelby had done well with his Cobra sports cars but he wanted to try racing a V8 Ford engine in a sports racing chassis on the West Coast. The end result was a Cooper-Monaco adapted by Shelby's team. They had been raced by Dave MacDonald and Bob Holbert but they had hit reliability and other issues so there was ground for development. The duo raced again in 1964 but MacDonald was killed at the Indianapolis 500 and Holbert retired from racing, so when Shelby bought three more new Monacos in 1964, he called

Ginther finishes second at the US Grand Prix. The larger-than-life Tex Hopkins is the man waving the chequered flag. *Lionel Birnbom*

on his old friend to initially develop the cars and then test them with the intention of racing the cars during the winter of 1964/1965. However, the racing hardly came about. Ginther appeared at Riverside alongside Bob Bondurant, Ed Leslie, Parnelli Jones and his soon-to-be-teammate at Honda, Ronnie Bucknum. Ginther finished seventh. But then nothing. Doug Nye's *Cooper Cars* only briefly mentions, "The team reappeared at Laguna Seca, less Ginther after a difference of opinion." This seems hardly surprising considering how combative 1964 had been for Richie at BRM, but not much more was mentioned as to the reason for the difference in opinion. Apparently Richie was annoyed beyond a reasonable level about something at Riverside during or immediately after the race, so either quit or was not selected again.

There were other sports car drives throughout the year, with only Le Mans, again in the Rover BRM coming about through his current employers. Perhaps his most notable result was at the Nürburgring 1000 Kilometres in a Porsche 904, when he finished in fifth place, sharing the car with Jo Bonnier.

One of the worst years of Richie's life was now over. It would be followed, immediately, by one of the best.

Belgian Grand Prix, 1964. *Gunther Asshauer*

Honda Accord

"Oh, those Honda people. Japanese people are the smartest people I've ever worked with. I felt incompetent as far as engines were concerned when I was around these people. It was a delight"
Richie Ginther

Belgian Grand Prix, 1965. *Gunther Asshauer*

Honda's original move into Formula One was very much down to the vision and drive of Soichiro Honda, the founder of the company which bore his name, who had seen his company do well in motorcycle racing and then wanted to replicate that in Formula One. Honda motorcycles were selling well but less so its cars.

The motorcycles were selling well especially due to savvy advertising. When Honda began to export to the United States motorcycle market, it teamed up with an advertising agency called Grey Advertising, using a slogan in a well marketed campaign of 'You meet the nicest people on a Honda'. This was deliberately targeted at a mass-market audience. For a long time, there were negative stereotypes of motorcyclists, such as Hell's Angels and so on, but this was an aimed campaign into every home. By the end of 1963 alone, Honda had sold 90,000 motorcycles. This advertising campaign was in tandem with its success in motorcycle racing as Mike Hailwood won the Isle of Man TT 125cc and 250cc races on a Honda, just two years after its first foray in the event.

Honda was still largely venturing softly into the car market in the United States by the time Ginther joined. Honda manufactured a T360 pick-up truck in 1963 which was swiftly followed by a Honda S360/500, a two-door convertible roadster. Indeed, they were still finding their feet somewhat in their homeland in terms of car development which made this project to race and win in Formula One even more remarkable. But Honda wanted sport to promote his cars as much as it had helped his bike sales.

Soichiro Honda had a personal involvement in the Formula One project, which was down to his racing background. The son of a blacksmith, Honda saw a Model T Ford in 1914 near his home which piqued his interest in cars. He worked in a garage before racing for a short while, before driving a turbocharged 8.0-litre aircraft-engined Ford at Tamagawa Speedway in 1936. He crashed and seriously injured his left eye. His brother was also injured and so Honda stopped his own racing career.

Honda was adamant about what he wanted for the car. He wanted a sixty-degree V12 engine, very much their own design but using the European engine model of four valves into each combustion chamber, but the difference with this engine was that it would sit cross-ways in the chassis, just like a motorcycle engine. In 1962, when the project was first mooted, the car's name became the Honda RA270. The 270 was deliberate as Soichiro Honda wanted 270 to be the engine horsepower target, much to the dismay of his designers and mechanics who had already achieved 210 at 11,800rpm, which was the highest engine horsepower at the time in Formula One. When the car was ready to his satisfaction, Soichiro Honda even drove the car on its first lap at his factory's research centre.

But the original plan for Honda was not to go for broke alone. In Christopher Hilton's history of Honda which was published in 1989, *Conquest of Formula 1*, he was able to interview Yoshio Nakamura and Ronnie Bucknum to some degree. Yoshio Nakamura takes up the original story: "Honda had won the World Championship on two wheels in 1961 and 1962 and this encouraged Mr Honda to start thinking about going into Formula One car racing. But it was only an idea and we made no announcement. But when the Swiss editor of a magazine, Gunther Molter, came to Japan to cover the Tokyo Motor Show in the autumn of 1962, he visited Honda and interviewed Mr Honda. During the interview, Molter said 'Does Honda have any intention of going into Formula One in the near future?' I was interpreting. In answer to the question, Mr Honda told me the company WOULD be in Formula One within a year. I asked him if he really wanted me to translate that, to which he said yes and so it became his formal comment on Formula One.

"We had been looking for chassis makers to whom we could supply the engine. That was why I went to Europe in 1963. I only personally knew Jack Brabham then, so I first went to Paris and asked Gerard Crombac, the journalist, to be my guide. I already had Brabham in mind as a partner but I did not make any decision. I returned to Japan and, less than a week after that, Colin Chapman of Lotus arrived. He said he wanted to put Honda's engine on his chassis. I was sort of at a loss because I still had Brabham in mind and all this was too sudden. But actually it sounded good. The driver was Jim Clark. We had nothing to complain about and no reason to reject the offer. I decided to accept it right away. Chapman came to the laboratory for three days and we talked over how we could put the engine on the chassis. According to the plan, Honda was to send a dummy of the engine to Lotus by December 1963 so that Lotus could make a monocoque and in February 1964 we were to send the completed engine to England and start testing.

"As we planned, by December, we had a dummy engine with an aluminium moulding – not just a wooden framework – and sent it to Lotus. In January we were about to start testing at Suzuka using a chassis similar to a Lotus chassis. We received a telegram from Chapman. It said, in short, Lotus were unable to go into partnership with Honda and that the situation of Lotus had changed. It went on that Coventry-Climax were affiliated to Jaguar and as Jaguar supported Lotus, they were unable to use Honda engines.

"At this point, it was too late to go into partnership with Brabham so we had no choice but to develop our own chassis. I was pretty angry, but I also had a feeling that I wanted to give it a try. We hurried to develop the chassis."

Nakamura was too much of a gentleman to say this, but other interviewees in the book (Gerard Crombac and Ron Tauranac) pretty much say that Colin Chapman never had any intention of running Honda engines in the Lotus but the fact that it was used either as a weapon or bargaining chip against Coventry-Climax to buck their ideas up or as a bluff so that no other team could get the chance to be offered the engines. Irrespective, Honda had decided to go it alone and got in touch with Ronnie Bucknum.

Ronnie Bucknum was, like Ginther, a Californian who had made his name in SCCA events on the West Coast. At the time of his surprise signing, he had made a name for himself as a mechanically sympathetic and capable driver in America, essentially the market Honda were really keen on initially.

Bucknum won on his debut at Pomona in 1956 when racing a Porsche 356 Speedster. He kept on winning in an array of cars including Healeys and an MGB. Bucknum had followed, however, in the same well-trodden path as not only Richie, but the likes of Phil Hill and Dan Gurney by winning races at Pomona, Santa Barbara (as an aside, Richie hated Santa Barbara; "At Santa Barbara it's difficult to drive a good race in a small-engined car. You sit there and drive like a robot; stop, turn, open the throttle, stop, turn, open the throttle") and Riverside. However, Bucknum's work was different to Richie's as he was a land surveyor whose employers, Land Engineering in Van Nuys, allowed him a lot of weekends off to go racing; winning made no difference in sales for Ronnie. But choosing Bucknum for Formula One was an immense risk as he had never tested, let alone raced, an open wheeled car. It seems the thinking was that if the car should under-perform due to Honda's lack of experience, then Ronnie was a perfect scapegoat. In Christopher Hilton's book *Conquest of Formula 1* which reviewed Honda's history, Ronnie Bucknum remembered thinking that the call from Honda was a prank: "I was twenty-eight years old, strictly an amateur with limited experience. I thought it was somebody joking with me and I was not particularly amused. I was invited to dinner at a very expensive Hollywood restaurant and I met a small, slender man who looked very young and spoke good English. When we sat down and he began to talk, I realised that this was for real."

In the same book, Nakamura gives more information about how a surveyor-cum-sports car racer got such a great drive. "Among the existing racing drivers, Phil Hill was the only one interested but his name was too big. We judged that it would be too difficult for Honda to have control over him. We looked for new drivers with potential in America, so we sent a telex to Honda America and asked them to look. They gave us a list of ten drivers. Amongst them, Ronnie Bucknum seemed the best suited, so I took the decision to hire him. When I first met him at Haneda Airport, he gave me the impression that he was a serious and hard working person. I sent him to Suzuka straight away on the night train. He drove the next morning. In those days the best lap of Suzuka was around three minutes but Bucknum recorded two minutes and fifty-four seconds which was just astonishing for us."

As it proved, Bucknum did not disgrace himself at all. Maybe his best performance was in his second race at Monza, Italy. He qualified ninth, but due to car issues started last. By lap two, he had passed four cars and soon overtook a number of established midfield runners, including Lorenzo Bandini, Jack Brabham, Innes Ireland,

Ronnie Bucknum and Richie. **The Grand Prix Library**

Jo Bonnier and Richie Ginther, all in one lap. No doubt this made a soon-to-leave-BRM Ginther excited about the possibilities that Honda could give him if something came about.

Sadly, Bucknum then had issues not only with the brakes, but also with the radiator spewing hot water onto Ronnie's goggles and the engine misfiring, while running in fifth, but both the car and Ronnie had shown real promise. But Ronnie, it seems, was very much a confidence driver and when Richie came and pretty much eclipsed him, he lost a lot of heart.

America was still quite resistant to Japanese products with memories of the atrocities of World War Two still resonant. Signing Bucknum to develop the car would not shake the United States car market by its foundations, but it would allow the team to work out, roughly, what level they were at, and more importantly in secrecy. Bucknum could travel freely and test freely, largely because being based in Japan shielded the team from the rest of the Formula One fraternity, but also because Bucknum was not part of the established group of personalities in Formula One. Not many top drivers would join a brand new team in its infancy, but they showed enough promise to entice Richie. Bucknum was always perfectly able, but he was not a potential grand prix winner. Ginther had the technical nous and racing experience and

Ronnie Bucknum and Richie. **Dr Benno Muller Archive/Jorg-Thomas Fodisch**

Richie and Bette Hill in younger days.
Dr Benno Muller Archive/Jorg-Thomas Fodisch

Dan Gurney (foreground, left), Denny Hulme and Richie discuss the Honda in the pits at British Grand Prix, Silverstone, 1965. Standing but crouched over to the right of Richie is Yoshio Nakamura. *Nick Faure*

was much faster than Bucknum. His reputation as both a non-car breaker and a car developer made him, for Honda, their perfect choice to lead the team and give them a true gauge of where their car really was in terms of development. By the end of 1964, they were already in discussions about him moving across.

Bucknum and Honda's start was hardly stellar. With Honda only joining towards the end of the season at the Nürburgring, Monza, and at Watkins Glen, Ronnie Bucknum qualified last (mechanical problems meant a start from the back), 10th and 14th respectively but three failures to finish were not a good start. Bucknum spun in the first race (Bucknum: "The steering failed. I hit the banking at 160km/h. I turned the wheel and nothing happened. Bar a banged knee, I was not hurt despite bouncing up a ravine"), Monza saw promise as mentioned already in this book whereas the latter race at Watkins Glen saw an engine mishap. But the team were still developing, and for 1965 managed to eke the horsepower up to 230 at 13,000rpm. The monocoque was also refined, streamlined and made stiffer. There was a genuine belief that with an experienced and fast driver, plus better reliability, that Honda could challenge for wins.

Ginther clearly was not fazed by their failures to finish in 1964. As he said to Pete Lyons in an interview for *Car and Driver* one year before his death; "At Ferrari and BRM, I'd no real desire to stay there. If someone did not have an open mind, then I was of no value to them." Honda courted Richie with the enticement of respecting all his previous work and giving him free reign to do what was necessary to reach the top. They would listen to him,

they would value him, would be open-minded and if Richie wanted something to help develop the car, then they had the resources to manufacture and fit it.

Ronnie Bucknum was among those having a quiet word with Honda about hiring Richie as he recalled to Christopher Hilton for *Conquest of Formula 1*: "Richie was a good friend and much more experienced than I was. I had followed his career and tried to learn from him. He went about everything very professionally and seldom had accidents. I pushed Honda hard to hire Richie. You see, when I was the only driver, I was doing all the testing and I had no basis for comparison, none at all because I had not driven any of the other cars on the grid."

BRM, as Rivers Fletcher recalled in an article in 1965, accepted as such that it was time for Ginther to move on; "It was right and proper that he should leave us to become a number one for another team, it just had to be. It has been proved many times that second drivers can only be second drivers for a limited period and if they develop into top driver material then they must have the right outlet; that outlet for Richie was not with us." Tony Rudd, in the BRM Volume 3 book, recalled, "As soon as Richie learnt that we had been speaking with Jackie Stewart, he talked to Mr Nakamura at Honda. Both Raymond Mays and myself spoke to Nakamura about Richie's qualities, which I still believed were admirably suited to a new or developing team. If his interest could be rekindled by a new challenge – and especially if he was an unchallenged number one driver – the information he could provide would be invaluable. Finally, all parties achieved an amicable agreement."

Richie gives a lift to Innes Ireland and Jo Bonnier at the French Grand Prix, Clermont Ferrand, 1965. **The Grand Prix Library**

Ginther tries out the bubble helmet.

Dr Benno Muller Archive/Jorg-Thomas Fodisch

The Honda crew around Richie's car before the 1965 Italian Grand Prix.

Steve Payne

Ginther recalled to Lyons: "The Honda was actually damned good for a first effort, but it was kind of sorrowful to see some of the things that could be done for it. I had mellowed out and learned to be more diplomatic about these things than I had been at Ferrari and BRM. It turned out to be rather difficult for Ronnie, because he had gone straight from racing sports cars into Formula One. He had the Honda F1 car handling like a production car. It was too soft in roll, so you had to wait to get it into a turn.

"So I got them to stiffen the suspension and by the end of the test at Suzuka two or three days later, the difference was something ridiculous, into the teens of seconds. They were all getting punch-drunk on what-ifs. Everybody was happy apart from Ronnie. He was taking it personally, but it was not his fault, dammit."

Yoshio Nakamura recalled to Christopher Hilton: "Ginther was a driver who could mature our cars. Bucknum was fast but he was not the one who could do what Richie could. In the beginning, I had thoughts of Ronnie winning races in cars Richie had matured because I judged that Richie could not win races. My idea was to let him concentrate on the maturing because he was more experienced than Ronnie and naturally became the number one driver. It made him extremely happy. Occasionally he demanded Ronnie's car if that had set a faster time."

The language barrier, which so frustrated Ginther at Ferrari, appeared not to be so much of an issue now four years on. Bill Huth, who owned Willow Springs International Raceway, recalled to *The Los Angeles Times* in 1991 the time that Honda used his relatively new track for testing and just how difficult development and feedback must have been for both the team, Bucknum and later Ginther: "The entire crew was Japanese, and Ronnie and I were the only ones who could speak English. Everything was done with hand signals, shrugs and smiles." Ginther also joked deprecatingly to Ed McDonough that there was another reason he got on with the mechanics so well; "They're all the same size as myself, I don't have to look up at people anymore! I don't need any seat adjusting or special seat fittings as the mechanics go into the car first and if they fit in, then so do I!"

The season started without Ginther and Honda. The RA272, their new car, was still in development, so the first race of the year at South Africa was sat out. Before the season started, though,

Richie at the Monaco Grand Prix, 1965. **The Grand Prix Library**

Honda had endured more misfortune when Bucknum broke his leg at Suzuka. The car suffered a broken steering spindle and Ronnie hit the steel guard rail at nearly 200km/h. The whole situation did not get an awful lot better at the next race. Monaco, the scene of so many of Richie's best moments saw him qualify 16th and last, and then he was out on the first lap when a half-shaft failed. He must surely have felt a little rueful to see his replacement, Jackie Stewart, take third place behind team-mate Graham Hill, who yet again won the Monaco Grand Prix. Yet despite this, he was described as elated and bubbling with enthusiasm about the car in an interview with Bob Thomas for *The Los Angeles Times*. "The crew are green, but we've been doing development work on the chassis and road handling. I really think that Honda has a chance this year."

Ginther was most impressed about Honda's ability when it came to engines. This was, after all, a man who was a mechanic and had done sterling development work in the past but as he explained to Pete Lyons in 1988: "Oh, those Honda people. Japanese people are the smartest people I've ever worked with. One time they asked me to draw the engine power curve I wanted onto a greenboard. So I said 'Take ten off the top, but give me twenty mid-range'. Well, they then gave me the twenty, but without losing any at the top. They were very pleased with that. I felt incompetent as far as engines were concerned when I was around these people. It was a delight."

Essential reading. Richie studying an article about cams at the Belgian Grand Prix, 1964. *Etienne Bourguignon*

On the grid at the Belgian Grand Prix, 1965. *Jack Fooshee/Walter Fooshee*

Belgian Grand Prix, 1965. *Sigurd Reilbach*

It soon became clear, though, that the RA272 performed better at high-speed tracks than low-speed twisty circuits. The next race at Spa Francorchamps for the Belgian Grand Prix saw Ginther relish the power his engine gave him, qualifying fourth. Ginther recalled to Pete Lyons that he saw how dedicated the team were that weekend: "During practice, the crankshafts broke in both cars, it was a design fault. Those suckers then designed new crankshafts, correcting the fault, overnight and sent three new cranks over as excess passenger baggage!" Ginther appeared, perhaps because the relationship with Jackie had now passed over a key stage of resignation that divorce was imminent, much more patient and easy going. Jackie, knowing the relationship was going nowhere and that racing was the priority, started a relationship with another man while Richie chose to concentrate on his career rather than the opposite sex. Richie was consistent and capable, despite somewhat going back four or five years, into a developing testing role as opposed to a racing one.

He saw the Belgian race through to finish sixth, within touching distance of Graham Hill in fifth. But that was the highlight of

the season going into the final race for the team. Perhaps to be expected, mechanical failures blighted the season and so, barring another sixth place, this time at Zandvoort for the Dutch Grand Prix, a promising year in terms of development had not seen the quantum leap yearned for. Ignition problems led to Richie's retirement at both the French Grand Prix and the Italian Grand Prix, whereas a light collision with Jackie Stewart at the American Grand Prix saw Richie struggle with suspension issues on his way to a seventh place finish.

Certainly fast starts had become a feature of Ginther and Honda's development. In the race at Zandvoort, Ginther led for two laps after a brilliant start and would have likely finished higher but for a couple of spins on the hairpin behind the pits. The British Grand Prix at Silverstone was also a turning point, when Richie qualified on the front row. He even led the Grand Prix, to give Honda their first laps led as a constructor, before retiring with engine problems. The speed was there, just not the reliability. All that would change in the last race of the year.

Richie at a wet Belgian Grand Prix, 1965. *Sigurd Reilbach*

Two more shots from a wet Belgian Grand Prix, 1965.
Jack Fooshee/Walter Fooshee

The grid line up before the 1965 US Grand Prix at Watkins Glen. The man in the pink jacket in front of the cars is starter and chequered flag man Tex Hopkins.
El Sol/Ed McDonough

Richie leads Dan Gurney at the 1965 United States Grand Prix. **Lionel Birnbom**

Richie at the British Grand Prix, Silverstone, 1965. **Ferret Fotographics**

Mexico's Day of the Red

"I sent a telegram to Honda Tokyo
echoing the words of Julius Caesar;
'I came, I saw, I conquered!'"
Yoshio Nakamura, Honda

Ginther is already off in the distance as the rest of the field try to catch him. *El Sol/Ed McDonough*

The Mexican Grand Prix of 1965 was held at the Ciudad Deportiva Magdalena Mixhuca, better known now as the Autodromo Hermanos Rodriguez, in Mexico City, named after Richie's former team-mate Ricardo Rodriguez and his brother Pedro Rodriguez. Ricardo Rodriguez, a frighteningly precocious talent, died at the tragically young age of 20 in a crash at the circuit that would later bear his name. Pedro Rodriguez would race in 54 grands prix between 1963 and 1971 for BRM, Ferrari, Lotus and Cooper, winning two of them and had incredible ability in wet-weather races. He was killed in an Interserie sports car race at the Norisring circuit on 11 July 1971, aged 31.

The high-altitude (7400ft) 3.2-mile track made this race significantly tougher on engines than most other races, normally the worst scenario for the team. However, the V12 powering both Ginther and Bucknum did not suffer as much as the other cars. Jim Clark in the Lotus and Graham Hill in the BRM both retired with engine failures. Ginther, who qualified third, had already got a reputation for being a good starter. The RA272, with its engine boost and quick acceleration was, in Ginther's hands, a first-lap rocket.

However, what is less known is the immense strain that Honda and Ginther were under coming into the race. Both 1964 and 1965 were littered with disappointments for the team and as much as Ginther had developed the team into potential winners, it had not come together for them. Jim Sitz remembers there was more going on behind the scenes: "I remember a few people saying that Richie had been somewhat unkind to Ronnie Bucknum. Bucknum would have been somewhat crushed by this as he looked up to Ginther from his days in California. However, I don't think it was a deliberate nastiness. Richie just felt, maybe correctly, that if they were going to win that the team should focus on him and his efforts and not Ronnie. Richie could be so focused he came across as a little bit nasty. Trouble was for Rich, this was HIS chance to lead, having been in the same position as Bucknum for so long. He just probably did not translate his experiences to how Ronnie was feeling."

Pedro Rodriguez, Richie and John Surtees at the 1966 Nürburgring 1000 Kms.
Ed McDonough

Bucknum, when talking to Christopher Hilton in 1989, shortly before Ginther's death, for the book *Conquest of Formula 1* admits things got strained: "We weren't doing well and naturally things got tense between Richie and myself, because we were both frustrated. It also got tense among the Honda people. But our friendship survived and even though our paths have gone differently since 1965 and I've only seen him once or twice, I still count him as a friend."

Ginther recalled to Pete Lyons in an interview for *Car and Driver* in 1988; "Honda had changed something in the fuel injection for this race; what, I'm not certain. It was their own system. We'd been there a week ahead of time, which really helped a lot. We got the mixture and the chassis right as a result." Two days before practice officially begun, Honda secured permission for an early test run and Richie went round the track at a decent pace, albeit on a track that was still drying out after recent rainfall.

Ginther took the lead at the start and never relinquished it. Although it nearly did not happen when the engine momentarily faltered and blipped before really firing up. When it did fire up, it actually came as a surprise to Richie as he told Pete Lyons: "In other races, I got off with the other cars but started to fade as I did not get quite enough wheelspin to get the engine up on step. This time, I put it down, man, and I was gone. I dipped the clutch, got wheelspin and I shot ahead of Dan Gurney and Jimmy Clark so fast, I sat up from my reclining position and looked over to Dan with a big grin on my face. He was surprised. I looked over at Jimmy, too, but he was looking straight ahead. I came off the line like a dragster. I was all by myself by the first corner. Out of the third turn, I looked in my mirrors, saw no-one there and thought that there had been an accident."

As Dan Gurney, who finished second, said to Peter Egan for Egan's obituary of Richie in *Road & Track* magazine, "That Honda could blow a tree down with its exhaust, it was such a staggering display of horsepower".

It was not just the engine that brought glory as the tyres played their part too. At the southern part of the track, between the Ese del Lago and the six subsequent Eses was a tight hairpin turn which Dunlop, now very experienced at racing, knew would cause their tyres problems, so they focused on grip rather than speed, but even then, grip remained a problem. Goodyear, in its first season of Formula One, learnt almost as they went along. Ginther and Bucknum actually benefited from this as unaware of the grip

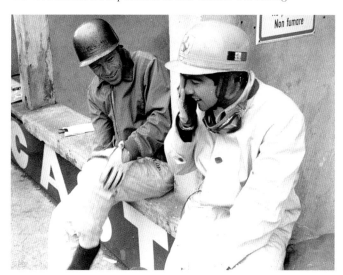

Richie and Ricardo Rodriguez share a joke at the 1961 Nürburgring 1000 Kms.
Ed McDonough

problems afflicting the Dunlop tyres, and with significant horsepower behind them, they pushed their cars much more than their Dunlop-shod rivals, their higher speed through the Eses also proving influential towards Ginther's win. Ginther takes up the story again with Lyons: "The chassis, tyres and engine all worked superbly. One change I had been asking for, we now had at Mexico, a fuel mixture control and I was able to hold my own out in front."

Initially Mike Spence, who passed Jackie Stewart early on, took up the challenge of chasing Ginther. By lap seventeen, Ginther had a six-second lead which had increased to seven seconds on lap nineteen. Spence, like many of his rivals, would not have been too worried about Ginther leading due to Honda's chronic reliability issues. But it soon became clear that it was going to be Richie's day of days. The list of retirees or issue-afflicted drivers was immense. Jim Clark, who started on pole, retired on the ninth lap. Graham Hill, Jackie Stewart, Jack Brabham, the exciting new talent Jochen Rindt, Bruce McLaren, home favourite Pedro Rodriguez, Lorenzo Bandini (who crashed trying to keep pace with Ginther) and many others retired or struggled.

Dan Gurney eventually passed Spence after 20 laps and had 40 laps to reel in the Honda seven seconds up the road and take victory in his Brabham. Or so he and everyone thought. Ginther, with half-a-mile's lead, could afford to relax a little and he was already nursing the engine at 11,000rpm rather than the maximum 12,000. Gurney was pushing his car in conditions where the car would have been screaming not to be pushed. By lap 35, the gap was down to five seconds. The only thing that could help Gurney was his team manager and team-mate, Jack Brabham, who was a lap down. Brabham had numerous mechanical issues with his car but was still capable of a decent speed. Aware of the situation of Richie coming up to lap him, he made his car as large as he humanly could, however Richie was not to be denied.

Ginther and Nakamura celebrate winning at Mexico. *Honda*

Ginther wryly remembered Brabham's efforts 23 years later to Pete Lyons: "I came up to lap Brabham on the straight behind the pits. He was going slowly, the son-of-a-bitch, waiting for me. They don't call him Black Jack for nothing. He moved over right, then left. I had to brake and change down a couple of gears. I stood on it, he did too and it became a drag race. I did not put my brake on until I was past him, and took the high line into the banked turn before the pits where Ricardo Rodriguez was killed, so it was a big no-no. I went around driving with one hand and gave him the bird. There's a bad bump off the banking and I just brushed the wall at the exit with the rear wheel."

Had these races been fully televised as they were some 20 years later, with repeated replays from every possible angle, Richie's pass would be up there in the pantheon of brilliant overtaking moves and be forever talked about. As it was, it was for Mexico City alone to watch as Ginther moved onto the outside of the famed Peraltada turn, the (as it was then) fourteenth and final turn of the circuit and akin to Monza's Parabolica, a blisteringly fast turn that led into the start-finish straight and drifted past Brabham.

Ginther kept the Honda going quickly but conservatively enough to keep Gurney, who was setting an incredible pace in pursuit, at bay, bringing the lead down from seven seconds on lap twenty to only two. Ginther said after the race that it put a bit of pressure back on him: "Sure, I knew he was coming, he made me work really hard. But I knew exactly what I was doing. I knew how much I could let him have, I did not do anything stupid. I could not let myself go too much in case I lost concentration. The car ran beautifully though, although I did have a tiny fuel leak. I could see Dan closing in but I knew he could not catch me. Making sure my car did not go sour, I was driving it well within itself and I knew I had more power to go to if I needed it. I had a fuel mixture control on the dashboard and I had it at lower rich to protect the engine, but I could alter the control to anywhere from full rich to full lean and the difference was 300rpm on the straight. My car was that much better than his."

Two laps before the end, as Ginther said above, there was a scare when fuel started leaking from the back of the car, but with Gurney also having to back off at the end as his car started having a few minor issues, Ginther passed the chequered flag in first place after 65 laps at an average speed of 94.28mph, eclipsing the average speed of Gurney's win in 1964.

"I still don't believe it, you can't imagine how I feel after having tried all these years," Richie exclaimed after the race. Once the celebrations had died down and fans and journalists had left him alone, Ginther got a Pepsi and went into Dan Gurney's pit to cheerfully express his delight that it was his day. Gurney, always a gentleman of the highest order, was graceful in defeat and delighted for his fellow American, even though the win for him had been so close.

The win was richly deserved. Ginther had done a herculean job of not only developing Honda's car, but his work had previously led Ferrari and BRM to Constructors' Championships as well. As for Honda, it transformed their profile from somewhat of a back-of-the-grid joke to a race winning car; a huge financial and publicity

Mexican Grand Prix, 1965. *Ferret Fotographics*

boost. As for Goodyear, it started a chain of immense success where they still remain, despite having not been in the sport since 1998, the dominant tyre manufacturer; 368 wins, 24 Drivers' Championships and 26 Constructors' Championships.

There was immense satisfaction across the board for Richie's win. The Mexican fans themselves remembered him well from the Carrera Panamericana days and there's a good probability that the warmness of their reaction was one consideration when Ginther moved to the country just under two decades later. Honda, too, from that day on, virtually worshipped Ginther for what he had done and never forgot it. Yoshio Nakamura said at the time "I sent a telegram to Honda Tokyo echoing the words of Julius Caesar; 'I came, I saw, I conquered!'" Nobuhiko Kawamoto, later Chief Executive Officer of Honda but at the time, one of the chief design engineers, recalled to Christopher Hilton for Hilton's *Conquest of Formula 1* book, "The victory in Mexico gave us the necessary punch to forge ahead and continue to invest in the automobile industry."

Kurt Zimmermann, who would later work for Richie as a mechanic at his racing team recalled; "Every year, Richie would be given a brand new Honda car by the company. That's how Honda paid respect to Richie." Cleo Davidson points out that even after Richie's death, they still honoured their former hero: "Honda Japan got in touch with Honda America to provide a car each year; we'd get a brand new one each year and we'd give the old one back to

them. But they very kindly let me keep the last one we were given for just over a year after his death."

Ronnie Bucknum, too, while obviously being overshadowed on the day, had a stellar drive himself. He finished fifth, but that did not quite tell the whole story as his right foot became so badly burned and blistered due to the intense heat, he had to use his left foot to brake, clutch and accelerate in the last quarter of the race; difficult enough in itself but in a racing car at around 150mph, this was some feat.

Ginther must have felt he had proved a number of people wrong with this win. There were many, especially at BRM, who thought he would never win. AF River Fletcher's article in *Sporting Motorist* which was especially written to mark Richie's win said: "Because of Richie's innate niceness, many of us thought that perhaps he would never reach the top, lacking perhaps the drive and toughness that would procure his car absolutely right for him, but there is, of course, more than one way to skin that winning race cat."

It would be easy to think that, after this win, the scene was set for a dominant 1966 as Honda and Ginther grew together. But the Mexican Grand Prix was the last race of the current 1.5-litre formula. From 1966, it would be 3.0 litres, engine capacity doubled with all the strains and development issues that ensued from such a change. Few would have expected that Ginther would have just five grand prix races left in his career.

Chapter Ten

1966 and All That

"A tread came off the tyre whilst I was travelling at around 185mph. By the time I hit the tree, though, I had brought the speed way down"
Richie Ginther

Richie being pushed by Cooper mechanics, International Trophy, Silverstone, 1966. *The Grand Prix Library*

or 1966, the engine capacity in Formula One was changed due to sports cars lapping faster than cars in the so-called pinnacle of the sport. Honda had to start again and develop their car. This time, the development was more involved and so Ginther had to find another drive in the meantime. Nobuhiko Kawamoto recalled to Christopher Hilton: "The new engine produced nearly 400bhp which was sufficient to run with other teams. We did not exceed that as there was a reduction in the efficiency of induction as the intake valves were reversed. Another problem was acceptable weight and size. This was entirely our fault. We had a preconceived idea that a 3.0-litre car had to be twice the size of a 1.5-litre car. Our car was, therefore, very fast on the straight due to its horsepower but had serious shortcomings on bends due to its weight and size."

Initially, the South African Grand Prix on 1 January 1966 was due to start the new 3 litre era. However so many teams were struggling, not only Honda, to have their cars ready that early, the race was downgraded to non-Championship status. As it was, only one 3.0-litre car made it; Jack Brabham's BT19 with a Repco V8 engine made its debut. The other entries were a variation of 2.8 litres (Prophet), 2.7 litres (Hulme, Hawkins, Anderson, Love, Tingle, Hume, de Klerk, Charlton and Puzey), 2.0 litres (Spence, Ginther, Ireland, Serrurier, Pretorious and Jeffries) and 1.5 litres (Bonnier and Arundell (back for the first time after his Reims crash). Jack Holme and Brian Reubenheimer had 1500cc Formula 2 engines in their cars – small wonder the race became a non-championship one with such a variation of entries.

Richie was entered by his nemesis at Monaco in 1961, Stirling Moss, who was now running a small independent team. Moss was on close terms to the British Racing Partnership (BRP) through his father and his former manager, Ken Gregory, and they fielded a 1964 BRP car (64/3, which was later bought by Jim Russell to be used in the film *Grand Prix*) with a BRM engine. Ginther qualified sixth, but, maybe caught out by the drizzle that had occurred just before the start, he lost the car at the Esses, colliding with Jo Bonnier, before limping back to the pits with terminal suspension damage. This short foray ended up being the last time a BRP car would race overseas in a competitive Formula One race.

Richie grimacing with effort. *Peter Darley*

He joined Cooper to drive their T81 Maserati V12 alongside their rising star, Jochen Rindt, for the first two World Championship races, plus potentially a few non-championship events before biding his time while he waited for the Honda RA273 to appear after moving aside for John Surtees. One week later, at the Monaco Grand Prix, there was a bit more encouragement as Ginther was running fifth, albeit in a race of high-attrition, before his own car developed transmission issues twenty laps from the end. Belgium saw a positive conclusion to his brief foray away from Honda with fifth place and two World Championship points, albeit three laps down.

But Belgium had not been the original destination of the conclusion of the agreement. The original plan had been for Ginther to compete at Reims, but Honda was now in a position for Ginther to start testing their new car in Japan, which he did for a while, sitting out the next four races at France, Britain, Holland and Germany. In any event, John Surtees became available to Cooper after the aforementioned falling out with Ferrari over his fitness (or alleged lack of it), so whether Ginther would have carried on with Cooper much longer is debatable. His time at Cooper was not particularly stellar, but it worked for both parties. He was also entered for the International Trophy at Silverstone but retired with overheating issues.

1966 also saw Richie heavily involved in another grand prix project whilst he waited for Honda – the film *Grand Prix* by John Frankenheimer had Richie and Phil Hill, among others, working as technical racing advisors. The project saw Richie work closely with Hill for the first time since 1961 but, by all accounts, they both had a job to do and did it professionally. Richie earnt $1500 for agreeing to be in the film, but also, crucially, would earn another $1500 being filmed in three grands prix. If Richie did not drive in three races, he would not get the money so this explains why he would have been particularly keen to secure the Cooper drive. In the end, Ginther only made it to three grands prix at Monza when Honda returned, which is where the last filming at a circuit took place. Richie's actual role, uncredited in the end, was that of John Hogarth, a driver in the Japanese Yamura team, based somewhat heavily on Honda.

Ginther in the Cooper-Maserati T81, Belgian Grand Prix, 1966. *Jack Fooshee/Walter Fooshee*

At one stage, there was even doubt Honda would be around at all in 1966; *The Austin American Statesman* was one of a few publications that mused about Honda's situation with their plans shrouded in secrecy: "Nothing is known except the Japanese are expected to be ready by the end of this season or the beginning of the next. They may even come up with a twenty-four cylinder engine."

As it happened, the Honda car was only available for three races and the first of them, the Italian Grand Prix, saw the most serious, and arguably only, life-threatening major crash of Richie's career. Before the race though Ginther was impressed with the car as he later recalled to Pete Lyons for *Car and Driver* magazine: "It was competitive right off and wow, that son of a gun was so strong. I got a good start, passed all but the leading car of Scarfiotti. I was reeling him in and got into his slipstream." Then disaster struck. On lap seventeen, when challenging for the lead of the race from Ludovico Scarfiotti, Richie left the circuit at the Curva Grande and crashed into the trees, and although he broke his right collarbone, as well as sustaining injuries to his pelvis and ribs, he was by all accounts lucky that he had not been killed. Despite his injuries, less than a month later, he competed at the American Grand Prix before competing in his last grand prix start, Mexico again.

In an interview with *The Los Angeles Times* on 29 September 1966, Ginther explained why the crash happened and how he had recovered so comparatively quickly: "Initially the doctors said that I could expect to be back in a racing car around six to eight weeks, so I'm delighted it was only three." (Ginther had, in fact, already got back to driving a car, when he drove Jack Nethercutt's Mirage sports car at a test at Willow Springs Raceway so that he could prepare for *The Times* Grand Prix at Riverside in October).

"It was unusual treatment. It was treatment they've [St Thomas' Hospital in Lambeth, London, where Ginther was flown to immediately after the crash; interestingly not hospitalised in Italy] used for rapid recovery that has been used effectively in England on such famous racing figures as Stirling Moss, John Surtees and Innes Ireland. The idea is to put your muscles right back to working. If the damage is such that it is pretty well supported by the muscle, the doctors have you moving right away. My arm, for instance, was moving the next day. But yes, it smarted a bit, there's no pampering!

"A tread came off the tyre whilst I was travelling at around 185mph. By the time I hit the tree, though, I had brought the speed

way down; I estimate it was travelling at 100mph when I went off the track and ploughed through a thick hedge; the hedge did me a favour as it took about 40mph off the speed when I hit the tree.

"I tried four laps on Sunday to see how I felt and I was thrilled. I really enjoyed it. I even induced oversteer to see if I could correct a spin. Well, I felt fine. Nothing hurt."

At Mexico, Richie remained competitive, qualifying third but, with one more year's experience of the circuit, Dunlop had prepared better and other teams had developed better than Honda. Nonetheless, fourth, still racked with pain after his off-track excursion 49 days earlier, was a creditable result, not least because he took a third World Championship fastest lap, with a lap of 1min53.75sec. Once again, Ginther made an outstanding start, taking the lead at the first corner and held it for the entire first lap, ahead of Jochen Rindt, Jack Brabham, Denny Hulme and John Surtees. Both drivers knew they were finishing as works Honda drivers as Ronnie Bucknum recalled to Christopher Hilton: "It was a bitter-sweet race meeting because we knew we were leaving. I remember sitting on the pit lane and John Surtees came up to have a little chat. He mentioned he was taking over and then spent a while in our pit having a look at the car."

Richie was, until his dying day, an immense fan of Honda and of his time there. In an interview with Bill Libby of *Car Life* magazine, Richie had a lot of praise for the Japanese outfit but was realistic about the team's prospects. "The Honda people have this spirit. The Japanese were new at racing and seemed to feel they had not yet made a place for themselves and proceeded hesitantly. They were technically far more advanced than their rivals in regards to powerplants, but far behind in the design of chassis.

The Honda group have other special problems and did when I was there. They have an unusual method of operation. Honda rotates people on its design staff and so forth to spread the experience and learning. Just about the time you get to seeing eye-to-eye with a key man, he's gone. Just about the time one of the key men gets a good hold on things, he's replaced.

Honda's goal is to be World Champion and it won't quit until that goal is attained. I don't know how long it will take Honda to get to the top, but I do think it will get tougher for them as time goes on. Changes in engine formula haven't helped. Honda was ahead of the rest on engines, but is rapidly losing its advantage in this area. Honda is still trying to catch up on chassis. But they are a very determined and very capable team."

Ginther was right, but Honda would not win as a constructor (unless you count a re-badged, re-branded Brawn 001 which won the 2009 drivers' and constructors' titles to be a Honda constructed car). As well as 1966, Honda had frustrations for the next two years. Its 3.0-litre car, as proved in Italy was definitely able but overweight and Honda failed to find the right balance. If anything, at least in Formula One, they succeeded a little better when they did not construct their own chassis; John Surtees winning for Honda but with a Lola chassis at Monza in 1967. In 1968, they had more trouble and, when Jo Schlesser was killed at the French Grand Prix at Rouen, it was the impetus needed for the marque to pull out of Formula One.

Richie Ginther, 1964. **Peter Darley**

As it happened, departure from Formula One actually led to a greater concentration on its road car business and saw the company grow and grow. The Honda Civic in 1972 was a massive best-seller. But the Japanese firm did not give up in Formula One and somewhat as in 1964, they came back quietly, choosing a back-of-the-grid team in Spirit with a young but capable driver in Stefan Johansson; again, if the project struggled, scapegoats were there. This time, though, they learnt from the experience and dominated the late 1980s with its units in the Williams and McLaren cars to win multiple world championships.

Honda's future was not the only thing that Ginther, who clearly was a very studious man in terms of engineering to pick things up, foresaw. In 1963, he spoke to Eoin Young about car sizes when John Cooper made a comment about the end of racing car design: "I think there's so far to go that you can't envisage an end yet. Racing cars have been getting smaller every year. When – and it is a when – they get the engine down to the width of a driver, it will then be the size of the driver that governs the width of the car." Four years later, Colin Chapman based the width of the monocoque of the Lotus 49 on Jim Clark's bottom.

And although it came much later than the monocoque development, Ginther also predicted a certain type of transmission: "There will be some form of constant speed or variable speed transmission, not one that you shift, but one that is automatic. If you had a constant-speed engine that was kept running at its most efficient point over a range of, say, 1000rpm and if you had a form of transmission that was infinitely variable and reversible, you could use it for both driving and braking power." Those comments were also from 1963; twenty years or so later, Patrick Head designed a continuously variable transmission, which replaced the car's conventional gearbox and allowed the engine to remain at optimum rpm during the entire lap, but it never made the grid due to changes in the rules. As such, it's slightly surprising considering his technical knowledge, that Richie never went into car design; maybe because the fact that he was not a studious man away from cars and would be working with extremely clever men with mathematical and scientific knowledge would have either leave Ginther feeling uncomfortable or maybe he would have clashed repeatedly.

Ginther had, since moving to Formula One, not been quite as regular in sports cars as he was in the 1950s. Through Ferrari, he competed at the Targa Florio, the Nürburgring 1000km, the 4 hours of Pescara and Le Mans. From 1962 onwards, Richie had normally appeared at Le Mans, the 12 Hours of Sebring, Daytona 24 Hours and normally because it went well with both seeing Jackie and Bret and was at the end of the year and after the F1 season, the 200 miles at Riverside. In 1966, he returned to the scene of some of his best drives but now in the Can-Am guise. In the only Can-Am race Richie ever participated in, he drove a Mirage. Jack Nethercutt had raced himself but wanted to build a car for other drivers to race against the best. He was able to fund the project through his role and contacts in the cosmetics industry. Designed by former aerospace engineer Ted Depew, the car was a neat design with a fantastic power-to-weight ratio. Had it come out a few years before, it would have likely done brilliantly. But by the time it made its debut,

Ginther (12) battles the Jochen Rindt/Nino Vaccarella car at the Nürburgring 1000 Kms, 1966. *MullerCologne*

competitors could take full advantages of wings, spoilers and high-downforce options to improve their cornering speed. The Mirage just could not cope well with the corners. Ginther, divorce almost through, and still in some pain from Italy, did the best he could but it's doubtful whether his heart was really in it, as he failed to qualify. His Can-Am record would forever read just one sole non-qualification.

By the end of 1966, though, Ginther was divorced. Jackie had decided that enough was enough and could not remain emotionally involved while Richie was racing. Jackie missed having a husband and a father around for Bret for day-to-day life, holidays or special occasions. Richie did, one year later, try to reconcile and rekindle the relationship but Jackie felt that Ginther was still too involved in racing. While he was involved, she thought, that any reunion would be short-lived. However, Jackie always remembered Richie with great affection when asked. Somewhat ironically, now he was actually divorced, 1967 was the first year that Richie planned to be predominantly based in America rather than Europe or Asia, with the Eagle team at Santa Ana in his home state of California.

Retirement from the Race

"I got back to my motel room and started thinking … there's got to be more to life than driving around in circles. Frankly, I had stopped enjoying driving … and felt it was a good time to quit"
Richie Ginther

Richie's last Formula One appearance – Monaco 1967. He failed to qualify. **The Grand Prix Library**

1967 is the first of the next 22 years that the facts and the myths about Richie Ginther get blurred. There is much fact, but some fiction, involved in terms of the sudden end of his career.

He started 1967 with an early attempt at Indianapolis ahead of his forthcoming season, to be largely spent driving for fellow American Dan Gurney in his All American Racers Eagle team. As part of a mandatory driving course for the forthcoming event for all rookie drivers to the Indianapolis 500, he drove a 153mph lap around the speedway. For a rookie test, this was pretty impressive. The slowest qualifier for the race some months later, after a number of intense qualification attempts was Al Miller, who drove 162.602mph, so Ginther definitely had the pace in his pocket.

Then it was confirmed in February 1967 that he would drive with All American Racers for all grands prix and the Indianapolis 500 and would also race at Sebring and Le Mans in a Ford Mark II.

On 4 and 5 February 1967, he raced the Holman Moody Ford GT40 MkII alongside Mario Andretti at the Daytona 24 Hours. However, the gearbox failed after 298 laps. It was the only time that Richie drove with Mario (two of the five World Championship American Grand Prix winners) but time together was short as Mario Andretti remembers: "I just did not have enough time with him. We were only together for the race. We never tested together or had dinner together or had any valuable time together outside the race car. It was a very quick weekend. You have to spend a lot of time with someone before you really connect and we did not have that. Unfortunately, I never saw him again. Usually when you drop out of a race, you split. You're done. It was not a fruitful race for me and I doubt it was for Richie too."

He appeared at the non-championship Race of Champions at Brands Hatch in March. Split into two heats, Ginther came third in the first heat, second in the second heat (both of these won by Gurney) but in the final itself, reliability problems led to him finishing eleventh as Gurney held off Lorenzo Bandini's Ferrari to win. All appeared well, and in essence it was.

Then came Monaco on 7 May, with Ginther surprisingly, and for the first time, failing to qualify for a grand prix, some 3.5 seconds

Ginther at the Race of Champions, Brands Hatch, 1967. *Peter Darley*

behind pole-sitter Jack Brabham. Monaco started the chain reaction of retirement as he recalled to *Autosport* magazine in 1977: "Monte Carlo was part of it. That was the next race after Brands and I did not qualify. I had a lot of problems in qualifying, sure, but I was upset by it. After all, I loved the place and had usually done well there. I never won it, but I was second frequently."

Shortly after that came qualification for the Indianapolis 500, Ginther's first attempt at his homeland's most famous race. In the end, he never made it to qualification. During practice, he parked the car and decided to stop racing there and then.

And this is where the mythology comes into play. Why did Ginther, winner of a grand prix just over a year ago, stop? It was said that he had personal problems that forced him to stop. It was said that he was so disgusted by Pedro Rodriguez being allowed to start at Monaco, even though he had posted a quicker time, that he decided to stop (as it happened, he would not have qualified even if Rodriguez had not started). It was said, certainly by newspapers at the time, that he quit because he failed to qualify for the Indianapolis 500.

Richie at Indianapolis Motor Speedway, 1967. *James R Gauerke/John Gauerke*

Richie at Brands Hatch, Race of Champions meeting, 1967.
Ferret Fotographics

Richie leads teammate and boss Dan Gurney and the Lotus of Mike Spence at the 1967 Race of Champions. *Mike Hayward*

Richie adjusts his car at the 1967 Monaco Grand Prix. *Ferret Fotographics*

In fact, it was for none of those reasons; better for the man to explain himself. He gave interviews at the time, but then expanded on them in later years. All of the following are Richie's words either told to the Associated Press, Nigel Roebuck, Rik Blote or Pete Lyons: "I had never been to Indianapolis before but I was fast in unofficial practice and I did not find it as much of a problem as I thought I would. But then I was sitting there in the car and I suddenly thought to myself 'What am I trying to prove, and for that matter, whom am I trying to prove it to?' Dan had a really good car. I think I was fifth fastest in initial practice. But when it came to the next stage, my first lap was fast, but my second lap slower and it kept happening. So I stepped out of the car and stopped. I said to Dan that I did not want to drive the car in the race and Dan, to his eternal credit, just said 'OK fine, I understand'. Quite honestly, I was moved by Dan's reaction. When you think of the money involved in getting that car there, well, I thought his understanding was remarkable.

"Well, I got back to my motel room and started thinking about it all again and again. There's got to be more to life than driving around in circles. Frankly, I had stopped enjoying driving to a degree and stopped acting like a pro and felt it was a good time to quit. One day I realised that it was becoming harder to concentrate and that I was not looking forward to the next race. If I was a racing driver and did not want to start that race, then it was time to get out. That was when I realised that if I kept up racing in the same vein, that I would

be doing a disservice to Gurney and that I could hurt myself and others seriously. I remember thinking that this was not fun anymore and that it is just a job. I decided to get out before I could not get out. I had a chance at that moment. If I kept going on with that mentality, then I would have got hurt.

"I'm retiring from racing in the sense that I'm not going to drive any more, but I intend to participate in the engineering and development of racing cars." (This line is significant; Richie had no real plans to walk away from the sport forever as some believed.)

Dan Gurney recalled pretty much the same reasoning, as recalled to Peter Egan in 1989: "Richie never actually made a qualifying attempt, he only did a practice with the car. He did not feel happy and just did not really want to run. He just reached that point in a driver's career when a driver says 'I don't desire to do this anymore," Evi Gurney, Dan's widow, said there was never any annoyance from Dan over the issue: "Richie told Dan that he did not feel comfortable on an oval and retired on the spot. This was a decision Dan understood and respected. After that, I only met Richie one more time – I think at Riverside 1970 – after that time I do not believe that Dan and Richie had much – if any – contact at all."

Ginther never really let on what led to that epiphany but certainly there had been a few factors in the last year. His marriage to Jackie had ended and the two had drifted apart and Jackie

Richie at Indianapolis Motor Speedway, 1967. *James R Gauerke/John Gauerke*

Richie in the Eagle, Indianapolis 500, 1967. *James R Gauerke/John Gauerke*

Richie Ginther and Dan Gurney, 1964. *Muller Cologne*

Richie was at the US Grand Prix in 1967 as a team member of Dan Gurney's Eagle team. Here he talks to his old team-mate Graham Hill. *Lionel Birnbom*

was now in another relationship. For a man who was so careful on the track and who had survived virtually unscathed during an incredibly deadly era in the sport, his injuries sustained at Italy must have been a significant jolt to the system. Of course, for many of his era, the loss of friends in crashes would have weighed deeply. Lorenzo Bandini had just died in a truly horrific crash, being burnt to death at the Monaco Grand Prix that Ginther had just failed to qualify for. Ginther didn't allow or want many people to get close to him, but he was, as noted by motor racing author Ed McDonough, "Often arm in arm with Bandini, they were good friends." Maybe Bandini's death was the final straw that broke the camel's back. While at Indianapolis, he learnt of Lorenzo's death (Bandini died from his burns three days after the crash) and Bandini's wife, Margherita, being hospitalised with shock and subsequently suffering a miscarriage. This would have brought back terrible memories of Jackie's two miscarriages. The 1961 Monaco Grand Prix had taught him that there was more to life than winning races and that must have gone through his mind. A ruptured fuel line during Indianapolis practice would have brought back memories of the North Witham fire in 1962. But as well as all this, he just wanted to enjoy life. He had been racing cars virtually full-time for some 15 years. Mindful perhaps that his father died aged only 50 years of age, and with Richie now rapidly approaching 40, it is only fair that Richie might well have wanted to explore more of life.

Later in 1967, he was interviewed by Bill Libby for *Car Life* magazine and the world away from racing was on his thoughts. "I'm getting to take another look at the world these days. I'm getting out and seeing what everybody else is like, I'm enjoying it. I'll get married again, I'm sure. I don't know who she'll be. Maybe it will be my ex-wife. Maybe someone I've never met.

"I haven't done well enough to get rich in racing, but I've made a good living at it. I've got some money put aside and I'll be able to take a deep breath and decide what I want to do now. I suppose I'll be able to stay in racing for a few years even though I've stopped driving. I have the experience and the mechanical know-how to help a team. But I don't know if I could hang on more than a few years. I learned on the track and in the pits. My actual education is very limited. This sport is becoming a sophisticated business. Once I'm no longer current, once I'm no longer going out there on the

track, feeling things out through practical experience, I don't know if I'll be able to remain for long. I hope I can stay though, I can't just turn around and walk away."

In an interview in 1972 with *Sportscar* magazine, Richie was asked if he regretted his retirement decision. "I had a lot of problems just then, including a divorce that I did not want. Maybe I could have continued driving, but if I had, maybe I would not be here now. What happened at Indianapolis was that I had bad vibes and that it was time to walk away." Rik Blote, later to be Richie's brother-in-law, recalls that Ginther told him that he wanted to do things at home that he could not have done whilst racing, specifically, watching Bret grow up and to live life fully.

To round up his driving career before we move onto the next part of Richie's life, what were his favourite tracks during his career? Well, in 1967, he largely kept it limited to Formula One tracks when he discussed his career with *Car Life* magazine: "Spa in Belgium is the most difficult I think. It is uphill and downhill with slow, difficult turns and high speed straights and serious consequences for any mistake you make. Monza in Italy is a tough course, especially because it is the fastest course. The Nürburgring in Germany is one of the slowest, but also one of the most trying. It has a lot of turns, which are difficult and a lot of sections that look alike, which makes it difficult to know where you are. I guess I like Reims in France least of all. It is mainly long straights with a couple of hairpin turns. I don't think you have as much pure racing there.

"I guess I enjoy Monaco most of all. It is not a fast course, but it is tiring and if you get sloppy, you may wind up putting your car in some shop or in the drink. Another point in favour of Monaco is that the race course, being right in town, is easily accessible. In many places just getting in and out of the course, battling traffic takes up considerable time and wears you out physically and mentally. At Watkins Glen, they had helicopters available to take us to and from the pits for a small fee, which was a blessing. I enjoyed racing at Watkins Glen very much. It has a fine, challenging course and the organisers treat you better than in most places."

1967 was not the last time Richie pulled on a crash helmet or sat in a racing car, but that part of his life was pretty much well and truly put to bed, certainly from a competitive point of view. But there would be many wins in motor racing to come for Richie.

Richie Ginther Racing

"Working for Richie was more like working with a good friend, he also helped me so much with my driving. He was so softly spoken and so patient. He gave me tons of good advice"
Elliott Forbes-Robinson, racing driver

Le Mans 1971 Richie Ginther Racing's car (34) is driven by Elliott Forbes-Robinson and Alan Johnson. *Elliott Forbes-Robinson*

Richie was not done with motorsport in its entirety. In fact, anything but. Despite no longer driving for Dan Gurney, Richie retained a good relationship with him and became Gurney's team manager for Indycar events. Richie was keen for his development and engineering skills to be transferred into a new role and initially became involved with his fellow American Grand Prix winner and his potential nemesis at Mexico in 1965. Both Gurney and Ginther celebrated a breakthrough win for All American Racers at the Rex Mays 300-mile race at Riverside in November, 1967. Ginther who had, after all, signed for the 1967 season, saw it through but with a host of different roles, including the above position, and that of a driving advisor, a technical advisor and, almost inevitably, a test driver, which he greatly enjoyed. He was certainly content by the end of the year as he recalled to *Car Life* magazine. "My know-how is being used to its utmost. Maybe I've finally found a home. I've really been given an interesting role in the organisation. I feel more a part of a real team operation than I ever have in the past. Everyone feels very patriotic about this, it's very inspiring."

Ginther had also kept links with former entrant John von Neumann. Richie was running a speed equipment business specialising in Porsche cars in Los Angeles in conjunction with von Neumann and the pair developed this to start running a racing team from 1968 onwards. Ginther would be supplying the racecraft knowledge and technical nous and von Neumann would be supplying the funds. Von Neumann's empire now spread not only through California, but across Nevada, Arizona and even Hawaii, but Ginther chose the Competition Motors headquarters in Woodland Hills as the base. Joining him on the team were Harold Broughton, a tuning specialist, Jack Pfluegler, who worked for Ferrari in California and Gary Pike. The drivers were SCCA C Division Champion Alan Johnson of Orange, California and Milton 'Milt' Minter of Santa Susana, California.

Ginther, in an interview with Shav Glick of *The Los Angeles Times*, was quite realistic and optimistic at the same time about the team's chances. "I admit our budget of $100,000 seems quite pikerish compared to some of the other teams with budgets of $300,000 to $500,000, but Porsche is essentially an engineering firm and it has been racing for many years, so we started from a much more solid basis than some of the others. We have a forty-foot van, two racing cars, a spare engine, a mechanic and myself. I hired Harold Broughton (who also drives the van) as our mechanic and then I took the two factory cars to Willow Springs to test drive them.

It takes a good deal of testing to understand the problems involved in setting up a car." (Ginther clearly seemed to relish getting behind a car to test it again as in his Ferrari days but in a different capacity now.) "I always make more changes to the chassis than the engine. More is gained through road holding than horsepower and reliability is most important. These two factors were responsible for Bruce McLaren's success in the Can-Am series and we hope to make our cars just as competitive in their C Production car class. We did not really take Alan Johnson away from the Don Burns Racing Team, it was just that Von Neumann felt an individual dealer in Burns could not compete with factory-supported teams on his own.

It takes money, big money to support cars in as competitive a series as the American Road Race of Champions series, but more than that, it is the way you go about it. Racing people have always been impressed by the way we operate. We think nothing of pulling the gearboxes out and changing the gear ratios right at the race. That is the way the European factories I was at (BRM and Ferrari) operate and I am drawing on my experience with them."

By this time, the sports car scene in America was blossoming; Can-Am (The Canadian-American Challenge Cup) had started in 1966 and quickly attracted some of the very best drivers around; Dan Gurney, Bruce McLaren, Phil Hill, Denny Hulme and John Surtees, to name just five.

The former Sports Car Club of America (SCCA) Chairman John Bishop had established the IMSA GT series which, like Can-Am, attracted top European racers and equipes. The attraction for Porsche to be involved was understandable. The US market was always a major market for Porsche who had been immensely successful with sales of both the Porsche 356 and then the Porsche 911, both of which had proven themselves in racing as fast and reliable cars. By 1970, the Sebring 12 Hour race and the 24 Hours of Daytona were attracting more and more European and International drivers and marques and with the fledgling but high-profile new series created, it was the perfect opportunity for Porsche to debut the 914.

Porsche by that time was in a position where, although its cars were of high speed, high quality and high comfort, they were also of high expense and the marque was concerned that the 911 was no longer the entry-level sports car of choice due to the cost, which was around $6500. Volkswagen also had concerns as, although the Volkswagen Beetle was doing brilliantly in the mainstream market, it had little in the way of sports car models and wanted, therefore, to diversify.

Ferry Porsche and Heinz Nordhoff of Volkswagen agreed a deal where a mid-engined sports car would be produced but in two different versions. Firstly there would be Volkswagen's Type 411 four-cylinder motor and Karmann chassis, which would be badged a 914-4 and sold as a Volkswagen-Porsche. Then there would be a 914-6 with a 2.0-litre, six-cylinder engine from the 911T. These would be assembled by Porsche. However, there were numerous start-up problems with both cars, with poor reviews and a quite heated debate about whether the 914-6 was actually a Porsche or not in the eyes of the purists. All of this was then compounded by Heinz Nordhoff's death from a heart attack in 1968.

Shortly afterwards, Josef Hoppen had just been appointed as Porsche and Audi's USA competition manager and the decision from above was to get the cars racing to show their potential. He was instructed to set up three different two-car 914/6 Porsche racing teams to compete in SCCA affiliated events in three different geographical areas of America for maximum sales and publicity coverage.

The chosen team would get $50,000 and cars to run in the C Production Class. Peter Gregg was chosen in the East; Art Bunker, Bob Hindson and Kendall Noah in the Midwest. In the West, the original target was actually Volkswagen Pacific but with Ginther in charge of the team. This shouldn't have been much of a problem as Ginther was already competitions manager for the marque through the dealership of von Neumann. Alan Johnson recalled to Roy Smith in Smith's *Porsche – The Racing 914s* book in a little more detail; "Jo Hoppen sent the car to the Volkswagen Pacific Porsche dealership of John von Neumann. I drove that first car at Willow Springs for a test and that's how Richie Ginther got involved. At the time, the car did not have the second mandatory roll bar, but the test was good and we looked forward to racing the car."

However, Volkswagen Pacific then asked for $150,000 from Hoppen as they complained that they would have to do all the development work. Hoppen, frustrated with the delay, eventually

chose Ginther to go it alone, Richie's renowned development and test work in years gone by being a big factor. Ginther and chief mechanic Harold Broughton worked on increasing the engine horsepower and making the car as light as possible to make full use of the car's handling ability, which included removing the windscreen, and before they fell foul of the SCCA, they even wanted to remove the rollbar. Broughton recalled to Casey Annis in an interview to *Vintage Racecar* in 2002: "By the time we were done with the car, there was nothing left of the engine that came with the car apart from the valve size and the displacement! Richie drove the car in a test, came back to the pits and said that in terms of its handling, it was the closest thing to a Formula One car that he had ever driven."

Richie never raced competitively again but would often test. Here he shakes down Jo Siffert's Porsche 917 at Road America. **The Grand Prix Library**

Richie at Road America, 1 May 1969. *Ronald Lathrop*

Richie and Elliot Forbes-Robinson at Santa Barbara. *Elliot Forbes-Robinson*

The operation got off to a flying start when, on 1 February at an SCCA event at Holtville, near San Diego, Johnson won the C Class event (Hollywood actor Steve McQueen won the A Class and overall race, but this was also a Ginther victory as Richie prepared and maintained his Porsche 908), albeit with a little luck as he told Roy Smith: "It was a damp track at the start and I chose to start with rain tyres whilst our main challenger, Jim Dittemore, chose dry tyres on what he felt was a drying track. As it turned out, rain tyres were a mistake; no more rain fell. I was losing two seconds a lap as there was no more rain after lap four and there were still thirteen laps to go. But when Dittemore had to pit with a loose wheel in his TR6, we were able to win the class. In the first race before that victory, we had a problem with too much advance and ended up burning a piston. At the end of February we fixed that by putting in a Bosch distributor and that worked just fine. For our next national championship race, we qualified on pole and won the race. Porsche were so impressed they sent Richie four more cars to set up and prepare for the two other regions. Richie fitted Teflon bushes, 21 and 22 millimetre torsion bars, Teflon front stabilisers and bearing modifications, all non-standard parts but they made the difference. Richie sent two over to Peter Gregg, but one was the original show car which we had problems with; I always thought that kind of funny. Two cars went to Art Bunker and we had two cars."

Johnson was clearly, understandably, a fan of the 914. In an interview with the *San Francisco Examiner* in 1970, he said that the cars prepared by Ginther handled better than any car he had ever driven: "It is extremely stable. It handled above and beyond my wildest dreams. I felt I could also take nearly any line I wanted out of Riverside's turn nine. It's an amazing race machine." It made Ginther's somewhat guarded comments before the Riverside race to the *Los Angeles Times* about the car's potential performance either a masterclass of smoke and mirrors or merely he humbly understated his ability to set the car up. "I know this will probably bring guffaws from our competition, but I honestly think that we are in a position of having to play catchup. The big problem at Riverside's long course is that it is a horsepower track. The driver to beat, in my opinion, is John Morton in his new Datsun Z car. The car has fantastic potential and has been very impressive in trial runs. Sure, they have some problems, but nothing that can't be solved, and if they do, John will be awfully tough to beat." In the end, Johnson won with ease.

Ginther-prepared cars would end up winning eleven national club events and all three championships; the Western Divisional Championship for Johnson, the Mid-Western for Bob Hindson, and the Eastern title for Gregg.

Ginther subsequently arranged a deal with Elliott Forbes-Robinson. Forbes-Robinson would agree to run the Porsche parts department in exchange for race experience in Ginther's Porsche 914-6 and Super Vee cars. Forbes-Robinson's father, of the same name, raced sports cars against Ginther in the 1950s and with the deal in place, Elliott effectively became Richie's protégé but he remembers Richie before driving for him. "The first time that I met Richie was actually when I was quite young as he was working as a mechanic where my father was working. It was later that I met him when he was driving for John von Neumann in the Cal Club races. I was going to the races with my family to watch my dad race.

"It was about 1968 when I started racing that I got to know him better, as he had cars entered in the same races that I was running. In 1968 I was asked by Richie to drive a 911S Porsche for him in B Production, the class that I was running in my 289 Cobra. He said that it removed the fastest car in the class and would be easier to win. I drove the car for him and continued later into the 914-6. While driving for him I lost my job at Technicolor [Elliott worked at Universal Studios' Technicolor division in the assembly department] because I was missing work to go to the races. Richie offered me a job at the shop handling the parts and sales for him. I took it and stayed there for a number of years."

In 1971, after a disappointing performance at Road Atlanta in the previous year's SCCA Road Race of Champions event, Porsche-Audi withdrew their support. Undaunted, Ginther ran the Porsche 914/916 GT cars in the US SCCA Production B Class as well as a factory-Porsche 911 at Le Mans for Johnson and Forbes-Robinson but an oil pump failure after eight hours ended their hopes. The iconic French 24-hour race had never brought much success for Ginther as a driver and his luck would not change as a team owner/ manager. Forbes-Robinson remembers the occasion with pleasure though: "The running of Le Mans in 1971 was so fantastic for a young driver who had only been driving for a couple of years. We got the car running quite well there enough to be fastest qualifier in the GT class. Unfortunately the car broke early and we did not have a good result."

Before the race, both Richie and John von Neumann were quite bullish about their chances of potentially embarrassing some of the factory Porsche cars. "Our idea is to prove to the Europeans that they are not always right. We're seven thousand miles away from the factory out here [here being Ontario Motor Speedway] and sometimes it's difficult to inspire what I call a level of respect from the home office. I have argued this with the Europeans but I've found them too self-centered to listen seriously. Yes, they may have built it, but it is our people who have evolved it and we won't be feeling belittled after Le Mans," said von Neumann.

Ginther, as always, was more circumspect than von Neumann: "It was a totally standard car; a forerunner of Porsche's 1972 promotion model when we picked it up. But they won't recognise it – on the inside, that is – when we get it back over there. I think the things we learned in the past year in C Production racing in the SCCA events against Datsun and Triumph will be a big help at Le Mans.

"Now in Europe, the tendency is to set every car up for the Nürburgring as it is an extremely tough course with a patched-up surface that can destroy cars. Le Mans, on the other hand, is smooth and fast, much like Riverside. Our car will be prepared with that in mind and I think the Europeans will do a double-take when Alan and Elliott start taking the corners at Le Mans."

At Le Mans 1971. From left to right: Richie, Cleo von Neumann, John von Neumann, Elliot Forbes-Robinson, Alan Johnson. *Elliot Forbes-Robinson*

After winning the Super Vee Gold Cup race at Laguna Seca, 14 October 1973. On the left is Joe Huffaker who built the engine. Richie celebrates on the far right. *Elliot Forbes-Robinson*

Von Neumann finished the interview with typical swagger: "It is great fun to be standing out on the course and seeing your car come around the corner and it's twice as much fun when that car is in first place. That is the sight that Richie and I expect to enjoy at Le Mans." To be fair to von Neumann, the context of first place is not known, with von Neumann it could well have been outright first but, in all likelihood, it should have been for their class. If the car had not retired then it would have stood a decent chance of winning its class as Johnson and Forbes-Robinson qualified 29th overall and came third in class only behind Jean-Claude Aubriet and Jean-Pierre Rouget in their Ecurie Leopard entered Chevrolet Corvette C3 and Greder Racing team principal Heini Greder and his co-driver Marie-Claude Beaumont, also in a Chevrolet Corvette C3. Johnson and Forbes-Robinson were the highest qualified Porsche 911 in the race and so it is quite reasonable to presume they would have won their class – and judging by the fact that eventual class winners Raymond Touroul and Andre Anselme in their Porsche 911 finished sixth overall but had qualified some way behind Johnson and Forbes-Robinson, a top five finish overall was quite possible.

1972 saw much success in the hands of Forbes-Robinson, the 914 winning in the E Class of the SCCA National Championships and during these few years of team management he also worked as a crew chief to Brian Redman when the Briton raced at the Mid-Ohio round of Can-Am in August 1969 in a brand-new Porsche 917. He also ran Jo Siffert in a 917/10 Can-Am car and, although Siffert finished fourth in the series in 1969, Ginther saw signs of improvement going forward: "Our problem next year will be to reduce the car weight by about 250lb. We will also probably install a Rootes-type supercharger onto the flat V12 engine to get more torque. We will be competitive".

Richie had spent a long time modifying the sharply shaped nose on the front of the car so that its handling and lack of ability to corner were significantly improved without losing the top speed of the car. Harold Broughton remembered to Michael Ling in *Automobile Quarterly* that Jo Siffert's ability to maximise the car's potential was extraordinary, but that Ginther was the best suspension tuner he had ever met.

Ginther had some experience already with Porsche. Here he races a Porsche 904/8 at the Nürburgring 1000 Kms, 1964. **Gunther Asshauer**

Some years later, Richie recalled to Rik Blote that one of the all-time highlights in his career was his work on the Porsches. "With a beaming smile, he told me of the time [this was when his workshops were preparing and running Porsches] that a delegation from Porsche in Germany came to see him, to figure out how come Richie's cars were going faster than the factory prepared ones. He did not tell me about the actual modifications he made, and it was only by talking to other people and reading articles that I later discovered his contribution to motor racing development was substantial."

Richie also helped Forbes-Robinson with his Super Vee efforts; Forbes-Robinson taking fourth place in the championship with two wins at Riverside and Portland. Super Vee was a formula powered by the 1600cc Volkswagen engines which developed up to 125bhp enabling the cars to go up to 140mph. The series was designed to try and let talented drivers without a big budget show their mettle and try and progress. Super Vee was initially recognised as a championship class in the United States by the Sports Car Club of America in 1971 and then it developed into a range of different series sanctioned either by the SCCA or the International Motor Sports Association (IMSA). Although the standard components from Volkswagen were used – for instance, transmissions, engines and braking systems – there was room for development, which was something that was right up Ginther's street.

Richie waxed lyrical about it in 1972 in an interview with *Sportscar* magazine: "It's a true international formula. Everything else, just about, is tied to one country. In Can-Am, you almost have to run a big American engine. In Formula 1, about the

only engine you can buy is British. It's the same in Formula 2, Formula 3 and Formula Ford. But with Super Vee, you can buy the basic parts just about any place in the world.

"It's also an ideal showcase for a young driver to make the long step up to Formula One. There aren't the same opportunities there used to be. When I was coming up, the sport was very different. We had the von Neumanns, the Edgars, the Cunninghams, the Parravanos of this world. If you showed ability, you got a chance to get a good ride. You could go to Sebring or Le Mans and measure yourself against the best drivers in the world. But now, there's no-one like the von Neumanns or the Edgars. I think Super Vee can offer that opportunity. If you can show the ability there, then you could make that step to Formula One."

Ginther was certainly right with this theory. It's worth remembering that Formula Super Vee produced a Formula One World Champion in Keke Rosberg and US Super Vee saw Bertil Roos (Forbes-Robinson's closest challenger for two years) make it to Formula One and Tom Bagley, Bob Lazier, Bill Alsup, Geoff Brabham, Al Unser Jr, Arie Luyendyk and Michael Andretti, to name just a few, enjoy success in CART or the Indianapolis 500.

There were other projects too; on 2 August 1970, Ontario Motor Speedway was dedicated and, as part of the weekend's festivities, a pro-celebrity race was held featuring Porsche 914-6s. While Ginther did not participate as a driver, both Richie and his race shop team did the preparation on all the cars. The likes of actors Kirk Douglas, Paul Newman, Steve McQueen, Robert Wagner and the astronaut Pete Conrad raced against the likes of racers Mark Donohue and Bobby Unser, who won the race in partnership with comedian Dick Smothers.

Ginther had lost none of his attention to detail as his former apprentice race car mechanic Kurt Zimmermann explains: "Richie was the consummate race car builder, he was involved in so much. He truly was one of a kind. Richie knew the perils of endurance racing and had us integrate four completely separate ignition systems, two separate fuel delivery systems, two separate radio systems and so on. The drivers could isolate problems while driving by toggling between systems." Richie ended up developing a number of suspension pieces for the Porsche which he could quite easily have marketed accordingly. But Ginther was not inclined to properly list and catalogue his items, let alone follow up the marketing thereafter. Perhaps the memories of how uncomfortable and fed up he was at the dealership before joining Ferrari preyed at the back of his mind.

Ginther had also not lost any of his fire and lack of tolerance for fooling. As a team boss he very much believed in team orders and discipline and would reportedly get even redder in the face when the drivers disobeyed his orders. Milt Minter would fly too close to the sun too often and was sacked by Richie. Richie's mechanic Kurt Zimmerman remembers the dispute. "When I asked about this, I was just told 'there was a disagreement'. But both men were strong headed individuals for sure. However Milt Minter did not own the car, so therefore had to agree to follow team orders, in fact, he had already agreed to follow team orders. When it came down to the team vs Minter, Minter decided to ignore team orders. I've met and known both men and they did not have the same ideas about racing."

However, it was a mark of Richie's overall character that although Milt, according to the *Automobile Quarterly* article, was furious at the time of his loss of income, he kept good relations personally with

Richie and when Minter later won a race against Richie and his team, Richie was the very first person to come and congratulate Milt.

For Elliott Forbes-Robinson, however, it was only good memories of his time at Richie Ginther Racing. "Working for Richie was more like working with a good friend, he also helped me so much with my driving. He was so softly spoken and so patient. He gave me tons of good advice. Most of all he taught me about car set-up and how to know what the car would want. Richie was a great friend of our family and the godfather of my first child. When he spent time with my kids at the race track they loved it, he was really good with them."

However the days of team ownership would soon end. Very much a perfectionist, Ginther was disappointed with himself when Forbes-Robinson was disqualified after appearing to dominate the 1972 SCCA American Road Race Championship E Production race. It had been a miscalculation rather than anything deliberate but it irked Ginther who felt he had let Elliott down. Forbes-Robinson remembers the situation well. "We were disqualified at the national championship race at Road Atlanta in 1972. It was because it rained. We had the car on the pole to the race by a good margin, and then on race day it rained. We used 7in wide wheels on the car but our rain tyres were mounted on 6in wheels. The car looked the same because the inch was on the inside. Not giving it a thought, we raced it as it was, and we were more than a second a lap faster than anyone else, but our track was too wide because of the narrower wheels. The SCCA would not listen to us or let us appeal and, in fact, the car that they gave the win to was late to the starting grid and told to start at the back or be disqualified! They refused and started from the front row, so it seems like SCCA did not want to have us win."

Kurt Zimmerman's copy of the Richie Ginther Porsche 911, complete with Richie Ginther Racing decal on the front. *Kurt Zimmerman*

RICHIE GINTHER
President

RICHIE GINTHER RACING, INC.
6110 WEST SLAUSON AVENUE
CULVER CITY, CALIFORNIA 90230
(213) 390-5144

Richie Ginther's business card.
Steve Payne

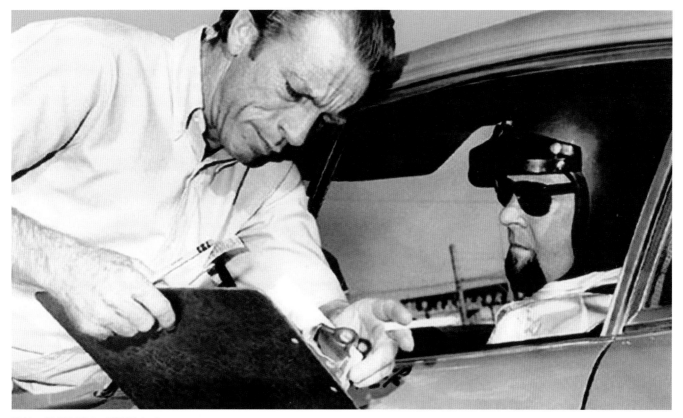

Richie with Milt Minter. **Milt Minter Jr**

But in truth, Ginther was already looking away from the sport.

In 1969, he had met Cleo (pronounced Clay-Oh) von Neumann, who at that time was still married to John von Neumann. Cleo, a stunningly beautiful woman of Dutch/Indonesian origin (her father was an oil executive for Shell, formerly known as the Royal Dutch Shell company, and he was based in Indonesia where she grew up), soon started an instant friendship with Richie, despite the seventeen-year age gap between them. Richie was now 39, Cleo just 22. The von Neumanns split up in the early 1970s and then at that point, the good friendship between Richie and Cleo developed into a loving relationship. Although Cleo did not really stay on good terms with her ex-husband, Richie did stay friends with John despite entering a relationship with his ex-wife.

The duo and Cleo's brother, Rik Blote, had already been discussing, back in 1972, doing a grand tour of America in a large motorhome with Richie keen to see more of life away from racing. As Blote recalls, "When I stayed with him at his house for about five days back in 1972, it was towards the end of an adventure trip for me. I had quit my job, flown to New York, bought a car and then went on to tour round the USA and Western Canada for three months. Back in 1972, such a thing was virtually unheard of. By the time I was with Richie I had covered around 14,000 miles and he was interested to hear about my route and the many places I had visited. It was at this time that he commented, 'Well hey, you've seen more of the country than I have!' He went on to say that he really liked the idea of touring round but that he would prefer to do it in a motorhome, to be more free and independent, rather than to have to

rely on finding motels each night the way I did. I remember agreeing that his idea was an even better way of doing it".

Already by this time Richie had become interested in all manner of non-motorsport pursuits. This included reading, art, music, books, animals and architecture as well as his real passion, Native American culture and history. Even while as a team patron, Richie was finding time to visit local archaeological digs and spent a huge amount of time there, uncovering artefacts that were well over 1500 years old.

Ginther stopped running the team at the end of 1973 and for two more years ran the parts business, taking it back over from Forbes-Robinson whose sports car career was now blossoming after proving his ability in the Ginther-prepared Super Vee cars. Forbes-Robinson concludes: "After driving for Richie for about five years through Porsche and Super Vee in SCCA club racing and some pro racing – winning almost every time we ran a Super Vee race because of the great car – I went on to drive the Super Vee for Grey Egerton after he bought it and his 911 in endurance racing. I left Richie Ginther Racing and became a full time race driver."

In 1975, Richie sold both his business and his house and finally got the chance to buy the motorhome and enjoy what had become the real passions in his life. Ginther was no businessman and never exploited his race car preparation and mechanical acumen very well. He was not one to bring a lot of attention onto himself so relief would have been a key aspect in choosing to sell. He had made no effort to relocate his business, which could likely have flourished, despite the commercial building it was in being condemned. Now was the time to really experience life to its fullest.

Reclusive Richie?

"I am not a recluse, I just value my privacy. I don't really follow racing unless a friend of mine is involved. Racing is in the past, however, and I believe in living in the present"
Richie Ginther

Cleo, Richie and Yoshio Nakamura at Rosarito market. *Cleo Davidson*

odern technology in all of its platforms has allowed opportunities for a number of retired racing drivers to stay in touch with the sport, enriching many historic festivals or reunions for drivers and fans alike. But there are some drivers who deliberately stay away from the sport. Some stay away due to painful mental or physical legacies, while for others, it's due to the fact they were never particularly gregarious when racing. Then there's a broad third category for whom racing was just one part of their life and once it was over, they left it behind and moved on.

Motor racing does not always seem to accept that. There's a recalcitrant side of it that does not appear to understand, as wondrous as racing is, that there's a whole world of possibilities elsewhere and subsequently, the so-called recluses often find a whole multitude of half-truths and rumours surrounding them.

This was very definitely the case with Ginther. He enjoyed an enriching, varied fifteen years or so that he had away from the sport until his death in 1989. But the key word above is away. There's more than one book and a few magazine articles that state he was a complete recluse living in a trailer in the desert. There were also various rumours with the rise of the internet, about his health, both physical and mental, and what caused his relatively early death. At least once or twice when meeting people, I was asked if Richie died early due to taking drugs, so it is clear that the misinformation spread quite widely.

One is somewhat reminded, when it comes to Richie and the impression of his post-racing life by so many people for so long, of the line from the end of John Ford's film *The Man Who Shot Liberty Valance*. In the film, James Stewart plays a senator, Ransom Stoddard, who sits down for an interview with a journalist and publisher, Maxwell Scott (played by Carleton Young). Stoddard forged an impressive, but somewhat dull, career based on shooting the outlaw Liberty Valance (played by Lee Marvin). Scott realises that the truth and Stoddard's reputation is based on a myth. He rips up his notes which prompts Stoddard to say, "You're not going to use the story, Mr Scott?'

Scott says 'No, sir. This is the West, sir. When the legend becomes fact, print the legend."

In other words, the better, juicier story, when transposing it here into Ginther's context, is that when discussing the grand prix heroes of yesteryear, you have the grand prix winner who became a drunken, drug addled bum in the desert. Folklore fits better because legends sell more or sound more exciting than facts. If you read numerous articles or books on Ginther, then the Indianapolis 500 in 1967 is the end of Richie's story. The clean-shaven, freckle-faced, crew-cut all-American hero becomes a long-haired moustached hippy who completely eschewed any form of human contact until just before his death. But in fact, another story just as rich and varied as his racing career was just beginning.

Ginther did not exactly turn his back completely on racing either. It is actually surprising to find how involved he was with the sport from 1973 to 1989. Maybe the difference was he was not as regular at historic events as Stirling Moss or Phil Hill, or did not

keep a high profile within the sport like Dan Gurney. But to say that he actually turned his back on the sport is largely misleading.

In fact, Ginther appeared in a number of high profile historic events. The United States Grand Prix West of 1976 at Long Beach was the third race of that amazing roller-coaster season, which was won by Clay Regazzoni in his Ferrari, his only win of the season. But prior to that, there was a five-lap Historic Antique Grand Prix with twelve racers. Jack Brabham appeared in his 1959 Cooper-Climax, Dan Gurney (who was also the competition director for the US Grand Prix itself) in a BRM, also from 1959. Then Innes Ireland in a Maserati 250F, Denny Hulme in a Cooper from 1957, Stirling Moss in a 1954 Maserati 250F and the great five times World Champion, Juan Manuel Fangio in his 1955 Mercedes-Benz W196. Carroll Shelby, Maurice Trintignant and Phil Hill also took part, but so too did Rene Dreyfus, then 70 years old and winner of numerous grands prix in the 1930s and the oldest driver (in the oldest car) was Pete DePaolo, the winner of the 1925 Indianapolis 500, and at the time of the event, just shy of his 77th birthday in a Bugatti T37. Ginther was entered to drive the second oldest car, a 1927 Bugatti T37A but in the end, only attended the event as a visitor. Dreyfus took over the Bugatti, his former car and Consalvo Sanesi was drafted in instead to drive a 1932 Alfa Romeo Monza.

In 1980, he turned up again at Long Beach for the grand prix. Unfortunately for the 1976 winner Regazzoni, it would be his last ever race. While driving an Ensign N180, his brakes failed on the main straight on lap 50 and he careered into the parked Brabham of Ricardo Zunino who had retired after an accident on the first lap and then into a concrete wall. He was paralysed from the waist down for the rest of his life, dying in 2006 in a car crash, at the age of 67. Before the race though, there were happier times. A bicycle race was arranged and a Formula Atlantic race supported the main event as did a ten lap Toyota pro/celebrity race which was due to feature Richie, Dan Gurney and Phil Hill alongside actors Gene Hackman and James Brolin and astronaut Pete Conrad. In the end only Gurney raced in the event, which was won by Parnelli Jones and the two former Ferrari team-mates simply enjoyed the event at their own leisure.

Richie appeared at the German Grand Prix in 1977 to commemorate the 100th win of a now-dominant Goodyear in Formula One, thoroughly enjoying meeting old friends, new fans and presenting Niki Lauda with a commemorative tyre for winning the race. He also drove at Riverside's 25th anniversary race, the Edward Diloreto Historic Can-Am Race, which was a preliminary event to the Can-Am race itself. He competed against George Follmer, Chuck Parsons, John Morton and Lothar Motschenbacher, racing a Porsche 914, in what would be his last racing event.

A few months prior to this saw him race at Monterey where he raced in a Porsche after being asked to by long-time friend, driver, team owner and car collector, Vasek Polak. Richie was also due to compete in a veterans race set up by Toyota at Riverside, in tandem with the Los Angeles Times/Toyota Grand Prix endurance event. It would have been (or rather was) a competition over 10 laps in a Toyota Celica GT Liftback between rookie drivers and veterans; as well as Richie were former Indianapolis 500 winners Sam Hanks,

Parnelli Jones, Rodger Ward and Johnnie Parsons, former land-speed record attemptee (among other things), Mickey Thompson and finally, his old Honda team-mate, Ronnie Bucknum. These veterans competed against a number of rookies as to who would come out on top; the experience or the youth. (Youth being relative in some cases; among those racing as a rookie was Phil Caliva, who made a number of attempts to qualify for the '500 but was 37 at the time of this race.)

In the end Ginther merely attended to catch up with Ronnie Bucknum and friends, leaving the racing to others with rookies John Paul Jr and Michael Chandler finishing ahead of the highest placed veteran, Parnelli Jones.

But even then Richie still stayed in touch with people and visited tracks. One of the last pictures of him in a racing car before the BRM reunion in 1989, is that taken by Peter Giddings, a regular historic racer for many years who met up with Richie in California for a historic race meeting. Ginther, who it has to be said looks well, is sitting, smiling beatifically, in Gidding's Talbot-Lago.

As well as all this, one of his most enduring friendships until his death was with Yoshio Nakamura, Honda's chief engineer, team manager and both Mr Honda and Mr Ginther's effective right-hand man at Honda. The two would meet up every year in Mexico and, although there was discussion of racing, this would take a back seat to Mexican food, the local market-stalls (especially in the market in Rosarito), wildlife and anything else that would take their fancy. Cleo and Richie once suggested to Yoshio in the late 1980s, that maybe Gardena, California, where Honda America were based, would be a better holiday destination, due to Yoshio's advancing age as it was nearer and much more comfortable. Yoshio adored Mexico and put a swift end to that suggestion. He kept life-long friendships, with regular meetings, with the likes of Carroll Shelby too and for some years, his motorhome rocked up near John von Neumann's home in Palm Springs.

Richie in Peter Gidding's Talbot Lago, 1984. *Peter Giddings Racing*

Ginther, however, always had a wry sense of humour and was very much his own man who did not really care what people thought of him and what he was doing out of racing. To somewhat lampoon those who thought he was a cave-dwelling hermit in the desert, he would seal any envelopes with stamps of a hermit crab. Cleo Davidson remembers one such incident where Richie definitely did attempt to eschew his past. "Rich and I headed up the cobblestone street where we lived, to join our closest neighbours at the local bar, for his birthday. Three of our other neighbours were there for the same reason. Whilst we were drinking and chatting, a complete stranger came over and asked Rich if he was Richie Ginther.

"'Yes,' Rich said, as he was not specifically asked if he was the racing driver, you see? Well, this stranger turned out to be a diehard fan. He started to rave on about every race he had seen Rich in. After a while Rich had had enough. After all, he was there celebrating a birthday with friends. 'I think you've mistaken me for someone else,' he said. 'But you said you were Richie Ginther!' The fan protested.

"Rich, deadpan, said; 'I lied'."

Ginther often said to a number of people about racing that, "It has been good to me and I have been good to it." But as he said in response to an article in *Autoweek* by Bill Lovell one January that had Richie down as 'missing' and living the life of a recluse: "I am not a recluse, I just value my privacy. I don't really follow racing unless a friend of mine is involved. Racing is in the past, however, and I believe in living in the present." Cleo Davidson recalls a similar answer should any fan or inquisitive visitor ask. "Nowadays I'm more interested in the flower that opened in my garden this morning than discussing my racing career." He would still meet up with old rival Dan Gurney on a couple of rare occasions with Gurney realising that, post-racing, their paths were going in different directions. As Dan, whose involvement in motorsport was still very active until virtually his dying day, said to Peter Egan in 1989, "When he left racing, he changed his whole way of life. Quite simply, he was no longer part of our world, he was part of *the* world."

Freed of commitments, Ginther went wherever he fancied, indulging in the luxury allowed to very few of having total freedom and not a care in the world. He took all the clocks out of the home as he did not want to be tied down or live his life by the clock any more, a hark back to his days at Douglas when the clock ruled the whole business. Very much his own man with his own interests, Ginther's only concession was to his son Bret. The two weren't exactly estranged but Bret had lived with his mother Jackie after his parent's divorce. Due to racing, Richie had not always had the quality time with his son either of them would have wanted thus far, so amends were made; another reason that racing took a back seat. Richie largely spent time in the motorhome by himself with Bret joining from time to time and Cleo from the late 1970s onwards.

In an interview to Nigel Roebuck of *Autosport* magazine at the German Grand Prix in 1977, Richie explained more about his life then and what led to it coming about. "What am I doing now? I've been asked that so many times this weekend and it's becoming a bit embarrassing. I'm not doing anything! But that was my choice, although not by my plan. A whole series of circumstances happened at the same time, in a sequence of time, and all they all pointed towards one direction, which was me being free. There were some problems with my business. It was successful but I had some problems like when they condemned my property.

"It really was a very successful company, a private company specialising in chassis development and components for the chassis and so forth. The stuff was not available anywhere else and thus it was very much in demand. But I had to move from where I was in Culver City because they condemned it solely so they could build a supermarket or some damn thing.

Then, right after that, someone came to the front door of the house that I'd lived in for fifteen years asking me if I wanted to sell it. You know, it seemed like someone was trying to tell me something! So, as it turned out, I made an arrangement with my company whereby I still have an interest in it and some income from it. I sold my house, carried the loan and have some income off that. So each month, I still have money coming in, and if I'm careful, I can live off that. The loans are 30 years long so that will last me until I die.

"So I dropped out, as it were. I bought a motorhome and I live in it. If I want some time at the ocean, then I drive down to the beach, park my motorhome and spend some time there. When I get tired of that and want to go to the desert, say, I just go, pull up and spend some time there. So that's the situation that I've been in. I've been living like this since 1974 and so long as I still enjoy it, there is nothing to make me do otherwise.

"I don't wear a watch anymore. I don't have a clock in my motorhome, not even a calendar! If I want to know what day it is, then I go and get a newspaper. However, I will admit that I do have a television in the motorhome but I honestly very seldom watch it. You see, the motorhome has a generator to keep all the batteries charged up and it's all self-contained. My only limitation really though is the lack of water I can keep on board. I carry a motorcycle on the back so if I run out of food or beer, then I just ride into the nearest town or village.

"I'm not lonely. I have friends that come and go and I often will go and see them. I have a son, who is now 15 and during his summer vacations, he and I generally go off somewhere. One time we both went to Canada on a three-month trip, just taking our time. It's a fantastic way of life; if things go your way to the point where you can do nothing, then that's what I'm doing; nothing. I do exactly what comes into my head, I'm very fortunate. I'm under no pressure, and I'm at peace with myself."

Richie's relationship with Bret was now different. Richie was able to be a father to Bret and taught him mechanical skills. Bret was starting to get interested in cars in his own right and occasionally took part in street racing in a Chevrolet Camaro which Richie had modified, although when Richie found out it was for street racing and not making the car generally better for day-to-day use, he was not best pleased.

The two Ginther males would also go motorcycle riding in the desert and Richie would encourage Bret when the younger of the two men got frustrated after the bike broke down that all mechanical failures can be fixed, providing sound reasoning prevailed. He

Yoshio Nakamura with Cleo and Richie's excited dog. *Cleo Davidson*

would drive the motorhome, a Fleetwood Tioga, to Jackie Ginther's house and visit (or pick up) Bret. Often when he did so, he would plant a rose at Jackie's house and for some time after his death, Jackie maintained a miniature rose that Richie once planted.

His intellect and forward thinking led to Richie being involved in different aspects of life; just because he was totally free did not mean he idled around. He was passionate about his archaeology, of course and his interest in America's past. Few things would excite him more than trying to discover more about the Folsom Site (also known as Wild Horse Arroyo) a major archaeological site about eight miles west of Folsom, New Mexico. It was excavated in 1926 and found to have been a camp where 23 bison were killed using tools, known as Folsom points. This site became famous as it was the first time that artefacts indisputably made by humans were found directly associated with faunal remains from an extinct form of bison from the late Pleistocene period. The information culled from this site was the first of a set of discoveries that would allow archaeologists to revise their estimations for the time of arrival of Native Americans on the North American continent. However, nothing was ever found (and still hasn't to this day) of the man or men who killed the bison and Ginther was particularly keen to discover more.

Another favourite archaeological haunt for Richie was the Calico Early Man Site, near Barstow, San Bernardino County, in the central Mojave Desert of southern California. Here, artefacts, tools, alluvial deposits and soil profiles aged the site to be home to humans around 14,400 to 18,000 years ago. It has also been home to immense amount of fossils including mammoths and sabre-tooth cats but it was ancient man that excited Ginther the most. (Note, in more recent years it has been suggested that the tools were shaped by geology and not humans so the jury is out about how long ago humans were at Calico.)

While ancient man was one interest, he was also passionate about America's future, becoming interested and deeply immersed in recycling, alternative energy sources and wildlife conservation, all before these became the important topics they are today. In short, he had a lot of interests and a lot of people to see. He was anything but a recluse.

A Whole New World

"He was a very likeable and interesting person and so different from the typical type one would expect to be a racing driver. The thing about Richie was that he was interested in just about everything"

Rik Blote, Richie's brother-in-law

Cleo and Richie at Bret and Catherine Ginther's wedding, 1982. *Cleo Davidson*

Many assumptions about Richie come from the feeling that, as a racer, it was only racing that he was interested in and all the worldly-wise and non-racing interests came in from 1974 onwards. In fact, Richie had developed an interest in things away from racing as far back as 1960 as he mentioned at the time to *Car and Driver*. "Whilst I've been at Ferrari, I've seen how interested the Europeans are in their history. It has made me very interested in the history of California and in particular, the Native Americans. Whenever we're home at California, we both like to go out and look at the old missions and trails."

Peter Miller in his 1963 article on Richie for *Men at the Wheel* also describes Richie's interest in archaeology, as well as gun collecting and riding his motorcycle, so it was a constant interest during racing, albeit not fully undertaken quite as much due to the demands of a full-time Formula One drive.

This interest appeared, according to Michael Ling's article in *Automobile Quarterly*, to start when Richie and Jackie got to know a Pasadena-based historian called Floyd Evans through dealings at the Ferrari salesroom. Evans was a keen photographer but also had a real interest in Native American culture and history, particularly of the Californian natives. Richie and Jackie travelled to various parts of California with Evans, studying arrow heads and other artefacts found in the desert sands. In the end, Evans made such an impact on both Jackie and Richie, that when it came to naming their child, Evans became Bret's middle name.

Ginther's interest and enthusiasm in the Native Americans remained constant for the rest of his life as already covered in this book. Ginther was not one (or certainly not in the 1960s) to have had an extensive book collection at his home, but he did set about buying as many books on Native Americans as he could. As well as this, in the late 1950s, Ginther was collecting gold coins and pistols too, so his interest in things away from racing started before he was even in Formula One, let alone after his motorsport days were over. Rik Blote always felt that Ginther was so knowledgeable about the Native American history that he could have quite easily become a teacher or certainly put his understanding of the subject to a wider use had Richie been inclined to.

But as keen as Richie was in Native American history, this was just one of a whole plethora of interests he now immersed himself in. Rik Blote, the brother of Richie's second wife Cleo, although a racing fan, now saw another side of Richie and described him thus: "He was a very likeable and interesting person and so different from the typical type one would expect to be a racing driver. The thing about Richie was that he was interested in just about everything. Chatting with him, a conversation could cover such diverse subjects as photography, history, aircraft design, the lifecycle of an insect and the migratory patterns of birds. It's what made him such an amazing person to be around. I think it may have been his wide range of interests that made him decide he wanted to do more in his life than solely motorsport.

"Those who could not understand this about him might have referred to him as 'going hippy', simply because he spent some time on archaeological digs, living in his beautiful motorhome,

An example of Richie's artwork. **Cleo Davidson**

or because he was interested in stuff they thought was weird, like Native American history, recycling, wildlife and its conservation and so forth. Not subjects normally associated with racing drivers, even today."

Richie was a talented artist and in particular had a passion for making jewellery. He designed brooches, belt buckles and bracelets, using the precious stones that he discovered on his journeys, such as malachite or turquoise and using his mechanical background and skills with welding torches and the like, then setting them in silver or occasionally he brazed them, creating Ginther's take on what the Native American's would have worn 1500 years prior.

But his main focus, after being accompanied by her for a few years in the motorhome was now Cleo, who was to become his second wife. They travelled to numerous places in the motorhome together, but two particular favourite haunts were Las Vegas, to take in the Siegfried and Roy magic show, and other entertainment and as converse a place as possible from Las Vegas was the Canyon de Chelly National Monument in Arizona, where Richie pursued his Native American interests. They settled on the Baja coast, near Rosarito, around 1980, building a home and garden virtually from scratch, funded in part by John von Neumann; another divorce proving very costly to him (firstly losing the Ferrari dealership to Eleanor and now funding a house for Cleo and Richie), although his great friendship with Richie softened the blow of another wife calling it a day on their marriage. Richie and Cleo would live in the Tioga motorhome while work continued although both of them got involved with labour around the house, reminding Richie somewhat of his time with Tony Rudd and his family some 25 years ago in their house.

Richie first met Cleo, as previously mentioned, in 1969 and there was "immediate attraction" between them recalled Cleo, and they had long conversations all through that first weekend.

"Rich and I became close friends in 1969. He had help me with garden projects, he turned me on to roses and when we all went dirt-riding on motorcycles, he was always the one who checked to see if I was all right (not my husband). He was also the one who came to the hospital with me to get a lump on my shoulder removed (not my husband). We were so close."

Ginther was very much in love and, with Cleo's soft and subtle encouragement, they discovered yet more experiences together. Richie became a committed and prodigious reader of books. Among his favourite were *The Lord of the Rings*, any books by James Herriot and William Stevenson's espionage novel *A Man Called Intrepid*, but Richie also concentrated on his rose garden at the home. He barely watched television, largely watching nature programmes when he did sit in front of the television. He had a lot of time for pets, as Cleo recalls. "He loved animals and creatures of all kinds. But he came to know and love cats through me, starting when we first met. He also had a sense of humour, quick and dry as toast. A neighbour in Baja had invited friends down for dinner and to spend the night. I don't recall why, but said neighbour had to go elsewhere, so we agreed to step in to feed and lodge the couple, whom we knew, but not well. The male was a song-and-dance man from Broadway musicals named Bob Wright, the lady his girlfriend. (Note – Bob Wright was a musical composer, probably best known for his work on the musical and then movie *Kismet*, with his writing partner George Forrest). I had made an Indonesian feast, but Bob kept staring at one of our cats, a big black Oriental named Kathmandu, who firmly believed he was a table decoration. Eventually Bob said firmly to Kathmandu; 'I'd like to know why you're lying in the middle of my dinner?' Without drawing breath, Rich said; 'He would like to know why you're eating in his bed'."

Richie, continuing to use his hands, even constructed a wooden coffee table for the home. The couple seemed to fit together nicely; although neither was a loner, they were happy in their own company with little time or tolerance for foolish people. They worked very closely together to find the right balance for them and also for any visitors or friends that remained close.

Richie's difficult maternal relationship had led to a lack of normal childhood experiences and thus, until Cleo, had never discovered

Richie with Kathmandu. *Cleo Davidson*

Winnie the Pooh. Richie took great delight in often quoting AA Milne's words and also had a great love of Tove Jansson's *Moomin* stories. A believer of the mystical and reincarnation, at least, in his later days, Ginther felt that he *was* Snufkin out of the Moomins (even going so far as to have a Snufkin hat) and it's not hard to see why going by the description of him in the books:

'Snufkin is a philosophical vagabond who wanders the world fishing and playing the harmonica. He carries everything he needs in his backpack, as he believes that having too much stuff makes life overly complicated. Snufkin is easygoing and carefree, and enjoys thinking about things. He always comes and goes as he pleases. He has plenty of admirers. Snufkin meets every new person and event with curiosity and a warm heart. The enigmatic Snufkin

Richie in later life, enjoying his pets and his garden.
Cleo Davidson

Ginther in Nepal with a Nepalese tour guide.
Cleo Davidson

One of the few Richie Ginther racing trophies known to be around – at the Bourne Heritage Centre in Lincolnshire. *Richard Jenkins*

does not avoid other people's company, but he does prefer to travel alone. On his journeys, he explores new places and tries his luck at fishing. Snufkin loves to go wandering at night and especially in the moonlight. He never asks the names of the new places he visits, but simply enjoys the journey itself.'

Ginther just kept adding interests into his already mixed bag: animals (cats, koi carp, pelican and whale spotting and in particular), railway tracks became a passion where he enjoyed putting pennies down, examining them keenly for how flat and elongated they had become once a train had driven over it. With Cleo's Indonesian upbringing they both enjoyed cooking and eating Indonesian food. One unfinished project was a cookbook the pair of them had planned called the *Racing Gourmet*. There were trips to discover more of the world, to Nepal and Thailand, where, as Cleo says, "He adored it there. He was always a bit mystical. I did say mystical and not a blathering phony loony, he just enjoyed the quiet mindset these places allowed." There had even been a little bit of talk between the pair about whether they would leave Mexico and go to live in Thailand.

Ginther always had quite a wry sense of humour but a mischievous side too when the mood took him, as Cleo recalls: "John Von Neumann's vice-president of Volkswagen Pacific and Competition Motors was a chap called Sam Weil Jr [note – Weil was actually also an editor of Road and Track magazine]. Weil was *very* OCD. All the items on his desk were just perfectly aligned. Rich would walk in and put one pen slightly out of alignment. The moment Weil came in, he would walk to his desk and straighten said item and it would wind him up. Rich's workshop for race cars was just across the street in Culver City, so he often roamed into Volkswagen Pacific. One day, he came over and saw Sam's spotless (of course) car with the window open, just a tiny crack.

"Carefully, Rich slid a dried leaf through the crack – well, it could have blown in – but twenty minutes later, Sam was roaring around the place; 'Where's Richie Ginther?! I know he put a leaf in my car!' However, I consider the best one with Sam to be in 1970. John von Neumann threw a party in Palm Springs, for all the dealers, and of course his top echelon of the company, which included Sam. Rich and I, already great friends, snuck out and put a bumper sticker on Sam's absolutely pristine Bentley. It read: LEGALISE POT, with a nice leaf beside it. Sam did not notice and drove all the way back, over 100 miles, to Los Angeles with it on!"

Their house was filled with flowers, art and books, jewellery created by Richie, and artefacts from their travels which jostled for attention in the roomy surroundings with five cats and a Mexican hairless dog. Proving he was thoroughly over his childhood hummingbird trauma, he built bird feeders to attract an array of birds to the home with the (successful) intention of attracting a number of hummingbirds. But there were no trophies, no driver suits, helmets, no racing photos and virtually no memorabilia of any racing links at all in the home.

Richie certainly used to keep racing memorabilia, at least up to when he sold his home and business. After that, he appears to have effectively given them to Bret and Jackie as he started his new life in the motorhome, which obviously would not have had space for

Richie and Cleo. *Paul Huf/Cleo Davidson*

everything. Chuck Miller recalls: "My friend lived across the street from Richie in the 1970s in Granada Hills. Richie invited him into his study and there were all of his trophies, the photo albums, large scale Honda F1 model, and Honda presentation miniature Samurai sword and helmet.

"The first time, however, that I saw this stuff was about the mid or late 1980s at the Auto Lit Fair in the Pasadena City College parking lot. A guy had a van parked and all he had on the van was a sign that read 'Richie Ginther stuff around back'. When I went back to rear doors there was the same stuff my friend had seen years ago except not in good shape. The guy said he was working to get some money for Jackie. The trophies were thrown in a big cardboard box, in a hundred pieces... sad. The sword and helmet was there as well. The next time I saw the stuff was at Ron Kellogg's place for a 'Thursday Car Night' meeting. I believe all that Ron had was some certificates, framed photos, and the leather albums. When I asked Ron about the big F1 model and the little presentation sword and helmet, he said he never knew about those items."

His time with Cleo was, undoubtedly, one of the happiest times in Richie's life. Although the time spent together was relatively short, every day was treated as if it were Richie's last and, if anything, that mindset actually enriched the time Cleo and Richie had together. Sadly, though, the ominous cloud of heart disease was always lurking in the background and it was now to take centre-stage.

The Final Lap

"[Richie] spoke only in a whisper with an ever-attentive Cleo by his side. The contrast between his wasted, slow-moving frame and the bounding vibrant energy of Moss and Gonzalez was quite shocking"

Chris Nixon, journalist

Richie being interviewed by Paul Foxall for the BRM reunion film. *Paul Foxall*

The heart disease that had, as mentioned, hung round like a shadow eventually started taking its toll on Richie. On many a photo or video, Richie is seen smoking and it is no secret that he enjoyed a drink, but all this needs to be seen in context. Firstly, it was a different era in Richie's day and there were far fewer health warnings. This, after all, was a generation, if you include those born just before Richie, that went through the horrors of World War Two and as a result were far more inclined to make the very most of the gift of life. Richie himself saw the deaths of numerous young men in Korea and so the 1940s to the mid-1960s were far more fatalistic days than they are now.

Of course, Richie had already outlived the likes of Jim Clark, Jochen Rindt, Graham Hill, Wolfgang von Trips, Lorenzo Bandini, Jo Bonnier, Pedro and Ricardo Rodriguez, Ken Miles and so many more. In addition to this, Richie was convinced that the hereditary congenital heart disease would kill him before he was 50 like it did his brother. If he was not going to live a long time, then why not enjoy it as much as he could?

It is a bit of a dangerous label to define someone as an alcoholic and though this word has been mentioned in two articles (Ling's article in *Automobile Quarterly* and Lynch's article in *Forza*), the feedback from friends at the time of his peak drinking spell in the late 1960s and through the 1970s largely suggest that Ginther was not totally reliant on alcohol and unable to function without it. However, to be totally balanced, many of the key people that knew Richie in the years of his biggest excesses are dead and also these were the years that Richie often spent some days by himself. Richie could well have been smoking a lot, drinking heavily and even smoking a few drugs for all we know, but without first-hand feedback, it would be unwise to speculate too much.

However, his first wife Jackie, in particular was concerned about him and felt he drank too much considering his heart condition and that appears to be the crux of the issue here, not that he drank a lot *per se*, but more that Ginther was never going to have as long as others on this earth so maybe he could have looked after himself a little better as a result of his heart disease. In Michael Ling's article in *Automobile Quarterly*, Bret was greatly concerned that the drinking Richie was partaking in was stopping Richie being both the man and father that he had wished for. Richie was unsure if working in medicine would suit his son but gave his blessing to follow whatever path lay ahead for Bret.

Michael Lynch, in his 2005 article 'Ginther's Travels' for *Forza* magazine, says that Richie's son Bret became a doctor after witnessing his father's declining health and in particular, the impact that a drink had on Richie. Certainly one of Bret's main focuses as a professor of emergency medicine (which he continues to this day in California) has been the impact of alcohol on the body and certainly Bret gave up a promising role in a national supermarket chain to become a doctor. As Bret is one of the few living people who knew Richie extremely well at that time, we must presume there was genuine cause for concern over Richie's drinking.

However, this book is not intended to take the moral high-ground and castigate Ginther for drinking and also, to be as balanced as I can, the majority of feedback received did not mention drinking at all.

Nobody involved with him in Formula One remembers him particularly the worse for wear at any time. It seems very clear that his dedication to the sport, especially when that dedication would lead to the end of his first marriage meant that he limited his drinking to the appropriate time and measures. He certainly was not a heavy drinker up to 1967. By the time he was living with Cleo, he had tempered his drinking somewhat, the excesses Richie might have had with one von Neumann (John) persuading him had vanished by the time another von Neumann (Cleo) had her own influence on Richie.

I suppose it depends on people's interpretation and definition of what an alcoholic is. In summary, though, it appears clear that for some years after 1967, Richie drank too much for comfort for some time, predominantly scotch more than any other drink. Jim Sitz recalls when I asked him about Richie's drinking; "Around 1983, I don't recall when, there was a time that I was very concerned that Richie looked run down and told my friend Jesse Alexander that we should drive down to Mexico and try and get help for him, or get him to see a doctor back home in California, but Jesse convinced me Richie had to have the desire to get better and live more healthily before we went down that way." However, this seems to be about the time Richie started suffering from stomach ulcers, so Richie's appearance may not have all been directly related to drink, even if the ulcers might have stemmed from it.

He was already a social drinker, as described in Peter Miller's pen-profile of him in 1963 for *Men at the Wheel*: "The fair-haired Ginther is a cigarette smoker and drinks wines and spirits." In discussion with *Car Life* magazine in 1967, he said "I've noticed there are girls and parties at many of the races I've raced. I like girls. I like parties." Crucially, he did also mention that he did not take part as much as others did due to preparing the car and a focus on what he had to do. Ginther was a thinker, serious about his sport and there was a time and a place to relax. As Augie Pabst said in the interview I conducted with him, "Richie was a thinker, not a drinker."

As a sideline, in 2000, Bret, who largely has stayed out of the limelight, was quoted in a number of national newspapers about the dangers of young people binge drinking after a particularly high spate of deaths of 18 to 25-year-olds. He reminded people of the importance of not drinking much at all unless they had built up a physiological tolerance to alcohol and explained the impact that drinking had on the body; specifically the brain and the heart.

However it is important not to make the correlation between Bret's comments in 2000 and his father's lifestyle some twenty or so years before; more pertinent is the fact, especially considering the date of the newspaper articles is that binge-drinking and deaths from it were on the rise. By 1999, nearly a quarter of 18 to 25-year-olds when surveyed, admitted they were binge drinkers. After all, in terms of the article, Bret was one of the more local experts asked for a quote of a growing problem in the country and was very much interviewed as a prominent medical expert and certainly not as the son of Richie. It's doubtful if the interviewer even knew of the relationship or even who Richie was.

Chapter Fifteen

Indeed, Bret hasn't really had that stigma, certainly not in motor racing terms, of being the son of someone more famous, of having to battle for recognition in his own right. Richie had a successful motor racing career. Bret has been a successful doctor, and both father and son have achieved great things in their own chosen field.

As Richie had moved on from the sport almost in its entirety, there was no pressure for Bret to go racing. It's certainly noticeable that, possibly due to the separation away from the sport that Richie had when Bret grew up, that the sons of Richie's former team-mates Phil Hill, Dan Gurney, Ronnie Bucknum, Graham Hill, John Surtees and Mario Andretti all went into the sport but Richie's son did not.

In 1977, Ginther suffered his first real health setback. When he returned to Europe as a guest of Goodyear's 100th win celebrations, he joined up again with Cleo, who was staying with her brother in France. John von Neumann was also in Europe and all of them met up at various locations in the South of France. Ginther had intended to visit some racing at the Paul Ricard circuit near Marseille. While out one night in St Tropez, the Ginthers and John von Neumann were returning to von Neumann's yacht when they heard arguing at one of their friend's harbourside bars. Upon checking, there were two football fans from England harassing the owner. The football fans then turned on the interlopers, swinging for Johnny von Neumann but Cleo and the bar owner hit one of the fans with a chair. Upon regaining his composure, the fan went to punch Cleo but Richie saw what was happening and put himself in front of Cleo to keep her safe. The punch knocked Richie out and he was taken to hospital in Switzerland at a later date to undergo facial surgery. However, for the last twelve years of his life, Richie had to live with a condition called tic douloureux (or its more correct medical name of trigeminal neuralgia), which is a disorder of a nerve in the face called the trigeminal nerve or fifth cranial nerve. This condition would often cause episodes of sudden, intense, stabbing or shocklike facial pain. Most of Richie's episodes would last seconds but occasionally they would rule him out of anything major for some minutes.

Whatever the reasons for Richie's decline, it was unfortunate that Richie's most high-profile – and last – appearance in the motor racing world was to commemorate BRM's 40th anniversary celebrations in September 1989. Unfortunate in the sense that no longer was Richie the carefree soul of even just a few years prior, but now a very frail and sick man. Cleo Davidson recalls that Ginther was convinced he would not make his birthday the month before. In the last couple of years of his life, Richie suffered three minor heart-attacks, all varying in severity, the most serious of the three occurring in 1988. He had also suffered for a long time from perforated stomach ulcers, which seemed to bother Richie more. So much so, he had surgery to treat them before being advised that heart-burn remedies would keep them under control (which they did).

In 1987, Rik Blote travelled with his family to the Ginther home in Baja. He had not seen Ginther for a year or so and noticed a small difference. "Richie looked rather tired throughout, but was still his usual self and we enjoyed going round the markets and, particularly, the tool shops/stands together."

The reunion at Donington Park came about after the documentary film maker Paul Foxall wanted to make a video about BRM in memory of Sir Alfred Owen, who died in 1975. Foxall worked for the BBC, Granada and many other companies, as well as being a freelance director, but always had a particular passion for motorsport and filmed a number of events or documentaries from the 1960s onwards. AF (Alec Francis) Rivers-Fletcher, a former racer at Brooklands and former riding mechanic to Malcolm Campbell was a man of many motorsport hats, but two roles significant to this documentary was that he was public relations manager for BRM for decades and he was a documentary film-maker himself. The duo got Richard Apsden involved as well to try and focus on the particular angle of how the documentary would play out.

David Owen, son of Sir Alfred, gave the project his blessing and this created a snowball effect. Tom Wheatcroft, then owner of Donington Park's motor racing circuit and a huge collection of motor racing cars, made the circuit and all his BRM cars available. David Owen suggested the best way to mark the video was a driver reunion. In his article 'Donington Déjà Vu' in *Thoroughbred & Classic Cars* in 1989, Chris Nixon spoke to another person involved with the project, Richard McCann. "Most people we spoke to thought it was a nice idea that could never be brought off. Of the surviving drivers, Juan Manuel Fangio and Froilán Gonzalez live in Argentina – about as far away from Donington as you can get. Richie Ginther was thought to be somewhere in Mexico and Dan Gurney lives in California, so not much closer. Stirling Moss and Jackie Stewart are easier to reach, but both so incredibly busy, so we weren't too hopeful of getting them either. However, when we finally made contact and asked if they would take part in what is essentially a tribute to Sir Alfred, they all said 'When do you want me at Donington?' David was very touched by this, for he did not realise just how strong the affection was for his father among BRM people."

There were reservations on what the journey would do to Ginther's body but, as Cleo says, "Rich was not feeling well at all, but he liked Paul Foxall and Richard Aspden who were organising the reunion for BRM. He felt that he would like to see some of the old drivers again and agreed to attend if they paid my fare as well. He was not at all happy, though, about being put back in a race car and told me once we returned to the hotel that he never wanted to sit in a racing car again".

Paul Foxall remembers, "Stirling Moss, Jackie Stewart, José Froilán Gonzalez and Damon Hill were easy to invite on board, but the reclusive Richie was another matter. In the end, I went to Mexico in March 1989 and with the help of some sparse directions from Phil Hill, managed to locate him and persuaded Richie to join the BRM party. As it was lunch time, we shared a few beers with Richie and Cleo, both of whom made us feel most welcome. Dick and I felt Richie looked rather frail so we hesitated to mention Donington. But in fact, persuading him turned out to be relatively easy. I think he and Cleo were so impressed that we'd come all the way from England, they felt obliged to go along with our request. Richie's only requirement was that Cleo should accompany him, which we fully agreed with."

Lesley Appel, Tony Rudd's daughter, who Richie had picked up from school in the Austin A40 all those years ago, recalls, "I only learnt about the reunion after Richie's death. Dad said he could not go as he was away but we would have both gone and I always thought that it did not occur to him to tell us about it. Mum and I nearly killed him! However, in hindsight, dad must have found out that Richie was not well, and probably did not tell us as he thought we were better remembering him as he was. Well, Mum and I did not agree, plus we would have loved to meet Cleo as well."

The reunion lasted a number of days in mid-September and October; Richie's time there was on 11 to 13 September 1989. Richie agreed to drive the car, the 1962 P57 V8 to be precise, but only for two very slow laps. He had no overalls, and nothing from his racing days, so in the end Paul Foxall leant him his own 1960s helmet and Dunlop overalls. He was so disappointed, according to Cleo as mentioned above, about how his health was stopping him perform that he said he never wanted to drive a racing car again. As mentioned already, he said to Cleo that the experience was his last in a racing car and he also said to Chris Nixon, "I will never do that again. The BRM was beautifully prepared but I felt like a fish out of water in it and I just humiliated myself. I could not live up to my own expectations and accomplish what a race driver is supposed to do. I really thought that I was going to enjoy driving in a race car again, but I did not. Even at the speeds I was going I was in way over my head. I hated it!"

John Sismey, who was at the reunion, remembers that "Richie was like a rag doll, he looked terrible. It took a number of us to help lift him in and out of the car, he was that weak." Certainly there was immense sadness, and obvious concern from all those present that Ginther did not enjoy the driving experience, especially in contrast, as Nixon puts it, to Jose Froilán Gonzalez's 'schoolboyish delight with everything'.

However it was not a total wipeout for Richie, Cleo and all involved. Paul Foxall takes up the narrative again. "He felt he had let everyone down and I assured him this was not the case. In spite of everything, he gave us a wonderful interview later, recalling how well he was treated by the BRM people. BRM always held good memories for him and he loved seeing and chatting with the old drivers and Bette Hill, as he liked Graham and her very much."

That evening there was a dinner at the Donington Thistle hotel, hosted by David Owen for sixteen people (to mark the V16), which included Richie and Cleo, Gonzalez and his nephew Julio, David Owen, Foxall, Nixon, McCann and Apsden, AF Rivers-Fletcher, John Sismey and former BRM mechanic and the man who felt Ginther's ire back in 1962, Cyril Atkins. Any grudge Ginther may have had for Atkins some 25 years earlier was long forgotten and all enjoyed a great night.

Ginther was also on form the next day, the second day of the reunion. As he was not driving, he seemed more amiable and was particularly delighted to meet Stirling Moss, who arrived on day two. Another enjoyable food fare was partaken at Tom Wheatcroft's private suite overlooking the Esses, where a cake and champagne was brought out to celebrate Stirling Moss's 60th birthday which was due imminently on 17 September.

After the celebrations had finished, the Ginthers travelled on 14 September 1989 to the Bordeaux region of France, Touzac, to be precise, where some of Cleo's family lived, to celebrate her father's

Richie in a racing car for the very last time at Donington Park, 1989. *Cleo Davidson*

The very last picture of Richie, one day before his death, overlooking the Lot valley. *Cleo Davidson*

birthday. Richie was still struggling with his health. Chris Nixon established as such in his article 'Donington Déjà Vu': "Frankly, I doubt anyone who saw Richie at Donington was surprised to hear of his death. The event was tinged throughout with the unspoken belief that he was a dying man, which indeed he was. Although ten years younger than Gonzalez, and also younger than Moss, Wheatcroft, Bette Hill and Rivers Fletcher, he looked older than all of them and his appearance was a terrible shock to those of us who had known him in the '60s.

"Clearly very weak, he spoke only in a whisper with an ever-attentive Cleo by his side constantly. The contrast between his wasted, slow-moving frame and the bounding vibrant energy of Moss and Gonzalez was quite shocking."

Rik Blote saw the duo just after Donington at his home in France. "They came to visit us here in France. I was shocked at his appearance when they arrived and realised that his heart condition must have deteriorated. He told me he had enjoyed meeting old friends at Donington though he had found driving the cars pretty scary. He knew things were bad with his health and I think his plan had been to make one last visit to see old racing friends, then one last visit to us but unfortunately he did not make it back to their home in Baja."

Cleo takes up the very final chapter of Richie's life. "Three days before his death, I did not like the colouring of his lips; they were pale and his fingernails were blue. I called a doctor who said that he has to go to a hospital immediately. Rich said to me 'You promised me years ago that you would never put me in a hospital to die and I'm not going now'. The doctor was insistent but I calmly replied that if he does not want to and his word is no, then I shall abide by that. He was feeling a little better on 19 September so we went for a little walk to a nearby village where a cat took a real liking to Rich and his safari jacket!

One day later, he dropped dead of a heart-attack. Rich was in the living room, looking through a book about Donington, where we had just been. I was leaning against the kitchen door, in the hall, so I could both see Rich and maintain a conversation with my mother, who was in the kitchen. Rich put down the book and walked over to me. He collapsed. I tried to catch him and fell to the floor with him, but I think he was already dead by the time he hit the floor. Just before he collapsed, his last words to me were 'Cleo, I think it's time'."

Chapter Sixteen

Richie Ginther's Legacy

"Richie was absolutely first-rate
as a driver and person.
He was a fine driver"
Lance Reventlow, team owner

Richie at Silverstone, 1963. *Steve Payne*

Ginther died on 20 September 1989, having made his 59th birthday a month before. He was cremated in his dragon robe and jeans. Richie wanted, according to Cleo Davidson, to be cremated "as he did not want someone finding, coming and then talking to his tombstone."

Although it has been over 50 years since he last raced in Formula One, he has not been forgotten, even if sometimes the memory banks need prompting. He is especially remembered with affection at Honda and Goodyear and, if anything, the aura of mystery he had around him after his racing career ended has somewhat kept interest in him going.

A mark of the impact Richie had is that I did not need to explain who Richie was to anyone within racing. What I mean by this is that sometimes, when writing or researching someone in motorsport, there may be pockets of people who remember a driver or a personality well, but not so much across the board. Not so with Richie. Everyone, even if they could not add much personally, had their own general recollection of Richie and thoughts on his racing ability.

When you look back at Richie's career, even if solely confined to Formula One, he achieved a lot. He raced for three of the biggest teams of their time, and raced for them at their peak. He helped two teams to Constructors' Championships in successive years (which is a feat not shared by many, in fact only three drivers have achieved this – Stirling Moss, Emerson Fittipaldi and Richie), won a grand prix (nor should this be sniffed at – at time of writing, only 14 percent of all grand prix drivers since 1950 have won a race), and, arguably one of the key achievements of his six-year Formula One career was surviving more or less intact the whole way through. It is also worthy of note that Richie was inducted in the Motorsports Hall of Fame of America in 2008.

It is natural that Richie will always be considered as one of the best number two drivers of his era, rather than the number one he so craved. At least his greatest success came as a number one driver. But arguably, when discussing his place in the pantheon of grand prix heroes, Richie shouldn't be placed in either category for if you are going to rank Ginther highly in any list of grand prix drivers, it should surely be that Ginther was one of the best test drivers of all time – certainly of his era. That sounds dismissive, but there are few drivers who had the ability to develop the cars as much as he did. As much as Richie owed Phil Hill for his breaks in motorsport, Phil Hill owed Richie for the work he did with Ferrari because, without it, Phil would never have been 1961 World Champion. Honda would more than likely never have won a race. Although John Surtees did sterling work there too, would Honda have still been around for him to join if Richie had not won in 1965? It's doubtful.

Richie must also be remembered as one of the very best sports car drivers of his era and certainly in America. It is quite easy to see an alternative scenario where, if Richie had not moved to Europe, that he would have continued to be increasingly successful in sports cars and quite possibly would have been remembered as one of Can-Am's leading lights, rather than the moribund effort that transpired in 1964.

Richie working on the car at the Race of Champions meeting, 1967.
Peter Darley

His legacy remains in a third area too, this one away from driving; that being his mechanical ability. He will forever be the inventor of motorsport's rear spoiler and his work with Porsche, and indeed during his sports car driving days, brought him, Porsche, Alan Johnson, Elliott Forbes-Robinson and many others much success. But one other legacy definitely remains through those who knew him and that's the ability to put racing to one side and explore the life around him. Many failed, and one of his colleagues, Willy Mairesse, could not even live without racing, committing suicide in 1969 when his injuries meant he had to retire from driving. Richie only learnt to embrace life to the full when reflecting on his divorce and how his marriage had effectively been ruined by racing, but boy, did he make up for it in the last twenty years of his life.

Richie's attitude towards racing, and in particular his sympathy with the car, were totally admirable but ultimately cost him wins. Had he been a true out-and-out ball-busting racer, then it is likely that Richie would have won more races, but would he have survived such a deadly era? Would we be remembering him like Ricardo Rodriguez, Wolfgang von Trips, Ludovico Scarfiotti, Lorenzo Bandini and so on as a talent lost too soon? Statistics don't always reflect careers accurately, but if you ignore the one win and look at the high amount of points finishes in an era of poor reliability, then that is a truly remarkable statistic for the era Richie raced in.

The motorsport commentator Murray Walker often used to say 'if is a very long word in Formula One; in fact, if is F1 spelled backwards'. If there had not been a second miscarriage at the start of 1964, could Richie, having had a brilliant 1963, have been a title contender for 1964? If the 1.5 litre era had not ended at the completion of the 1965 season, Richie would have been a title contender for 1966. But he never dwelled on this and certainly had no regrets from a racing point of view.

There will be plenty of people, I hope, reading this book who may not have fully appreciated who Richie Ginther was and what his driving ability was. Before I started this project, I was one of them. I hope to have guided them accordingly and, for those who do remember him and his career, that this has rekindled their own memories. I'll end with a few words of summary, which did not quite fit into any other part of the book, either given to me directly from some of those closest to him, or where those who have since passed away have commented (not always accurately in terms of Richie's life), before letting Richie have the final word.

Rik Blote: "Richie truly was an individual who was very much his own man. What he told me is what he enjoyed the most was developing the cars to make them go faster."

Jim Sitz: "Richie was a sweet guy but got a bit hardened by grand prix racing, which led to his divorce. Racing became the biggest thing in his life. As much as he loved Jackie, racing was just too all consuming for him."

Augie Pabst: "Seems to me that the divorce or arguments affected him as a person, him as a driver. I think if it had not happened, or he was not married at the time, he could have done better. I lost track of Richie, I think he was badly hurt and affected by the loss of his marriage."

Carroll Shelby: "He was a straight-shooter, you always knew where you were with Richie. He was always in the shadow of Phil Hill. People didn't recognise him for what he could be – not only in driving. He was an excellent mechanic, as honest and straightforward as anyone you'll see and extremely talented – I cared very much for Richie."

Sir Stirling Moss: "He was a little fella – smaller than me – but quick: he and I shared the lap record at Monaco in 1961. He wasn't flamboyant, he was a clean, competent driver and a nice bloke – like most Americans who came into F1 he wasn't ruthless. I don't think he had an enemy in the world."

Three of America's best racing drivers; Richie, Phil Hill and Dan Gurney.
The Grand Prix Library

Roy Salvadori (former grand prix driver and later Cooper team principal): "He was good to race against – most American drivers were very civilised. He was a rather unusual guy, easy to get along with when I drove with him in the Cooper team but I don't think many people knew him well. He was respected, well-liked and dedicated to racing, but I'm told he was shocked by getting back into a car when he came back and he stayed away from them after that."

David Piper (former grand prix and sports car driver): "He was great fun, one of a group who came over with Phil Hill in the late 1950s to do the European scene – they were the first Americans we

Monaco Grand Prix, 1964. *Etienne Bourguignon*

German Grand Prix, 1963. *MullerCologne*

got to know. He was a very good driver, very popular and a charming chap – a bit like Masten Gregory. I don't think he made a lot of money and towards the end of his life he had a tough time. But he was a good ambassador for the USA."

Lance Reventlow: "Richie was absolutely first-rate as a driver and person. He was a fine driver."

Ed McDonough (author of many books including *Ferrari 156 Sharknose*): "I am so pleased to have been able to meet Richie, especially when he was with Honda. He was held in high regard by those who raced hard against him, and was perhaps the best development driver of all time, certainly of the period. And he was a real person with all that implies."

Kurt Zimmerman: "Richie's legacy is that he knew how to build race cars from scratch and how to optimise them. He committed his life to racing and gave Honda and Goodyear their first F1 wins. Richie took care of the cars, did not waste them and he finished most of his races. He was very brave, but had a lot of close calls and somehow survived to tell about it when at the time most did not survive.

"Richie was highly underrated, highly misunderstood, highly introspective and did not seem to care about slamming the press and many others including myself. In terms of his legacy, his abrasiveness cost him a lot in terms of recognition and partnerships. But if you search through racing history, you will find his name or picture around the drivers almost everywhere. It's amazing, considering their personalities, that he was able to work directly

with Enzo Ferrari for so long. In the end, virtually all the car manufacturers have failed to give him the credit he deserves for his commitment and contributions."

Roy Lunn (former American Motors Corporation Head of Engineering): "Richie was one of the finest ever development drivers in the world."

Tom Schultz (motor racing author and historian): "Way back in the 1960s I had the thought, which I still hold today, that Ginther was a very valuable development driver. To me it is no coincidence that Ferrari came right in 1961, BRM in 1962, and Honda in 1965."

Phil Hill: "I think it's a bit unfair that he did not win more races. He was certainly an underrated driver. He was a very good test driver and his technical knowledge helped him as a racer."

Cleo Davidson: "I am happily married again now but I must admit I miss Rich dearly, he was the kindest person I ever knew. He was my jewel of many colours."

As for Richie, he could be outspoken. He famously said about the much-loathed Lotus 40 sports car, after driving the car at the *Los Angeles Times* Grand Prix in 1965 (his only race for Team Lotus), "It's a Lotus 30 with ten more mistakes." But he could be very modest. He was certainly more the latter in 1967, when, newly retired, he was reflecting about his career: "One thing I have learned is that there is some good and some bad in every organisation. I have done the best I could for everyone I drove for." But overall, he was his own man and he lived his life the way he thought best. As Richie said, "Life is not a rehearsal."

Appendix: Race Results

The World Championship race results have kindly been put together by Steve Hirst, however the author has put them in the same format as the other races for consistency. Only actual appearances have been included. Races where Ginther was on the entry list but did not appear to make any tangible attempt to race or qualify are not listed below. Some of the information of Ginther's early races is sparse to say the least, but the author has tried to compile as comprehensive a list as possible with whatever information can be found and with as accurate and detailed information as is possible. If anyone can advise of any missing or incorrect information then should the book be re-printed, amendments and additions will naturally take place.

Dutch Grand Prix, 1961. *Gunther Asshauer*

Date	Race	Circuit	No	Car	Entered by	Qualified	Race Result	Notes
8.4.1951	Sandberg Hillclimb	Sandberg, Sierra Pelona mountains	2Jr	MG TC 2 Junior Ford V8	Bill Cramer	n/a	5th (Best Time)	
27.5.1951	SCCA Pebble Beach Cup	Pebble Beach	82	MG TC 2 Junior Ford V8	Bill Cramer	14th	33rd	Did not finish
27.5.1951	SCCA Pebble Beach Handicap Road Race	Pebble Beach	82	MG TC 2 Junior Ford V8	Bill Cramer	14th	3rd	
23.11.1953	Carrera Panamericana	Carrera Panamericana on Mexican public roads	4	Ferrari 340 Mexico Vignale Coupe	Allen Guiberson	n/a	DNF	Accident on Lap 2. Phil Hill co-drove
23.11.1954	Carrera Panamericana	Carrera Panamericana on Mexican public roads	20	Ferrari 375 MM	Allen Guiberson	n/a	2nd	Phil Hill co-drove
6.2.1955	Singers Owners' Club Hillclimb	Aguora		Austin-Healey 100	Richie Ginther	n/a	1st in class	29.66; 1st in Stock Austin-Healey class
13.2.1955	California Sports Car Club Willow Springs Modified + 1.5 Race	Willow Springs	80	Austin-Healey 100	Richie Ginther	not known	8th	
13.2.1955	California Sports Car Club Willow Springs Production + 1.5 Race	Willow Springs	80	Austin-Healey 100	Richie Ginther	not known	8th	
17.4.1955	SCCA National Race	Pebble Beach	not known	Austin-Healey 100	Dave Forman	not known	5th	
1.5.1955	Preliminary Production Race	Minter Field, Bakersfield	66	Austin-Healey 100	Richie Ginther	not known	8th	
1.5.1955	SCCA National Race	Minter Field, Bakersfield	66	Austin-Healey 100	Richie Ginther	not known	12th	
4.9.1955	California Sports Car Club Production Race Under 1500cc	Santa Barbara	211	Porsche 550	John von Neumann	3rd	3rd	
22.10.1955	California Sports Car Club Torrey Pines 6 Hours	Torrey Pines	11	Porsche 356	Eric Buckler	not known	9th	Buckler co-drove
13.11.1955	SCCA National Race	Glendale	311	Ferrari 500 Mondial	Manning J Post	not known	7th	
26.2.1956	SCCA Palm Springs Sports Car Race	Palm Springs	211	Porsche 356 Carrera	Richie Ginther	not known	DNF	Retired due to brake failure
18.3.1956	SCCA Stockton Sports Car Race	Stockton Airfield	211	Porsche 550	John von Neumann	not known	1st	Won after 33 laps, 116.356km
22.4.1956	SCCA National Race	Pebble Beach	211	Porsche 550	John von Neumann	not known	DNF	Reason for retiring unknown
19.5.1956	California Sports Car Club Preliminary Production Race	Minter Field, Bakersfield	211	Porsche 550	John von Neumann	not known	2nd	
20.5.1956	California Sports Car Club Production Race #1	Minter Field, Bakersfield	211	Porsche 550	John von Neumann	2nd	5th	
20.5.1956	California Sports Car Club Production Race #2	Minter Field, Bakersfield	211	Porsche 550	John von Neumann	not known	2nd	
3.6.1956	SCCA National Race	Eagle Mountain	211	Porsche 550	John von Neumann	not known	DNF	Reason for retiring unknown
3.6.1956	SCCA National Race	Eagle Mountain	211	Porsche 550	John von Neumann	not known	1st	Won after 15 laps, 70.006km
23.6.1956	California Sports Car Club Preliminary Production Race	Pomona	211	Porsche 550	John von Neumann	not known	2nd	
24.6.1956	California Sports Car Club Production Race #1	Pomona	211	Porsche 550	John von Neumann	not known	1st	Won after 40 laps, 128.747km
24.6.1956	California Sports Car Club Production Race #2	Pomona	211	Porsche 550	John von Neumann	not known	DNF	Retired due to Richie suffering a nose bleed
1.7.1956	SCCA San Francisco Regional Race	Buchanan Field	211	Porsche 550	John von Neumann	not known	2nd	
8.7.1956	SCCA Los Angeles Regional Race	Santa Maria	112	Ferrari 500 Mondial	John von Neumann	not known	5th	
8.7.1956	SCCA Los Angeles Preliminary Regional Race	Santa Maria	211	Porsche 550	John von Neumann	not known	3rd	
8.7.1956	SCCA Los Angeles Regional Race	Santa Maria	211	Porsche 550	John von Neumann	not known	1st	Won after 21 laps, 111.527km

Date	Race	Circuit	No	Car	Entered by	Qualified	Race Result	Notes
18.8.1956	California Sports Car Club Preliminary Production Race	Paramount Ranch	211	Porsche 550	John von Neumann	not known	1st	Won after 10 laps, 32.187km
19.8.1956	California Sports Car Club Production Race #1	Paramount Ranch	211	Porsche 550	John von Neumann	2nd	1st	Won after 36 laps, 115.873km
19.8.1956	California Sports Car Club Production Race #2	Paramount Ranch	211	Porsche 550	John von Neumann	not known	3rd	
1.9.1956	California Sports Car Club Preliminary Production Race	Santa Barbara	211	Porsche 550	John von Neumann	not known	2nd	
2.9.1956	California Sports Car Club Production Race #1	Santa Barbara	211	Porsche 550	John von Neumann	not known	7th	
2.9.1956	California Sports Car Club Production Race #2	Santa Barbara	211	Porsche 550	John von Neumann	not known	7th	
8.9.1956	SCCA 4 Hours of Road America	Road America	23	Cooper T39	Lance Reventlow	not known	4th	Reventlow co-drove
9.9.1956	SCCA 6 Hours of Road America	Road America	23	Cooper T39	Lance Reventlow	not known	DNF	Reventlow co-drove; Reason for retiring unknown
30.9.1956	Sacramento Sports Car Race	Sacramento	211	Ferrari 500 Mondial	John von Neumann	2nd	2nd	
20.10.1956	California Sports Car Club Preliminary Production Race	Pomona	211	Porsche 550	John von Neumann	not known	2nd	
21.10.1956	California Sports Car Club Production Race	Pomona	211	Porsche 550	John von Neumann	not known	DNF	Retired due to an accident
4.11.1956	SCCA National Race	Palm Springs	211	Porsche 550	John von Neumann	4th	3rd	
7.12.1956	Governor's Trophy	Windsor Airfield, Nassau, Bahamas	88	Ferrari 857 S	Carroll Shelby	not known	6th	
7.12.1956	Preliminary over 2000cc Race	Windsor Airfield, Nassau, Bahamas	88	Ferrari 857 S	Carroll Shelby	not known	not known	
9.12.1956	Nassau Trophy	Windsor Airfield, Nassau, Bahamas	88	Ferrari 857 S	Carroll Shelby	not known	DNF/39th	Reason for retiring unknown
19.1.1957	California Sports Car Club Preliminary Production Race	Pomona	249	Aston Martin DB3S	Joe Lubin	not known	4th	
20.1.1957	California Sports Car Club Production Race	Pomona	249	Aston Martin DB3S	Joe Lubin	not known	2nd	
10.2.1957	National Sports Car Day Race	New Smyrna Beach	not known	Ferrari 750 Monza	Tony Parravano	not known	2nd	
10.2.1957	National Sports Car Day Sportscar Race	New Smyrna Beach	not known	Ferrari 750 Monza	Tony Parravano	2nd	DNF/22nd	Retired due to faulty flywheel mountings
9.3.1957	California Sports Car Club Preliminary Production Race	Paramount Ranch	49	Aston Martin DB3S	Joe Lubin	not known	3rd	
10.3.1957	California Sports Car Club Production Race	Paramount Ranch	49	Aston Martin DB3S	Joe Lubin	not known	3rd	
23.3.1957	12 Hours of Sebring	Sebring	28	Ferrari 500 TRC	Temple Buell	27th*	10th	Howard Hively co-drove. *Before 1964, starting places were decided on highest cubic capacity to lowest
7.4.1957	SCCA Los Angeles Regional Race	Palm Springs	211	Aston Martin DB3S	Joe Lubin	5th	3rd	
18.5.1957	California Sports Car Club Preliminary Production Race #1	Santa Barbara	88	Porsche 550	John Edgar	not known	4th	
18.5.1957	California Sports Car Club Preliminary Production Race #2	Santa Barbara	211	Aston Martin DB3S	Joe Lubin	not known	DNF	Retired due to a spin
19.5.1957	California Sports Car Club Production Race #1	Santa Barbara	88	Porsche 550	John Edgar	not known	3rd	
19.5.1957	California Sports Car Club Production Race #2	Santa Barbara	210	Aston Martin DB3S	Joe Lubin	not known	6th	
26.5.1957	The Luther Burbank Rose Festival Sports Car Road Races	Cotati	169	Porsche 550	John Porter/ Menagerie Aadvark	9th	5th	
26.5.1957	The Luther Burbank Rose Festival Sports Car Road Races Class Handicap	Cotati	not known	Denzel	Wolfgang Denzel	5th	5th	
8.6.1957	SCCA National GT Haybale Championship Race	Lime Rock	not known	Ferrari 250 GT	Richie Ginther	not known	1st	Won after 15 laps, 36.210km
23.6.1957	Le Mans 24 Hours	Le Mans	29	Ferrari 500 TRC	Los Amigos	25th*	DNF	Retired due to water pump failure, lap 129. Francois Picard co-drove. *Before 1963, starting places were decided on highest cubic capacity to lowest.
27.7.1957	California Sports Car Club Preliminary Production Race	Pomona	7	Ferrari 500 TR	Richie Ginther	not known	6th	
28.7.1957	California Sports Car Club Production Race	Pomona	7	Ferrari 500 TR	Richie Ginther	not known	3rd	
31.8.1957	California Sports Car Club Preliminary Production Race	Santa Barbara	211	Ferrari 625 TRC	Richie Ginther	not known	1st	Won after 10 laps, 35.406km
1.9.1957	California Sports Car Club Production Race	Santa Barbara	211	Ferrari 625 TRC	Richie Ginther	not known	2nd	
21.9.1957	California Sports Car Club Preliminary Production Race	Riverside	211	Ferrari 410 Sport	John Edgar	not known	5th	
22.9.1957	California Sports Car Club Production Race	Riverside	211	Ferrari 410 Sport	John Edgar	not known	1st	Won after 26 laps, 137.036km
6.10.1957	SCCA San Francisco Regional Race	Sacramento	211	Ferrari 500 TR	John von Neumann	not known	4th	
19.10.1957	SCCA San Diego Regional Preliminary Production Race	Hourglass Field, San Diego	211	Ferrari 500 TR	John von Neumann	not known	2nd	
20.10.1957	SCCA San Diego Regional Production Race	Hourglass Field, San Diego	211	Ferrari 500 TR	John von Neumann	not known	2nd	
26.10.1957	California Sports Car Club Preliminary Production Race	Pomona	211	Ferrari 500 TR	John von Neumann	not known	2nd	
27.10.1957	California Sports Car Club Production Race	Pomona	211	Ferrari 500 TR	John von Neumann	not known	2nd	
3.11.1957	SCCA National Sportscar Race - over 1500cc	Palm Springs	211	Ferrari 410 Sport	John Edgar	3rd	6th	

Appendix: Race Results

Date	Race	Circuit	No	Car	Entered by	Qualified	Race Result	Notes
10.11.1957	SCCA National Sportscar Race	Laguna Seca	190	Ferrari 857 S	John von Neumann	4th	5th	
17.11.1957	SCCA National Sportscar Race	Riverside	211	Ferrari 410 Sport	John Edgar	not known	5th	
1.12.1957	Nassau Tourist Trophy	Oakes Field, Nassau, Bahamas	88	Ferrari 410 Sport	John Edgar	5th	2nd	
6.12.1957	Governor's Trophy Preliminary Production Race	Oakes Field, Nassau, Bahamas	29	Ferrari 250 TR	John von Neumann	not known	6th	
6.12.1957	Governor's Trophy	Oakes Field, Nassau, Bahamas	88	Ferrari 410 Sport	John Edgar	not known	5th	
8.12.1957	Nassau Trophy	Oakes Field, Nassau, Bahamas	88	Ferrari 410 Sport	John Edgar	not known	5th	
8.12.1957	Nassau Memorial Trophy	Oakes Field, Nassau, Bahamas	88	Ferrari 410 Sport	John Edgar	not known	2nd	
8.2.1958	California Sports Car Club Preliminary Production Race	Pomona	211	Ferrari 500 TR	John von Neumann	not known	1st	Won after 10 laps, 32.187km
9.2.1958	California Sports Car Club Production Race	Pomona	211	Ferrari 500 TR	John von Neumann	not known	1st	Won after 44 laps, 141.622km
2.3.1958	SCCA Arizona Regional Production Race #1	Phoenix	211	Ferrari 500 TR	John von Neumann	not known	1st	Won after 40 laps, 100.000km
2.3.1958	SCCA Arizona Regional Production Race #2	Phoenix	211	Ferrari 500 TR	John von Neumann	not known	2nd	
2.3.1958	SCCA Arizona Regional Production Race #1	Phoenix	5	Scarab MK 1	Lance Reventlow	n/a	n/a	Attempted in practice only
22.3.1958	12 Hours of Sebring	Sebring	17	Ferrari 250 TR	John von Neumann	13th*	DNF	Retired due to gearbox failure, lap 168. Von Neumann co-drove. * Before 1964, starting places were decided on highest cubic capacity to lowest.
13.4.1958	SCCA Los Angeles Regional Race	Palm Springs	171	Ferrari 250 GT Berlinetta	George Reis Jr.	1st	1st	Won after 12 laps, 54.074 kms
11.5.1958	SCCA Hawaiian Regional Production Race #1	Dillingham Air Field, Hawaii	6	Cooper T39-Climax	Bill Woodward	2nd	3rd	Woodward competed in the practice, Ginther raced
11.5.1958	SCCA Hawaiian Regional Production Race #2	Dillingham Air Field, Hawaii	211	Ferrari 500 TR	John von Neumann	1st	3rd	
1.6.1958	California Sports Car Club Production Race	Santa Barbara	211	Ferrari 250 TR	John von Neumann	not known	3rd	
15.6.1958	SCCA San Francisco Regional Race Production Cars over 1500cc	Laguna Seca	11	Ferrari 625 TC	John von Neumann	not known	1st	Won after 30 laps, 128.747km
15.6.1958	SCCA San Francisco Regional Race Production Cars over 1600cc Race #1	Laguna Seca	71	Ferrari 250 GT Berlinetta	John von Neumann	not known	1st	Won after 25 laps, 76.444km
15.6.1958	SCCA San Francisco Regional Race Preliminary Production Car Race	Laguna Seca	71	Ferrari 250 GT Berlinetta	John von Neumann	not known	1st	Won after 12 laps, 36.693km
28.6.1958	California Sports Car Club Preliminary Production Race	Riverside	171	Ferrari 250 GT	John von Neumann	not known	1st	Won after 6 laps, 30.035km
29.6.1958	California Sports Car Club Production Race #1	Riverside	171	Ferrari 250 GT	John von Neumann	not known	1st	Won after 15 laps, 79.059km
29.6.1958	California Sports Car Club Production Race #2	Riverside	211	Ferrari 860 Monza	John von Neumann	not known	2nd	
3.8.1958	SCCA San Francisco Production Car Race	Minden	211	Ferrari 250 TR	John von Neumann	not known	3rd	
30.8.1958	California Sports Car Club Preliminary Production Race	Santa Barbara	112	Ferrari 250 TR	John von Neumann	not known	2nd	
31.8.1958	California Sports Car Club Production Race	Santa Barbara	112	Ferrari 250 TR	John von Neumann	not known	2nd	
12.10.1958	USAC Road Racing Championship Race	Riverside	211	Ferrari 250 TR	Ferrari Representatives of California	9th	5th	
8.11.1958	SCCA San Francisco Regional Preliminary Production Race	Laguna Seca	211	Ferrari 250 TR	John von Neumann	not known	2nd	
9.11.1958	SCCA San Francisco Regional Production Race	Laguna Seca	211	Ferrari 250 TR	John von Neumann	not known	3rd	
23.11.1958	California Sports Car Club Production Race	Pomona	102	Ferrari 500 TRC	Jack Nethercutt	3rd	2nd	
31.1.1959	California Sports Car Club Preliminary Production Race	Pomona	211	Ferrari 335 Sport	Ferrari Representatives of California	not known	3rd	
1.2.1959	California Sports Car Club Production Race	Pomona	211	Ferrari 335 Sport	Ferrari Representatives of California	3rd	1st	Won after 25 laps, 139.369km
21.3.1959	12 Hours of Sebring	Sebring	70	Ferrari 250 GT California	Scuderia Ferrari	65th*	9th	Howard Hively co-drove, finished 1st in Grand Touring Class. *Before 1964, starting places were decided on highest cubic capacity to lowest
26.4.1959	Gran Premio d'Avandaro	Avandaro, Mexico	21	Ferrari 625 TRC	John von Neumann	6th	5th	
3.5.1959	2nd Annual Lago de Guadalupe	Lago de Guadalupe, Mexico	21	Ferrari 625 TRC	John von Neumann	not known	1st	Won after 30 laps, 120.218km
20.6.1959	California Sports Car Club Preliminary Production Race	Hourglass Field, San Diego	211	Ferrari 250 TR	Eleanor von Neumann	not known	1st	Won after 8 laps, 23.176km
21.6.1959	California Sports Car Club Production Race	Hourglass Field, San Diego	211	Ferrari 250 TR	Eleanor von Neumann	not known	1st	Won after 25 laps, 72.420km
19.7.1959	USAC Kiwanis Grand Prix	Riverside	211	Ferrari 412 MI	Eleanor von Neumann	1st	1st	Won after 47 laps, 246.230km
27.9.1959	USAC Road Racing Championship Race	Vaca Valley	211	Ferrari 412 MI	Eleanor von Neumann	2nd	14th	
11.10.1959	USAC Road Racing Championship Race	Riverside	211	Ferrari 412 MI	Eleanor von Neumann	1st	DNF	Retired due to oil pressure, lap 35

Date	Race	Circuit	No	Car	Entered by	Qualified	Race Result	Notes
4.12.1959	Governor's Trophy	Oakes Field, Nassau, Bahamas	53	Ferrari 412 MI	John von Neumann/John Edgar	not known	DNF/18th	Reason for retiring unknown, lap 5
4.12.1959	Governor's Trophy Preliminary Production Race	Oakes Field, Nassau, Bahamas	53	Ferrari 412 MI	John von Neumann/John Edgar	not known	2nd	
6.12.1959	Nassau Trophy	Oakes Field, Nassau, Bahamas	53	Ferrari 412 MI	John von Neumann/John Edgar	not known	DNF/45th	Reason for retiring unknown, lap 25
31.1.1960	Buenos Aires 1000kms	Buenos Aires	2	Ferrari 250 TR 59/60 Fantuzzi Spyder	Scuderia Ferrari	3rd	2nd	Wolfgang von Trips co-drove
26.3.1960	12 Hours of Sebring	Sebring	7	Ferrari 250 TR 59/60	North American Racing Team	7th *	DNF	Retired due to water and oil leak, lap 123. Chuck Daigh co-drove. *Before 1964, starting places were decided on highest cubic capacity to lowest
8.5.1960	Targa Florio	Piccolo Circuito delle Madonie	202	Ferrari 250 TR 60	Scuderia Ferrari	n/a	DNF	Retired due to accident, lap 5. Cliff Allison co-drove
22.5.1960	Nurburgring 1000kms	Nurburgring	3	Ferrari Dino 246 S	Scuderia Ferrari	not known	DNF	Retired due to oil pressure, lap 13. Ludovico Scarfiotti co-drove
29.5.1960	Monaco Grand Prix	Monte Carlo	34	Ferrari Dino 246P-60	Scuderia Ferrari	9th	6th	Classified but had gearbox failure towards the end of the race
6.6.1960	Dutch Grand Prix	Zandvoort	6	Ferrari Dino 246-60	Scuderia Ferrari	12th	6th	
26.6.1960	Le Mans 24 Hours	Le Mans	10	Ferrari 250 TRI/60	Scuderia Ferrari	10th*	DNF	Retired due to gearbox failure on lap 204. Willy Mairesse co-drove. *Before 1963, starting places were decided on highest cubic capacity to lowest
3.7.1960	French Grand Prix	Reims	28	Scarab S4 02	Reventlow Automobiles Inc	20th	DNS	Did not start due to a blown engine
1.8.1960	Silver City Trophy	Brands Hatch	40	Ferrari 246 S	Scuderia Ferrari	13th	9th	
4.9.1960	Italian Grand Prix	Monza	18	Ferrari Dino 246-60	Scuderia Ferrari	2nd	2nd	Led 24 World Championship laps
2.10.1960	Gran Premio di Modena	Modena	26	Ferrari Dino 156 - Tipo 178	Scuderia Ferrari	6th	2nd	
16.10.1960	Grand Prix of Riverside 200 Miles	Riverside	211	Ferrari 625 TRC V12	Ferrari Representatives of California	4th	DNS	Did not start due to a blown engine
16.10.1960	Grand Prix of Riverside 200 Miles	Riverside	64	Ferrari 412 MI	Fred Knoop	4th	DNF	Retired due to gearbox failure. Pete Lovely qualified car, Ginther drove the car in the race
25.3.1961	12 Hours of Sebring	Sebring	15	Ferrari 250 TRI/61	Sefac Automobile Ferrari	24th*	2nd	Giancarlo Baghetti, Willy Mairesse and Wolfgang von Trips co-drove. *Before 1964, starting places were decided on highest cubic capacity to lowest
25.3.1961	12 Hours of Sebring	Sebring	27	Ferrari Dino 246 SP	Sefac Automobile Ferrari	13th*	DNF	Retired due to steering arm. Von Trips co-drove. Richie and von Trips then co-drove Baghetti and Mairesse's car. *Before 1964, starting places were decided on highest cubic capacity to lowest
30.4.1961	Targa Florio	Piccolo Circuito delle Madonie	164	Ferrari Dino 246 SP	Sefac Automobile Ferrari	n/a	DNF	Retired after Phil Hill had accident on the 1st lap.
14.5.1961	Monaco Grand Prix	Monte Carlo	36	Ferrari Dino 156/61	Sefac Automobile Ferrari	2nd	2nd	Led 13 World Championship laps. Achieved joint fastest-lap.
22.5.1961	Dutch Grand Prix	Zandvoort	2	Ferrari Dino 156/61	Sefac Automobile Ferrari	3rd	5th	
28.5.1961	Nurburgring 1000kms	Nürburgring	4	Ferrari Dino 246 SP	Sefac Automobile Ferrari	not known	3rd	Von Trips and Olivier Gendebien co-drove
11.6.1961	Le Mans 24 Hours	Le Mans	23	Ferrari Dino 246 SP	Sefac Automobile Ferrari	1st*	DNF	Retired due to running out of fuel, lap 231. Von Trips co-drove. *Before 1963, starting places were decided on highest cubic capacity to lowest
18.6.1961	Belgian Grand Prix	Spa-Francorchamps	6	Ferrari Dino 156/61	Sefac Automobile Ferrari	5th	3rd	Achieved fastest lap.
2.7.1961	French Grand Prix	Reims	18	Ferrari Dino 156/61	Sefac Automobile Ferrari	3rd	15th/DNF	Classified but retired due to engine failure and oil pressure, lap 40. Led 3 World Championship laps.
15.7.1961	British Grand Prix	Aintree	6	Ferrari Dino 156/61	Sefac Automobile Ferrari	2nd	3rd	
6.8.1961	German Grand Prix	Nurburgring	5	Ferrari Dino 156/61	Sefac Automobile Ferrari	14th	8th	
15.8.1961	Grand Prix of Pescara	Pescara	12	Ferrari Dino 246 SP	Sefac Automobile Ferrari	1st	DNF	Retired due to steering failure, lap 10. Baghetti co-drove
10.9.1961	Italian Grand Prix	Monza	6	Ferrari Dino 156/61	Sefac Automobile Ferrari	3rd	DNF	Retired due to engine failure, lap 23. Led 7 World Championship laps
23.4.1962	Glover Trophy	Goodwood	2	BRM P57	Owen Racing Organisation	6th	10th	
28.4.1962	BARC 200	Aintree	12	BRM P57	Owen Racing Organisation	4th	DNF	Retired due to gearbox failure, lap 22
12.5.1962	Daily Express International Trophy	Silverstone	2	BRM P57	Owen Racing Organisation	4th	DNF	Retired due to accident at Club, lap 4
20.5.1962	Dutch Grand Prix	Zandvoort	18	BRM P48/57	Owen Racing Organisation	7th	DNF	Retired due to accident when hit by Trevor Taylor, lap 71
3.6.1962	Monaco Grand Prix	Monte Carlo	8	BRM P48/57	Owen Racing Organisation	14th	DNF	Retired due to accident on 1st lap due to throttle issue. Marshal Ange Baldoni killed as a result of accident. Initially attempted to qualify in the BRM P57 but had gearbox problems so switched cars
17.6.1962	Belgian Grand Prix	Spa-Francorchamps	2	BRM P57	Owen Racing Organisation	9th	DNF	Retired due to transmission failure and gearbox issue, lap 22
24.6.1962	Le Mans 24 Hours	Le Mans	11	Aston Martin DP212	David Brown	4th*	DNF	Retired due to broken oil pipe, lap 78. Graham Hill co-drove. *Before 1963, starting places were decided on highest cubic capacity to lowest
1.7.1962	Grand Prix Internationale de Reims	Reims	4	BRM P57	Owen Racing Organisation	9th	DNF	Retired due to gearbox failure, lap 31

Appendix: Race Results

Date	Race	Circuit	No	Car	Entered by	Qualified	Race Result	Notes
8.7.1962	French Grand Prix	Rouen-les-Essarts	10	BRM P57	Owen Racing Organisation	10th	3rd	
21.7.1962	British Grand Prix	Aintree	14	BRM P57	Owen Racing Organisation	8th	13th	Suffered electrical pump and throttle issues
5.8.1962	German Grand Prix	Nurburgring	14	BRM P57	Owen Racing Organisation	7th	8th	
1.9.1962	Oulton Park Gold Cup	Oulton Park	18	BRM P57	Owen Racing Organisation	1st	DNF	Retired due to broken piston, lap 31
16.9.1962	Italian Grand Prix	Monza	12	BRM P57	Owen Racing Organisation	3rd	2nd	Had engine failure in original car in qualifying
7.10.1962	United States Grand Prix	Watkins Glen	5	BRM P57	Owen Racing Organisation	2nd	DNF	Retired due to engine failure, lap 35
15.12.1962	Rand Grand Prix	Kyalami	4	BRM P57	Owen Racing Organisation	5th	DNF	Retired due to gearbox failure, lap 36
22.12.1962	Natal Grand Prix	Westmead	4	BRM P57	Owen Racing Organisation	2nd	3rd	
29.12.1962	South African Grand Prix	East London	4	BRM P57	Owen Racing Organisation	7th	7th	
23.3.1963	12 Hours of Sebring	Sebring	25	Ferrari 250 GTO	Rosebud Racing Team	23rd*	6th	Innes Ireland co-drove. *Before 1964, starting places were decided on highest cubic capacity to lowest
30.3.1963	Lombank Trophy	Snetterton	2	BRM P57	Owen Racing Organisation	2nd	5th	
15.4.1963	Glover Trophy	Goodwood	2	BRM P57	Owen Racing Organisation	5th	DNF	Retired due to engine failure, lap 28
27.4.1963	BARC 200	Aintree	2	BRM P57	Owen Racing Organisation	5th	4th	
11.5.1963	Daily Express International Trophy	Silverstone	2	BRM P57	Owen Racing Organisation	8th	DNF	Retired due to gearbox failure, lap 7
26.5.1963	Monaco Grand Prix	Monte Carlo	5	BRM P57	Owen Racing Organisation	4th	2nd	
9.6.1963	Belgian Grand Prix	Spa-Francorchamps	8	BRM P57	Owen Racing Organisation	9th	4th	
16.6.1963	Le Mans 24 Hours	Le Mans	00	Rover-B.R.M. Turbine	Owen Racing Organisation	49th	7th (Not classified)	Finished 7th on the road, but due to being an invited entry, could not be officially classified. Given special award akin to class win for first turbine car to finish. Car started after all other cars, hence qualification position
23.6.1963	Dutch Grand Prix	Zandvoort	14	BRM P57	Owen Racing Organisation	6th	5th	
30.6.1963	French Grand Prix	Reims	4	BRM P57	Owen Racing Organisation	12th	DNF	Retired due to a stone hitting his radiator, lap 4
20.7.1963	British Grand Prix	Silverstone	2	BRM P57	Owen Racing Organisation	9th	4th	
4.8.1963	German Grand Prix	Nurburgring	2	BRM P57	Owen Racing Organisation	4th	3rd	Led one World Championship lap
8.9.1963	Italian Grand Prix	Monza	10	BRM P57	Owen Racing Organisation	4th	2nd	
21.9.1963	Oulton Park Gold Cup	Oulton Park	2	BRM P57	Owen Racing Organisation	3rd	2nd	
6.10.1963	United States Grand Prix	Watkins Glen	2	BRM P57	Owen Racing Organisation	4th	2nd	
13.10.1963	Grand Prix of Riverside 200 Miles	Riverside	211	Porsche 718 RS 61	Precision Motor Cars	24th	DNF	Retired due to broken rod, lap 29
13.10.1963	1 hour of Riverside Race	Riverside	211	Ferrari 250 GTO	Otto Zipper	not known	5th	
20.10.1963	Monterey Pacific Grand Prix	Laguna Seca	211	Porsche 718 RS 61	Otto Zipper	14th	7th	
27.10.1963	Mexican Grand Prix	Mexico City	2	BRM P57	Owen Racing Organisation	5th	2nd	
28.12.1963	South African Grand Prix	East London	6	BRM P57	Owen Racing Organisation	7th	DNF	Retired due to broken driveshaft/transmission failure, lap 43
21.3.1964	12 Hours of Sebring	Sebring	36	Porsche 904 GTS	Precision Motor Cars	17th	37th	Ronnie Bucknum co-drove
18.4.1964	BARC 200	Aintree	4	BRM P261	Owen Racing Organisation	6th	DNS	Did not start due to a crash prior to the race
10.5.1964	Monaco Grand Prix	Monte Carlo	7	BRM P261	Owen Racing Organisation	8th	2nd	
24.5.1964	Dutch Grand Prix	Zandvoort	8	BRM P261	Owen Racing Organisation	8th	11th	
31.5.1964	Nurburgring 1000kms	Nürburgring	126	Porsche 904/8	Precision Motor Cars	4th	5th	Jo Bonnier co-drove. Took class win in P 2.0 Class
14.6.1954	Belgian Grand Prix	Spa-Francorchamps	2	BRM P261	Owen Racing Organisation	8th	4th	
22.6.1964	Le Mans 24 Hours	Le Mans	11	Ford GT40	Ford Motor Company	2nd	DNF	Retired due to gearbox failure, lap 63. Masten Gregory co-drove
28.6.1954	French Grand Prix	Rouen-les-Essarts	10	BRM P261	Owen Racing Organisation	9th	5th	
5.7.1964	Reims 12 Hours	Reims	5	Ford GT40	Ford Motor Company	2nd	DNF	Retired due to gearbox failure. Masten Gregory co-drove
5.7.1964	Grand Prix de Reims	Reims	22	Lola T55 Cosworth	Midland Racing Partnership	15th	DNF	Retired due to an accident, lap 31
11.7.1964	British Grand Prix	Brands Hatch	4	BRM P261	Owen Racing Organisation	14th	8th	
2.8.1964	German Grand Prix	Nürburgring	4	BRM P261	Owen Racing Organisation	11th	7th	
9.8.1964	Gran Premio di Pergusa	Pergusa, Enna	14	Lola T54/55 Ford 116E	Midland Racing Partnership	4th	7th	

Date	Race	Circuit	No	Car	Entered by	Qualified	Race Result	Notes
23.8.1964	Austrian Grand Prix	Zeltweg	4	BRM P261	Owen Racing Organisation	5th	2nd	
29.8.1964	BARC Tourist Trophy	Goodwood	28	Ferrari 250 GTO	Eric Portman	21st	9th	
6.9.1964	Italian Grand Prix	Monza	20	BRM P261	Owen Racing Organisation	9th	4th	
4.10.1964	United States Grand Prix	Watkins Glen	4	BRM P261	Owen Racing Organisation	13th	4th	
11.10.1964	Los Angeles Times Grand Prix for Sportscars	Riverside	92	Cooper King Cobra Ford	Shelby American Inc.	7th	7th	
25.10.1964	Mexican Grand Prix	Mexico City	4	BRM P261	Owen Racing Organisation	11th	8th	
28.2.1965	Daytona 2000 Kilometres	Daytona International Speedway	72	Ford GT40	Shelby American Inc.	2nd	3rd	
27.3.1965	12 Hours of Sebring	Sebring	10	Ford GT40	Ken Miles	4th	DNF	Retired due to broken rear suspension, lap 37. Phil Hill co-drove
30.5.1965	Monaco Grand Prix	Monte Carlo	20	Honda RA272	Honda R and D Co.	17th	DNF	Retired due to transmission and driveshaft failure, lap 0. Actually started in 16th due to Ginther being a guaranteed starter as number one driver for Honda. Rindt, who qualified 16th was subsequently a non-qualifier
13.6.1965	Belgian Grand Prix	Spa-Francorchamps	10	Honda RA272	Honda R and D Co.	4th	6th	
27.6.1965	French Grand Prix	Clermont-Ferrand	26	Honda RA272	Honda R and D Co.	7th	DNF	Retired due to ignition failure and fire, lap 9
10.7.1965	British Grand Prix	Silverstone	11	Honda RA272-K1	Honda R and D Co.	3rd	DNF	Retired due to ignition failure, lap 26
18.7.1965	Dutch Grand Prix	Zandvoort	22	Honda RA272-K1	Honda R and D Co.	3rd	6th	Led 2 World Championship laps
12.9.1965	Italian Grand Prix	Monza	20	Honda RA272-K2	Honda R and D Co.	17th	14th/DNF	Classified, but retired due to ignition failure, lap 56
3.10.1965	United States Grand Prix	Watkins Glen	11	Honda RA272-K2	Honda R and D Co.	3rd	7th	
24.10.1965	Mexican Grand Prix	Mexico City	11	Honda RA272-K2	Honda R and D Co.	3rd	1st	Led all 65 World Championship laps. Won after 65 laps, 325.00km
31.10.1965	Los Angeles Times Grand Prix for Sportscars	Riverside	30	Lotus 40 Ford	Team Lotus	11th	DNF	Retired due to gearbox failure, lap 28
1.1.1966	South African Grand Prix	East London	7	BRP-BRM V8	Stirling Moss Racing Team	6th	DNF	Retired due to accident, lap 8
6.2.1966	Daytona 24 Hours	Daytona International Speedway	87	Ford Mark II	Holman and Moody	6th	DNF	Retired due to gearbox failure, lap 329. Bucknum co-drove.
16.5.1966	Daily Express International Trophy	Silverstone	5	Cooper T81 Maserati	Cooper Car Co.	7th	DNF	Retired due to overheating, lap 5
22.5.1966	Monaco Grand Prix	Monte Carlo	9	Cooper T81 Maserati	Cooper Car Co.	9th	DNF	Retired due to broken driveshaft, lap 80
5.6.1966	Nurburgring 1000kms	Nurburgring	12	Ferrari Dino 206 S	Ferrari s.p.a.	9th	3rd	Pedro Rodriguez co-drove
12.6.1966	Belgian Grand Prix	Spa-Francorchamps	18	Cooper T81 Maserati	Cooper Car Co.	8th	5th	
19.6.1966	Le Mans 24 Hours	Le Mans	27	Ferrari 330 P3 Spyder	North American Racing Team	5th	DNF	Retired due to gearbox failure, lap 151. Rodriguez co-drove.
4.9.1966	Italian Grand Prix	Monza	18	Honda RA273	Honda R and D Co.	7th	DNF	Retired due to accident caused by blown rear tyre, lap 16
2.10.1966	United States Grand Prix	Watkins Glen	12	Honda RA273	Honda R and D Co.	8th	7th/DNF	Classified, but retired due to transmission failure, lap 81
23.10.1966	Mexican Grand Prix	Mexico City	12	Honda RA273	Honda R and D Co.	3rd	4th	Achieved fastest lap. Led one World Championship lap
30.10.1966	Canadian-American (Can-Am) Challenge Cup LA Times Grand Prix for Sportscars	Riverside	2	Mirage Mark I A Oldsmobile	Jack Nethercutt	40th (DNQ)	n/a	
5.2.1967	Daytona 24 Hours	Daytona International Speedway	5	Ford Mark II	Ford Motor Company (Holman and Moody)	5th	DNF	Retired due to gearbox failure, lap 298. Mario Andretti co-drove
12.3.1967	Race of Champions – Heat 1	Brands Hatch	6	Eagle-Weslake T1G 103	Anglo American Racers	3rd	3rd	
12.3.1967	Race of Champions – Heat 2	Brands Hatch	6	Eagle-Weslake T1G 103	Anglo American Racers	3rd	2nd	
12.3.1967	Race of Champions Final	Brands Hatch	6	Eagle-Weslake T1G 103	Anglo American Racers	2nd	10th	
7.5.1967	Monaco Grand Prix	Monte Carlo	10	Eagle-Weslake T1G 102	Anglo American Racers	DNQ	n/a	Qualified in 18th place, only 16 starters. Officially classified as 19th in qualifying as Pedro Rodriguez, who qualified 19th, started 16th due to being a guaranteed starter due to being the number one driver for Cooper
31.5.1967	Indianapolis 500	Indianapolis Motor Speedway	42	Eagle 67 214-Ford	All-American Racers	DNQ	n/a	Withdrew from qualifying after rookie test and time trials
6.7.1969	California Sports Car Club Rally	Los Angeles-Huntington Beach	not known	not known	not known	n/a	not known	
10.10.1976	Historic Antique Grand Prix	Long Beach	n/a	Bugatti T37A	Robert Sutherland	n/a	Did not Race	
21.8.1982	Monterey Historic Automobile Race	Monterey	not known	Porsche 917/10	Vasek Polak	n/a	not known	
3.10.1982	Edward Diloreto Historic Can-Am Race	Riverside	not known	Porsche 914	not known	n/a	not known	

Bibliography

BOOKS

BRM – A Mechanic's Tale by Dick Salmon. Published by Veloce Publishing, 2006

BRM – The Saga of British Racing Motors Volume 2: Spaceframe Cars 1959-1965 by Doug Nye and Tony Rudd. Published by MRP Publishing, 2003

BRM – The Saga of British Racing Motors Volume 3: Monocoque V8 cars 1963-1969 by Doug Nye and Tony Rudd. Published by MRP Publishing, 2008

Conquest of Formula One by Christopher Hilton. Published by Patrick Stephens, 1989

Cooper Cars by Doug Nye. Published by Osprey Publishing, 1983

Forghieri on Ferrari by Mauro Forghieri and Daniele Buzzonetti. Published by Giorgio Nada Editore, 2013

Grand Prix 1964 by Louis T Stanley. Published by Doubleday Press, 1964

Grand Prix Ferrari: The Years of Enzo Ferrari's Power 1948-1980 by Anthony Pritchard. Published by Veloce Publishing, 2014

Inside Track – Phil Hill, Ferrari's American World Champion – His Story, His Photography by Phil Hill, Derek Hill, Steve Dawson and Doug Nye. Published by The Grand Prix Library, 2018

It was Fun! By Tony Rudd. Published by Patrick Stephens, 1993

Meister Brauser; Harry Heuer's Championship Racing Team by Tom Schultz. Published by Dalton Wilson Fine Books, 2019

The Moomins; The World of Moominvalley by Tove Jansson. Published by MacMillan Children's Books, 2017

Porsche – The Racing 914s by Roy Smith. Published by Veloce Publishing, 2016

Scarab – Race Log of the All-American Specials 1957-1965 by Preston Lerner. Published by Motorbooks International, 1991

Southern Californian Road Racing by Tony Baker. Published by Arcadia Publishing, 2019

Vintage American Road Racing Cars 1950-1970 by Harold W Pace and Mark R Brinker. Published by Motorbooks, 2004

MAGAZINES/JOURNALS

Autocourse – Tester to the Prancing Horse by Jerry Sloniger, 1961/1962 (Autocourse is now a book but in its first year, it was published in magazine form)

Automobile Quarterly – Richie, We Hardly Knew You! by Michael Ling, Vol.40, no 2, May 2000

Autosport Magazine – Whatever Comes into my Head by Nigel Roebuck, 2/3/1978 and Race of my Life by Chris Nixon, 15/3/1990

BRM Association Magazine – BRM Cavalcade by Paul Foxall, August 2019.

Car and Driver – Ginther's Goal: Go Fast! by Steve McNamara September 1961 and Whatever Happened to Richie Ginther by Pete Lyons, 1988

Car Life – Richie Ginther by Bill Libby, September 1967

Classic and Sports Car – When the Music's Over by Rik Blote, October 2006

Classic Car Magazine – Donington Déjà Vu by Chris Nixon – December 1989 and Quick Thinking by Eoin Young, March 2001

Forza – Four Great Years in the Life of Richie Ginther by Jonathan Thompson, Fall 1997, and Ginther's Travels by Michael T. Lynch, June 2005

Men at the Wheel – Richie Ginther by Peter Miller, 1964

Motorsport magazine – Ronnie Bucknum (December 1965), Looking Back with Peter Arundell (Jul 1984), No Regrets with Phil Hill (October 1994), Legends: Phil Hill by Nigel Roebuck (December 1997), Legends: Richie Ginther by Nigel Roebuck (March 1999), Honda, Team of Dreams (August 1999), Legends: Giancarlo Baghetti by Nigel Roebuck (Jan 2003), One Hit Wanderer by Richard Heseltine (December 2005), Stirling's Day of Days (May 2011) and Year of the Shark by Anthony Pritchard (November 2011)

Road & Track – Richie Ginther by Murray Roche, January 1960 and Richie Ginther 1930-1989 by Peter Egan, January 1990

SCCA Sportscar Magazine – Richie Ginther by James T. Crow, July 1972.

Sporting Motorist – The Success Story of Richie Ginther by A. F. Rivers Fletcher, December 1965

Sports Car Journal – Speed Portraits – Richie Ginther, November 1957

Sports Illustrated – 22/3/1976

Vintage Racecar – Identity Crisis by Casey Annis, June 2004, Remembering Richie by Art Evans, July 2009 and Fast Lines: Ginther's Honda by Pete Lyons, April 2011

NEWSPAPERS

Austin-American Statesman; 18/1/1966

Baltimore Sun; 11/2/1968

Binghampton Press & Sun Bulletin; 8/8/1969

Boston Globe; 1/1/1967

Chicago Tribune; 7/7/1963

Cincinnati Enquirer; 27/11/1969

Graham Hill (10) leads Richie Ginther (22), Jim Clark (6) and Dan Gurney (16) at the 1965 Dutch Grand Prix. *Nationaal Archief (Dutch National Archive)*

Greenwood Index Journal; 29/7/1967
The Guardian; 15/2/1977 and 22/9/1989
Honolulu Star Bulletin; 7/3/1958
Indianapolis Star; 23/9/1957
Kokomo Morning Times; 16/6/1967
Los Angeles Times; 5/9/1955, 26/2/1957, 9/6/1957, 20/07/1959, 8/10/1959, 10/10/1959, 17/1/1960, 10/5/1962, 4/10/1963, 10/10/1963, 15/3/1965, 25/10/1965, 29/9/1966, 21/11/1968, 28/5/1970, 25/5/1971, 27/3/1976, 29/3/1980, 30/9/1981, 7/8/1988, 22/9/1989 and 28/6/1991
(The Los Angeles Times has given permission for two excerpts from two articles to be used; 'Ginther Returns to Raceway Following Amazing Recovery' by Bob Thomas, Copyright © 1966, Los Angeles Times and 'Richie Ginther Makes Full Circle in Racing' by Shav Glick, Copyright © 1968, Los Angeles Times. Used with Permission.)
The Observer; 20/5/1962, 16/9/1962
The Paducah Sun; 26/10/1965
Pasadena Independent; 6/6/1961
Philadelphia Inquirer; 27/11/1967
Reno Gazette; 21/10/1984
San Bernardino County Sun; 16/6/1958, 2/2/1959 and 16/6/1967
San Francisco Examiner; 20/11/1958 and 29/11/1970
Santa Cruz Sentinel ; 17/4/1964
Valley News; 8/5/1954, 14/8/1956, 29/8/1957, 31/3/1960
Wilmington Daily Press Journal: 30/10/1957

WEBSITES
www.conceptcarz.com – Ginther Finally Gets It! by Jeremy McMullen, 16/8/2013
www.the-fastlane.co.uk/formula2/index.html
www.oldracingcars.com
www.racingsportscars.com
www.sportscartv.com

Index

About the Author

Nurburgring 1000kms, 1966. *El Sol/Ed McDonough*

Although this is the first book Richard has written, he has been involved in motor racing research for over 20 years. In November 2002, his opus on what former grand prix drivers did after their time in the public glare was over – *Where Are They Now?* – was published online at www.oldracingcars.com to go perfectly hand-in-hand with the attempts of ORC's founder, Allen Brown, to trace former racing cars. Feel free to pay the site a visit and find out more. On the section Richard works on, there are almost 3000 names, covering over 100 years of the Indianapolis 500 and 70 years of World Championship Grand Prix racing.

Richard has also helped a number of authors and historians with their research, including Donald Davidson at the Indianapolis Motor Speedway and especially so with Peter Higham and his *World Encyclopaedia of Racing Drivers*. Richard is also listed as a key source in *Auto Racing Comes of Age: A Transatlantic View of the Cars, Drivers and Speedways* by Robert Dick (2013) and by the same author in 2019 with his book *Auto Racing in the Shadow of the Great War*.

Richard, who has followed motor racing since 1985, lives in Hertfordshire with his wife and three children.

The author Richard Jenkins. *Amy Jenkins*